The Reapportionment Puzzle

The Reapportionment Puzzle

Bruce E. Cain

UNIVERSITY OF CALIFORNIA PRESS

Berkeley / Los Angeles / London

University of California Press
Berkeley and Los Angeles, California

University of California Press, Ltd.
London, England

Printed in the United States of America

1   2   3   4   5   6   7   8   9

Library of Congress Cataloging in Publication Data
Cain, Bruce E.
    The reapportionment puzzle.

    Includes bibliographical references and index.
        1. Apportionment (Election law)—California.
2. Apportionment (Election law) I. Title.
JK8768.C33   1984   328.794'073452   83–18077
ISBN 0–520–05028–2

Contents

List of Figures and Tables   ix

Preface   xi

1
Introduction   1

    Themes of This Study   4

ONE: THE POLITICAL NATURE OF
REAPPORTIONMENT

2
A Simple Matter of Demography   9

    The Tabula Rasa Method   10
    The Incrementalist Method   15
    Methods of Containing Ripples   22
    The Collapse of Old Seats   27
    Conclusion   30

3
Aesthetic Considerations   32

    A Hypothetical Case   34
    Hypothetical Cases and Real-World
    Constraints   43
    The Intrinsic Value of Compactness
    Reconsidered   50

4
The Consistency of Good Government Criteria   52

        The Value of Good Government Goals   54
        Equal Population Considered   55
        Respect for City and County Lines   60
        Preserving Communities of Interest   63
        Protecting Racial and Ethnic Communities   66
        Competitive Districts   67
        The Consistency of Good Government Criteria   68
        The Ordering of Good Government Criteria   73
        Fairness as Seats-Votes Ratio   74
        Conclusion   77

TWO: THE POLITICAL REAPPORTIONMENT
EXAMINED

5
A Tale of One Reapportionment   81

        Technical Considerations   83
        The Republican Strategy   87
        The Hispanic Lobby   90
        The Breakdown of the Bipartisan Coalition   97
        Reaction to the Bill   101

6
What Legislators Want   104

        Case 1: The "Give Me What I Need Only"
        Syndrome   105
        Case 2: "His County's Keeper"   107
        Case 3: "Hedging Your Bets"   109
        Case 4: "Nickel and Diming"   110
        Case 5: "There's No Place Like Home"   112
        Case 6: "Constraint from the Top"   113
        Case 7: "On Being Vigilant"   115
        Basic Principles Concerning Legislative
        Preferences   115
        Reversing the Downsian Model   117
        Conclusion   119

7
Bargaining and Legislative Reapportionment   120

    A Typology of Bargaining Positions   121
    Trades with Intervention   127
    What Makes Legislators Effective Bargainers?   132
    Conclusion   134

8
The Staff and Data of Reapportionment   135

    Institutional and Quantitative Approaches
    Compared   136
    Ways of Assessing Partisan Effects   138
    Conclusion   146

9
Gerrymanders   147

    The Partisan Gerrymander   148
    The Party's Decision to Implement a Partisan
    Gerrymander   151
    Individual Legislators and the Partisan
    Gerrymander   154
    Pluralist Tensions and the Partisan
    Gerrymander   155
    Partisan Plans and the Distribution of Power   157
    The Bipartisan Gerrymander   159
    The Rules of a Bipartisan Gerrymander   160
    A Party's Decision to Pursue a Bipartisan Plan   162
    The Affirmative Action Gerrymander   166
    The Twin Sins of Dispersion and
    Concentration   168
    Determining Sufficient Levels of Strength   171
    Pluralist Tensions and the Affirmative Action
    Gerrymander   174
    Conclusion   177

10
Reform in a Pluralist Setting   179

    The Choices of Reform   181
    Improving Legislative Reapportionment   188

Index   193

List of Figures and Tables

FIGURES

1.	Demonstration of a Simple Reapportionment Procedure	10
2.	The Effect of Constraints	11
3.	A Displacement Example—I	17
4.	A Displacement Example—II	18
5.	Illustration of Linear Ripple	20
6.	Dispersing a Ripple	21
7.	Absorbing Area on Several Borders	21
8.	Illustration of Circular Ripple	23
9.	County Lines and Displacement	24
10.	Using Population Variance to Minimize Displacement	25
11.	An Example of Seat Collapse	28
12.	Hypothetical State	36
13.	Model Plan with Compact Lines	36
14.	Extreme Partisan Remedy	38
15.	Moderate Partisan Remedy	39
16.	Communities of Interest Respected	40
17.	Minorities United	41
18.	Final Plan	42
19.	Partisan Distribution of Assembly Seats in Los Angeles County	45
20.	Los Angeles County, 1980 Black Population	47
21.	Los Angeles County, 1980 Hispanic Population	48
22.	Seat Shares by County	49
23.	Variations of Voters by Seats in the Assembly	58
24.	Changing Incentives of Seats	158
25.	Dispersion of Minorities	169
26.	Concentration of Minorities	170

27.   Seats with Nonvoters Included   173
28.   Seats with Nonvoters Excluded   173

TABLES

1.   Displacement Example   26
2.   Possible Connections Between Compact Shapes
      and Good Government Values   35
3.   Value of Vote with Different Deviation Levels   57
4.   Advantages of Single and Multiple
      Representation   62
5.   Redistricting Values   69
6.   Equity and Number of Voters   76
7.   Typology of Seats   121
8.   Complementarity of Trades Between Seat Types   124
9.   Classification of Assembly Seats by Types   125
10.   Breakdown of Trades in Assembly
      Reapportionment   127
11.   Sample of Short Printout Provided to Members   138
12.   Projections for Some Los Angeles Districts   140
13.   Probability of Holding Seats at Various Levels of
      Registration   142
14.   Simulated Races for the 39th Assembly District   144
15.   Number of Democratic Wins by District   145
16.   Impact of Territorial Gains on District
      Partisanship   156
17.   Percent Registered by Minority and Non-
      Minority Categories   168
18.   The Institutional Choices of Reapportionment
      Reform   182
19.   Representation Characteristics and
      Redistricting Values   186

Preface

Reapportionment is a murky and dimly perceived process for most political observers. The eyes of even the most dogged journalists frequently glaze over at the mere mention of the term. Only those who are directly affected by it—the politicians, their staff, and some party officials—and those who make political reform their profession ever really manage to get excited about reapportionment.

This is not difficult to understand. The process of drawing new district lines is very technical, involving a mass of numbers, maps, and geographical esoterica. It requires enormous attention to detail in order both to execute a plan and to try to understand the implications of one that has been proposed. And as if this were not enough, those who would enter into this process must come to grips with its generally disreputable image. Would you really want your sister to marry a gerrymanderer?

This is a book based on my observations and experiences as a reapportionment consultant in California in 1981. As such, I hope that it will provide a clearer view of the difficulties inherent in the redistricting task and of the political process behind line drawing. The point of this book is to show political scientists, their students, and informed members of the public that reapportionment is much more central to other issues of politics and representation than they had hitherto thought. Most have some vague sense that reapportionment is important, but they do not see clearly how it is related to the rest of the political process.

I became involved in reapportionment because it so happened that I was captain of the divisional softball team at Caltech, and one of our players was an attorney, Walter Karabian, who had been majority leader for the State Assembly in the early 'seventies. The Assembly had just finished a two-year speakership struggle and was looking for someone who had not been tainted by involvement with one side or the other, and who had the technical background to handle the job of directing the staff operations and drawing up plans. Karabian, and his friend and my colleague Dan Kevles, arranged a meeting for me and Richard Alatorre, the newly appointed Chairman of the Assembly Elections and Reapportionment Committee. With their help, I managed to persuade Richard that I was the man for the job, and I was appointed in January 1981.

It was always my intention to write a book based on my experiences, but I am grateful to a colleague, Burton Klein, for urging me to initiate the project as soon as I could and for giving me an idea about how to focus it. I would also like to thank Walter Karabian and Dan Kevles for acting as my agents in securing this position. My intellectual debts are extensive. On the practical side, I must thank first and foremost my mentor in real politics, Richard Alatorre, whose insights and wisdom suffuse this book. In addition, my numerous discussions with Jim Wisley and Jim Tucker, both members of the reapportionment staff, were extremely valuable in very different ways. Two of my colleagues read the early drafts with unusual care and had an enormous impact on the book per se: Roger Noll helped me organize it more clearly and gave me many useful ideas, and Will Jones gave my manuscript an unusually detailed reading and critique. Dan Kevles, John Ferejohn, and Morris Fiorina helped me think about the general issue of whom the book was addressed to and how best to do it. In addition, Bob Bates, Bernie Grofman, Ken McCue, Matt McCubbins, Carl Lydick, and Morgan Kousser read and commented on the second draft in very useful ways. I also managed to persuade my wife Anne and my parents to read and react to portions of the manuscript. Georgeia Hutchinson and Irene Baldon worked long and hard to prepare the book. Needless to say, I owe a great deal to all these people.

1

Introduction

Legislative reapportionment has few friends and many enemies. Its critics maintain that for legislators to vote on an issue that so vitally affects their own careers creates a conflict of interest. The district lines drawn by reapportionment can determine the strength of an incumbent's position and the chances of his or her political survival. They can also influence who runs against an incumbent and how much money will have to be spent on both sides. Given these stakes, legislators cannot help analyzing plans from the perspective of how they are personally affected. As Common Cause explains, the "guiding principle for most incumbent legislators has been self-protection," and "all too often, incumbents give in to the pressure to manipulate district lines for personal or partisan benefit." Under such conditions, Common Cause argues, it is not surprising that legislators will attempt "to draw lines that perpetuate their positions of power within the status quo."[1]

Other descriptions of the process of legislative reapportionment are equally unflattering. Bob Moretti, a former Speaker of the California State Assembly, has said of it that "quite simply, it is the most political, most crass, most selfish act that any legislator ever engages in."[2] Some have been appalled at how tough-minded and selfish legislators become where their districts are concerned: "The unsavory scenario never changes much, decade in and decade out. . . . Reapportionment is hardball politics at its zenith. Whoever has the advantage—Demo-

---

1. Common Cause, *Toward a System of "Fair and Effective Representation"* (Washington, D.C.: Common Cause, 1977), p. 17.

2. Quoted in "The Year of the Gerrymander," *North East Bay Independent and Gazette*, January 11, 1981.

crats or Republicans—is going to play for keeps."[3] Though some legislators try to mask the conflict of reapportionment in the rhetoric of public interest, others, like State Senator H. L. Richardson, are quite honest about what reapportionment means to them: "Fairness, impartiality, registration balance, justice, community interest, equal representation, equality, all of these considerations become so many words in a dictionary, they have little or no relationship to where the lines are drawn. The prime consideration is how to 'Fadargol' (a political word meaning to mess) the foe and fur line your friend's future."[4]

When legislators concentrate on their own and their friends' political futures instead of on the public interest, critics say that legislative reapportionment can have several pernicious effects. One is that by predetermining the outcome of an election through political gerrymandering, legislative reapportionment diminishes the impact that any one voter can have on an election either by voting or by volunteer campaign activity. Robbing voters of the incentive to participate in the electoral process contributes to voter apathy and alienation. Another alleged adverse effect is that it makes legislators "less responsive to the political interests of their entire constituency." When legislators can reapportion their seats so as to make themselves less vulnerable, they will be less attentive to their constituents and will work less hard. This means, in effect, that legislative reapportionment undermines their incentive to be responsive. Finally, some have even argued that legislative reapportionment weakens political parties "by allowing them to field weak candidates."[5] This follows from some of the earlier points. As districts become less competitive, they can be held by less able, less diligent, and less hardworking politicians. The hope is that abolishing legislative reapportionment would restore the incentives necessary for quality representation.

It is not surprising, then, that many people feel that the time is long overdue for reform. In the words of one California newspaper, "there must be a less seedy way to conduct this confusing decennial rite so steeped in geography and hypocrisy."[6] But if reapportionment is to be taken out of the hands of the legislature, to whom should the task be assigned? Opinions vary greatly on these questions.

One school of thought is the "nonpartisan" or "take the politics out of reapportionment" approach. The essence of this line of thinking is to purify reapportionment by giving it to apolitical or impartial observers. Ronald Reagan, for instance, proposed that reapportionment be

---

3. "Reapportionment Woes," *The Sun* (San Bernardino), September 24, 1981.
4. "Richardson Report," *Firebaugh–Mendota Journal*, September 3, 1981.
5. Common Cause, *Toward a System of "Fair and Effective Representation,"* p. 24.
6. "Joe Scott on Politics," *Los Angeles Herald-Examiner*, September 20, 1981.

given to "a blue-ribbon citizens' committee on the basis of what is good for the people, not just for the party that happens to be in power."[7] Many have faith that the computer can solve the redistricting dilemma by introducing a technical, impartial, and even scientific tool. One editorial writer, for instance, has said, "I wish we would bring in three computer scientists and have them draw the lines without regard for party, race, or creed."[8] To aid the apolitical commission and its computer, it has been proposed, first, that they be given strict guidelines of reapportionment criteria to follow—such as compactness, competitiveness, equal population, respect for city and county lines, preserving communities of interest, and the like—and, second, that they be denied the use of political information. Not giving the commission political data would ensure that it would not be swayed by political considerations. The outcome might accidentally favor one party over the other, but since the process would be blind to political considerations, it would therefore be fair, or so those who hold this position argue.

A second school of thought on reform accepts it as inevitable that political interests cannot be excluded and tries to contain partisan mischief by various devices. There are several variations on this theme. The most common is the bipartisan commission proposal. A bipartisan commission would allow the parties to fight over the political consequences of reapportionment, but would make it more difficult for one party to impose a plan that was unfair to the other party. This proposal would have the virtue of taking redistricting out of the hands of those who stand to gain or lose personally and putting it into the hands of those who, while cognizant of the political questions, would not be themselves directly affected.

Another version of this second line of reform is the "political formula" solution, first proposed by the distinguished reapportionment scholar Robert Dixon and most recently advocated by the political scientists Grofman and Scarrow.[9] The idea behind this is that the best way to resolve the unseemly struggle of redistricting is to formulate a measure of political fairness and then select from the plans submitted by various parties and interest groups the one that best meets this measure. The norm of fairness they propose derives from the concept of an

---

7. "Slaying the Gerrymander," *San Jose Mercury*, September 28, 1981.

8. "So Let the Computers Do It," *San Diego Daily Transcript*, September 22, 1981.

9. Richard Niemi and John Deegan, Jr., "Competition, Responsiveness, and the Swing Ratio," *American Political Science Review*, 72:4 (December 1978), 1304–1323; Guillermo Owen and Bernard Grofman, "A New Approach to the Seats-Votes Swing Relationship" (Social Science Research Report, School of Social Sciences, UC–Irvine, September 1981); Edward R. Tufte, "The Relationship Between Seats and Votes in Two-Party Systems," *American Political Science Review*, 67 (1973), 540–547; and Douglas Rae, *The Political Consequences of Electoral Laws* (New Haven: Yale University Press, 1971.)

impartial distribution of seats to votes. For a given number of votes, the political system should reward a party with a given number of seats. The ideal distribution would look like an S-shaped curve on which a party would get slightly less than its rightful share of seats below 50 percent of the vote and slightly more than its rightful share of the seats above 50 percent of the vote. By generating as many plans as possible and measuring the political consequences of each, there would be a range of plans, from which the one that most closely approximated the ideal S-shaped curve would be chosen. The attraction of this approach is that it confronts the question of political fairness directly and suggests an impartial way of determining whether a plan meets that criterion. It emphasizes what the participants in reapportionment consider fair, which is whether the outcome rather than the process per se is just.

Finally, there are hybrid versions of reform that mix elements from several different approaches. For instance, Common Cause and the Republicans put an initiative on the ballot in California in 1982 that called for a commission that would have been partly bipartisan—with representatives from both parties for the State Assembly, Senate, and U.S. Congress—and partly nonpartisan—with four members of the commission appointed by the senior members of the state appellate court. It would have also provided for judicial review if the commission could not come to agreement.

As the preceding discussion indicates, the criticisms of legislative reapportionment are extensive and serious, ranging from alleged violations of the conflict of interest principle to a weakening of the democratic electoral process itself. This study takes a closer look at these criticisms and suggests some counterbalancing considerations that may have been overlooked in the public debate.

Themes of This Study

There have been many fine studies of the legal issues surrounding redistricting.[10] There have also been several studies of the policy and political impact of reapportionments since *Baker v. Carr*, ad-

---

10. The list of articles on this topic is extensive. The reader is best advised to see the bibliography in Bernard Grofman and Howard Scarrow, "Current Issues in Reapportionment" (Working Paper, School of Social Sciences, UC–Irvine, January 1981). The classic study in this area is Robert G. Dixon, Jr., *Democratic Representation and Reapportionment in Law and Politics* (New York: Oxford University Press, 1968). I am much persuaded by his view of reapportionment in that study and in "The Warren Court Crusade for the Holy Grail of 'One Man, One Vote,' " in Nelson Polsby, ed., *Reapportionment in the 1970's* (Berkeley: University of California Press, 1971), pp. 7–45.

dressing the central question of whether reapportionment matters.[11] There are a few excellent, comprehensive studies on the details of software and data construction and, more generally, on the impact of computers on the whole process.[12] By contrast, there has been less discussion of how reapportionment plans are formulated in a legislative setting and what considerations come into play.[13] This is an unfortunate omission, since an understanding of how a legislative reapportionment actually works and how a plan is actually put together is crucial to any discussion of reform. This book attempts to throw light on these aspects of reapportionment, aspects that have been assumed rather than studied. The book is neither a defense of the status quo nor an apology for the California reapportionment. Rather, it endeavors to show that the reality of reapportionment is more complex and morally ambiguous than critics and reformers commonly suppose, and that the public's hopes for reform should be tempered by knowledge of the tangled web the Supreme Court has woven.

In particular, this study will address two related topics. One is why reapportionment should be regarded as a political question, when a political question is defined as one that creates disputes between contending groups and parties in a society. It is most desirable that disagreements in a democracy be limited to issues that do not involve the fundamental rules of the game. A society should be able to disagree about policies without disagreeing about how to resolve its disagreements; or to put it another way, it should agree about how to disagree. Disagreement over reapportionment is particularly unsettling because it is about the rules of political conflict. When one party gets an advan-

11. Good critiques and summaries can be found in Timothy G. O'Rourke, *The Impact of Reapportionment* (New Brunswick, N.J.: Transaction Books, 1980); and David Saffel, "The Policy Consequences of Reapportionment," in Bernard Grofman, Arendt Lijphart, Robert B. McKay, and Howard A. Scarrow, eds., *Representation and Redistricting Issues in the 1980s* (Lexington, Mass.: D.C. Heath, 1982). Also extremely useful is William E. Bicker, "The Effects of Malapportionment in the States: A Mistrial," in Nelson Polsby, ed., *Reapportionment in the 1970's* (Berkeley: University of California Press, 1971), pp. 7–45. One of the strongest statements for the potential policy effects of redistricting is Gordon E. Baker, *The Reapportionment Revolution* (New York: Random House, 1967).

12. The Rose Institute has put out several good summaries of the computer technology. See especially the chapter on "Computerized Redistricting" and Appendices A through E in *California Redistricting* (Claremont, Calif.: Rose Institute of State and Local Government, 1980) for details on census materials and computers. Another useful study is Terry B. O'Rourke, *Reapportionment: Law, Politics, Computers* (Washington, D.C.: American Enterprise Institute for Public Policy Research, 1972).

13. One participant who has published his insights into the politics of redistricting is Leroy Hardy. See especially his "Considering the Gerrymander," *Pepperdine Law Review*, 4:2 (1977), 243-284; and Leroy Hardy and Charles P. Sohner, "Constitutional Challenge and Political Response: California Reapportionment 1965," *Western Political Quarterly*, 23:4 (December 1970), 733-751.

tage out of reapportionment, it seems as though it has rigged the rules of the game in its favor, and this violates an intuitive sense of fair play. To treat reapportionment as a political question is to abandon the idea that political and reapportionment issues can be separated. It is not assumed in a political reapportionment that there is one and only one solution that all participants can agree to. Instead, it provides a framework for disagreements to be discussed and ironed out to the extent possible. Inevitably, there will be winners and losers. The reapportionment plan that is formulated politically cannot pretend to be the "best" plan. It is simply the one that enjoyed the broadest consensus, for whatever reasons.

The second and related question this study explores is how an actual political reapportionment worked. It will be apparent that the first part of this study applies universally to all reapportionments, since it discusses the many factors that must be considered in making reapportionment decisions. What is said there is as relevant to Texas or New York as to California. But what is said in the second part of the book has to be considered a case study. The institutions of reapportionment vary considerably across the country, and these variations will affect which legislators have the most power, the role of the Speaker, the importance of staff operations, the degree of cooperation between the two parties, the kinds of constitutional criteria that must be observed, and so on. Even so, a case study of the California experience provides the reader with valuable insight into how a political treatment of reapportionment works, even if the exact nature of the political institutions may vary across states. The discussions of the kinds of requests that legislators make, the choices that legislative leaders face, the methods of persuasion at the disposal of those leaders, and the principles of gerrymandering are relevant to the experiences of reapportionment nationwide.

The final chapter returns to the issue of reform and tries to make some suggestions about what is and is not a realistic expectation. Being realistic about reapportionment does not mean that one has to be fatalistic about the prospects of improvement: it means aiming for what will work rather than for what is hopelessly utopian.

PART ONE

The Political Nature of Reapportionment

2

A Simple Matter of Demography

On the face of it, reapportionment seems quite simple. Since all of the seats in the houses of a state legislature or in a state's Congressional delegation must have equal populations, the reapportionment task is to draw the boundary lines of a specified number of districts so that each is as close to some ideal number as is practical. The ideal population is the state population divided by the number of seats in the legislature. So defined, the problem is not political but technical, in the sense that determining the ideal population is an arithmetic exercise and figuring the size of the districts requires no more than knowledge of, and skill in, the use of census data. Objective calculations of this sort should not provoke a great deal of controversy. The districts either have equal populations or they do not.

By contrast, the practice of redistricting is quite complicated. A great deal of time and money is spent on drawing and analyzing plans. Reapportionment staffs collect immense amounts of data and build or purchase sophisticated computer systems to aid them in their tasks. The legislators themselves sit through numerous meetings, arguing about various proposals and bargaining for a better seat. The legislative leadership, too, must devote time to putting together the votes for a bill, time that some would say could be better spent on more pressing policy matters. Even after a bill is passed, the reapportionment struggle continues. Aggrieved parties bring suit against the legislature to invalidate the plan, with the consequence that reapportionment can be fought in the courts for years. In the end, both the participants and the public grow weary of this struggle, and quite naturally people begin to question whether all of the bother was necessary.

In principle, it seems possible to make reapportionment a simple, technical exercise. Why has it not been so? One answer may be that

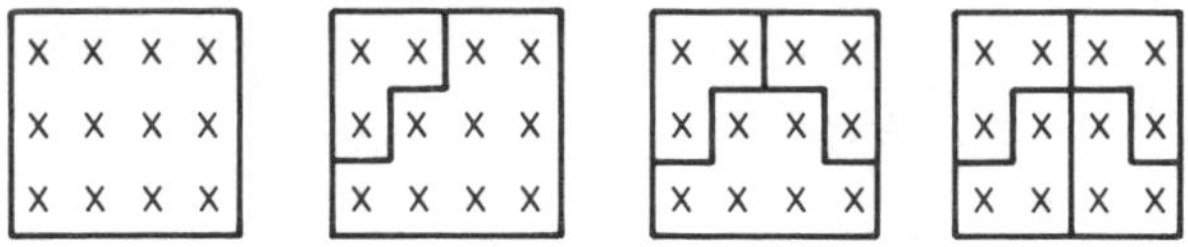

FIGURE 1   *Demonstration of a Simple Reapportionment Procedure*

simple methods have been innocently overlooked. A more cynical reason may be that politicians and party activists have felt threatened by their potential impact. In either case, approaches to reapportionment that concentrate on the simple technical task of creating a specified number of equal districts deserve close examination.

The Tabula Rasa Method

The simplest approach to reapportionment may be called the Tabula Rasa method. This method, as its name is intended to suggest, starts with a clean slate: abolishing the old districts and building from scratch. As an example, assume that a state with twelve people must be apportioned into four districts of three people each. Disregarding the old district lines, which may have contained populations ranging from one to four, one simple approach would be to pick a corner of the state at random and start the construction of new seats from there. Each new district must have three people in it and be contiguous and as compact as possible, which rules out districts with disconnected parts and sprawling contorted shapes. The procedure begins by putting together the three people nearest the upper corner of the state into one district (see Fig. 1). After the first district has been created, the second one can be constructed from three more people, and so on until all four seats are defined. The process is so simple that a computer program has been written to do it in an automated fashion; by flipping a switch, the districts can be drawn almost instantaneously.[1]

Obviously, a large number of district plans could be drawn on the basis of population alone. The addition of compactness and contiguity requirements restricts the choice somewhat—the person in the upper left-hand corner cannot be linked with the person in the lower right-

---

1. See, for instance, the following: Edward Forrest, "Apportionment by Computer," *American Behavioral Scientist*, 8 (December 1964), 23–35; James B. Weaver and Sidney Hess, "A Procedure for Nonpartisan Districting: Developments of Computer Techniques," *Yale Law Journal*, 73 (1963), 288–308. Some programs have tried to include a political component as well, such as Stuart S. Nagel, "Simplified Bipartisan Computer Districting," *Stanford Law Review*, 17 (1965), 863–899.

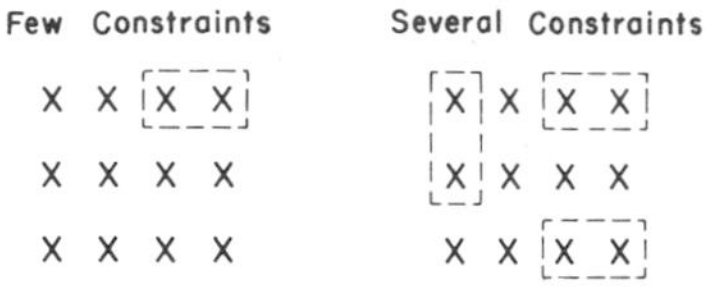

```
 Few  Constraints          Several  Constraints

 X   X  ⌈X  X⌉            ⌈X⌉ X  ⌈X  X⌉
        ⌊_ _⌋             |  |    ⌊_ _⌋
 X   X   X   X            |X| X   X   X
                          ⌊_⌋
 X   X   X   X             X   X  ⌈X  X⌉
                                  ⌊_ _⌋
```

FIGURE 2   *The Effect of Constraints*

hand corner—but there are still many possibilities, depending upon which corner the apportionment starts from and how the first districts are built. There will be more freedom of choice with the first districts than with the last ones, since by virtue of having completed n-minus-one districts, the nth seat will have been completed as well. Sometimes what is left over comes as a surprise to the reapportioner, particularly if the plan starts in the area of greatest interest and leaves the area of least interest to last. For this reason, a plan will evolve iteratively. The lines of the first district must be changed if the last district in the first edition of the plan turns out to be unsatisfactory.

As an example, assume that we have only to meet the requirements of population equality, contiguity, and compactness, but change the distribution of the population in the state slightly so that the district that remains in the lower right-hand corner after we have started in the upper left-hand corner is extremely noncompact. If the districts are constructed in a sequential manner, it is possible to make three of them compact and then discover that the fourth is noncompact. This discovery requires having all the pieces in place, or at least being able to visualize all the pieces being in place at the time the first choices are made. However, this sort of iterative or simultaneous solution of districts is certainly within the capacities of a computer and can even be done quite quickly by an experienced reapportioner.

The range of choices available can be restricted somewhat by the introduction of additional redistricting criteria, such as respect for city and county lines or for communities of interest (see Fig. 2). For instance, if the two people in the upper right-hand corner were in the same city or county, then they would have to be treated as a unit, thus eliminating all combinations that split the two. The more such constraints, the fewer the number of choices available to the computer or to the reapportioner. Were the people in this example grouped into compact three-person counties, there would be a unique solution to the problem. The constraining effect of criteria such as respect for city and county lines is thus the key to the formalist or "good government" solution to gerrymandering. By putting forward formal requirements about shape, respect for city and county lines, and communities of interest, some reformers hope to narrow the permissible range of choices available to the would-be gerrymanderer so that it becomes impossible to draw an unfair plan.

Clearly, to make this strategy of reform work there must be some ordering of the criteria to resolve conflicts that might arise among them. The issues surrounding such conflicts will be considered later. For the moment, assume that there are no such conflicts or that where they exist they can be resolved with some rule. What problems arise with this simple Tabula Rasa approach?

The most obvious one is that by starting from scratch, as in the examples given so far, and ignoring old boundary lines, the result is likely to be a radical change in the electoral system. A number of incumbents, for instance, could lose their seats if the new lines accidentally grouped their homes in the same district, or severed them from the voters and activists with whom each had developed ties over the years. Some might argue that this would be desirable, and that a redistricting process that protected incumbents would be pernicious per se.[2] This view can be criticized on several grounds. First, it ignores the fact that the incumbents have been duly elected by the voters in their old districts, and that a commission or computer program that removed a large number of them from their seats would in effect be depriving those voters of their elected representatives. It is hardly consistent with democratic theory to argue that a government whose legitimacy depends on duly elected representatives should permit their unnecessary and arbitrary removal. It would seem more consistent with the principles of democracy if voters were allowed to the greatest extent possible to keep their elected representatives.

Second, this anti-incumbent posture is inconsistent with the desire of reformers to see the quality of people entering politics improve. If there is a dearth of qualified people in public office in America today, then the threat of arbitrary removal every ten years hardly seems the best way to induce good people to run for office, especially in the elections immediately preceding a reapportionment. Good people will prefer jobs where quality work is rewarded, not where an arbitrary lottery determines the fate of one's career.

Further, radical change is likely to disrupt the organizational ties that have developed over the years among the activists in a given district. The experience of working together on various campaigns often creates an informal local party structure that would be weakened if districts were greatly altered, because the incentive for local activists to cooperate with one another often depends upon sharing common political

---

2. Common Cause, *Toward a System of "Fair and Effective Representation"* (Washington, D.C.: Common Cause, 1977), pp. 21–24.

campaigns. Given the well-documented fragility of the American party system, this blow to grass-roots organization could have serious consequences.[3] It would mean that activists would have to establish new ties, and this would take some time. The failure to nurture stable grass-roots organizations would in turn facilitate the media-centered, direct-mail orientation of American campaigns. Since parties on the left have traditionally depended on organization to offset the wealth and power of parties on the right, a weakening of the grass-roots party structure would also give an advantage to the wealthier, better financed, and more media-oriented candidates of the right.[4]

Finally, a major disruption of the political landscape might also increase the expense of running campaigns and profoundly affect the behavior of incumbents. Taking incumbents out of known areas would force them to spend more money and time on developing name recognition in the newly formed districts. Name recognition for most legislators comes with frequent visits to his district, going to every constituency function he can, doing a great deal of casework, getting out many newsletters, grabbing headlines whenever possible, etc.[5] None of these activities particularly improve the policymaking of legislatures. Unnecessarily removing incumbents from known areas would result in their diverting more staff resources to constituent matters at a time when many observers question whether too many resources are being channeled in that direction already.

A good illustration of the pitfalls of the Tabula Rasa approach is a proposal for California redistricting that was authored by Dr. Richard Morrill of the University of Washington under the auspices of the Rose Institute. Morrill, a geographer, was chosen for his impartiality and his lack of knowledge about California politics, and he drew his lines in accordance with the standard formal criteria of compactness, contiguousness, equal population, and respect for minority communities, but without knowledge of where incumbents lived and how commu-

---

3. See the following works on the subject of the decline of party organizations in America: Austin Ranney, *Curing the Mischief of Faction: Party Reform in America* (Berkeley: University of California Press, 1975); and idem, "The Political Parties: Reform and Decline," in Anthony King, ed., *The New American Political System* (Washington, D.C.: American Enterprise Institute, 1978), pp. 213–247. The relationship between this and party voting is explored in Morris P. Fiorina, "The Decline of Collective Responsibility in American Politics," *Daedalus*, 109:3 (Summer 1980), 25–41.

4. This argument is made in Maurice Duverger, *Political Parties* (London: Methuen, 1954).

5. Richard Fenno, *Home Style: House Members in Their Districts* (Boston: Little, Brown, 1978); and Bruce E. Cain, John A. Ferejohn, and Morris P. Fiorina, "The Roots of Legislator Popularity in Great Britain and the United States" (Social Science Working Paper 288, California Institute of Technology, October 1979).

nities had historically been linked to one another.[6] Even the press release that went with the maps and data for the proposed plan failed to indicate which incumbent was intended to go in which seat. Indeed, the press and the legislators had to spend several days puzzling over the maps before they could figure out how the old seats matched up with the new ones and what would be the fate of various legislators. When the confusion was finally cleared up, the press discovered that the plan had abolished the districts of seven incumbents (six Democrats and one Republican), including that of the newly elected Speaker of the Assembly, the first Black ever to hold that office. In short, the blind impartiality of Morrill's plan would have effectively wiped out one of the most significant racial achievements in the history of California politics!

In addition, several counties objected that Morrill's plan ignored the historical traditions of their areas and tied them with communities of incompatible interests. Contra Costa County, in northern California, was particularly upset that its northern border had been grouped in the same Assembly district with counties across the Bay. The regional newspaper, the *Contra Costa Times*, reacted bitterly:

> In previous editorials, the Times has pointed out the dangers of an overly political approach to reapportionment: the often-demonstrated tendency to gerrymander to protect the interests of parties and individual office holders. Here, we are dealing with the other extreme—and it's just as bad.
>
> In fact, it's worse, because in addition to being illogical, it's impractical. We are, after all, dealing with political subdivisions and politicians, and anyone seriously contemplating a proposal to redraw district boundary lines must take that into consideration.
>
> The Rose Institute plan looks like it was drawn by a computer mole: someone so immersed in the statistics that are the lifeblood of his machine that he never sees the light of day and the reality that goes with it. . . .
>
> Everyone is allowed one mistake, but by letting this monstrosity out of the bag—academic exercise or not—the Rose Institute has discredited itself.[7]

To summarize, the costs of the Tabula Rasa approach are the costs of making radical changes in the electoral system. These are increases in the cost of conducting elections, in the time representatives must spend reestablishing themselves, and in the effort to restore the grassroots strength of local party organizations. These costs must be weighed against the benefits of new faces in the legislature and, for a period of one election at least, some lessening of the incumbency ad-

---

6. "Landmark Model Redistricting Plan Released" (Rose Institute news release), June 16, 1981.

7. "Lots of Promise, Punk Results," *Contra Costa Times*, June 19, 1981.

vantage. The Tabula Rasa method is likely to appeal only to those with a Rationalist's confidence that all the consequences of a radical departure from the status quo can be understood and calculated.

The Incrementalist Method

A redistricting method that requires less confidence in one's ability to predict the consequences of a major departure from the status quo—in short, a more Burkean approach—would be more incrementalist[8] in orientation, respecting the status quo and its nonobvious advantages to a greater degree. The essence of this approach is that each seat starts from a position of surplus or deficit and trades with other seats until it reaches the ideal population level—that is, the level achieved by dividing the total population by the number of seats. A surplus is defined as population in excess of the ideal: for instance, if the ideal population is 100, and a district has 135, then it is over by 35. People in the reapportionment trade call this "overage." A deficit is defined as the amount by which a seat is under the ideal population: if the ideal is 100, and a seat has a population of 75, it is under by 25. This is sometimes called "underage." Districts with a surplus must shed population to get down to the ideal, and those with a deficit must pick up population to get up to the ideal. Hence, there must be trades between the seats that are over and those that are under in order to make the state balance.

This approach has certain advantages over the Tabula Rasa approach. If the status quo districts were originally drawn on sound principles, then this plan, which respects the old lines, will have a leg up on drawing districts that observe county and city lines and respect communities of interest. In addition, the historical and informal ties that have developed among party activists, the representative, and local government officials will not be unnecessarily broken. By means of trades between established districts, the districts can adapt to change while preserving as much of the status quo as possible. In this way, disruption to the electoral system can be minimized.

If the status quo is to be changed in a manner that absolutely minimizes disruption, certain rules must be followed to the extent possible. The first rule is that seats should have to pick up and lose only what they need. If a seat is over by fifty-three people, it should have to lose

---

8. I have borrowed this term from the organizational process literature, where it means determining the direction of an organization by small incremental decisions. See James March and Herbert Simon, *Organizations* (New York: John Wiley, 1958); and Herbert Simon, *Models of Man* (New York: John Wiley, 1957).

no more than fifty-three people; and if it is under by fifty-three people, then it should have to pick up no more than fifty-three people. To pick up or lose more would seem to complicate the trading process and unnecessarily disrupt the status quo.

A second intuitive rule of fairness is that every city and county should get the number of seats that its population supports. If the ideal population is 100, and county A has a population of 200, then it makes sense that it should get two seats. For it to get three seats is to give county A more representation than it deserves, and to give it one seat is to deprive it of a seat. A corollary of this principle is that if a county or city loses population, then it should not gain representation; and conversely, if a county or city gains population, then it should not lose representation. A second corollary is that if a city or county has less than the population required for one seat, then it should not have multiple representation. To the extent possible, city and county splits should occur when the population dictates that there should be more than one seat. This follows from the previous principle that no unit should get more representation than its population merits.

These principles make a lot of intuitive sense both from the viewpoint of a plan that minimizes disruption to the political process and of justice to the individual cities, counties, and seats involved. Though it seems intuitively fair that counties and cities get only the number of representatives that their populations warrant, and that seats should gain and lose only what they need to gain and lose, adhering to these principles is unfortunately not as simple as it might first appear. Reapportionment would be easier if each seat could somehow be considered in isolation from the others. When interest groups and individual members of the legislature present their proposals to the Reapportionment Committee, they will typically say something like "I need ten thousand people to bring my population up to the ideal, and since there are ten thousand people in this area, just give me this area and I will be fine." In a similar way, the press in rural counties will frequently use their county's population as a baseline for admissible change.

For instance, Sonoma County in Northern California had a population of 299,827 according to the 1980 census figures. This meant that it had enough people to justify one whole Assembly district (with an excess within the allowable range of deviation) and half of a State Senate and Congressional seat. The fact that it had been divided into several districts in the past seemed unfair to some residents. In the words of a local newspaper: "We think a good case could be made for Sonoma County being a 'community of interest' and thus have its own legislators. We have the population. Now all we need is a fair-minded Legislature willing to cast partisan politics aside and willing to abide by the

A	50
B	100
C	100
D	150

FIGURE 3 *A Displacement Example—I*

dictates of Proposition 6."[9] The problem was that in order to keep Sonoma whole, other counties such as Marin would have to be split. One
columnist noted the dilemma and commented that for "eight years Sonoma County officials have been moaning about the 1973 redistricting
which chipped the county into three Assembly districts, two Senate
districts and two Congressional districts. And now Marin County leaders are rallying to battle against another havoc of redistricting." "The
trouble is," he observed, "it may be impossible to make both counties
happy. For Marin County to be politically happy, Sonoma must be
halved. And vice versa."[10]

Every shift in reapportionment has a potential effect up and down
the state. Plans for particular seats or regions ignore the needs of seats
in other areas, whereas the final plan cannot ignore the interrelation-
ship between different areas of the state. In the end, there must be a
specified number of districts with populations within a certain range.
To achieve this, the reapportioner must understand the impacts that
changes in one area have on another.

Central to this problem of adjustment is the issue of population ripples and displacement. The concept of a ripple is that population that
is left over or borrowed from one district to help another will cause displacement for neighboring districts. Deficits and surpluses can cascade
from one district to the next until all districts in the state are affected.
Consider a very simple example. Imagine four seats each abutting its
neighbor at one border. The ideal population is 100 people, and they
have an initial population that is distributed as shown in Figure 3. If
each seat is considered in isolation, A needs to pick up fifty people, and
D needs to lose fifty people; B and C are already ideal. The displacement
required by demographic changes is fifty for A and D, and zero for B
and C. Typically, B and C are aware of this fact and have come to expect
that they will not be required to suffer much displacement. They will
consider A's and D's problems to be A's and D's, not theirs. However,
since A and D are not contiguous, a trade cannot be made between

9. "We Should Have Our Own Lawmakers," *Press Democrat* (Santa Rosa), January 14,
1981.

10. Pete Golis, "Capitol Notebook," *Press Democrat* (Santa Rosa), March 29, 1981.

A	75
B	75
C	100
D	150

FIGURE 4   *A Displacement Example—II*

them. It is clear that all four seats must make trades if their populations are to be equalized. This means that B and C must each accept displacements of fifty people each.

The first example illustrates how interdependent changes between contiguous districts can be. However, in the actual process of reapportionment, the legislator's or county's sense of hardship is frequently exacerbated by the compounding of initial deficits upon ripple deficits. This can easily be seen by changing our example slightly. In Figure 4, both A and B are under, C is at the right population, and D is over. A takes twenty-five from B, and by so doing adds to the displacement by that amount. Now B must not only recover the twenty-five people from his initial deficit, but must also get an additional twenty-five people to compensate for the trade with A. The second deficit can be called a re-apportionment deficit, since it is created by the redistricting ripple. Note also that C must now pick up fifty people from D even though C was at the right population. C's displacement is greater than A's even though A starts with an initial deficit while C does not. This will often prove to be quite irksome to C.

In addition, displacement can be aggravated further by strategic trades. A strategic trade is one that is dictated neither by the initial deficit nor by the population ripple. Going back to Figure 2, assume that B was a marginal Republican seat and C was a strong Republican seat. If the B seat were to be made safer, it might take an additional trade of ten people over and beyond the fifty already being exchanged, making the total displacement for both sixty. This obviously increases the burden on C, who will probably resist losing so many people when he had a strong seat to begin with and no initial deficit. In this sort of situation, the perspectives of the reapportioner and the reapportioned are likely to diverge.

Defining displacement as the number of new people a seat must pick up, there are three sources of displacement. They are:

1.   The initial deficit or the number of people needed to get back to the ideal population.

2. The reapportionment ripple, or deficits caused by the absorption of an incumbent's territory by another seat.

3. The strategic trade for the sake of political, racial, or community of interest reasons.

The key to preserving the simple rule of the least change possible is to minimize displacement as much as possible. However, some amount of displacement is necessary for almost every seat. The court causes the first source of displacement (i.e., the initial deficit) by refusing to ignore population shifts. Most actors in the reapportionment drama accept the necessity of this displacement. The second sort of displacement is also caused by the court, but it is a secondary result of initial deficits and surpluses in other seats, and for that reason it is less obvious to participants in the reapportionment process. Depending upon how the ripple is channeled, this form of displacement can be moderated to some degree, but it is rare for a seat to escape ripple displacement completely. The last sort of displacement is the one the reapportioner has the most control over, so that minimizing it is the best way to lessen disruption. However, some strategic displacement is necessary to accomplish even good government goals such as compactness and respect for cities, counties, and communities of interest. For instance, after taking care of the initial deficit and the ripple effects, it might be possible to avoid an additional city split by taking a small number of people from another seat. This adds to the incumbent's burden of displacement, but improves the plan in terms of a good government criterion.

The examples used so far illustrate the linear ripple where the flow of the ripple can only go in two directions. A good real-life example of a linear ripple is the California coastline. Since the court masters in 1973 respected the coastal range as a natural boundary, the reapportioner was constrained to draw districts that are piled one on top of the other in the fashion previously described. The map in Figure 5 shows how the coastal districts 28, 29, 35, 36, and 38 are all divided from the central valley by a range of mountains. Four of these five districts had populations in excess of the ideal and therefore had to lose people. Ignoring for the moment any ripple that might have spilled out of the San Francisco area in the north into the coastal area, it is easy to see how ripple effects add to displacement. If the 28th Assembly District (AD) gave its surplus 22,000 population to the 29th AD, then the 29th would be over by 66,000. The 35th AD would then pick up not only the 19,000 that it needed but an additional 45,000, which would have to be passed on to the 36th AD, putting it over by 78,000 and the 38th over by 108,000, or more than three times its initial surplus. Since respecting communities

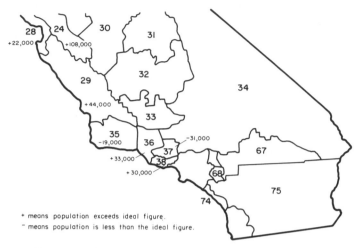

FIGURE 5   *Illustration of Linear Ripple*

of interest ruled out crossing the mountains into the valley to get rid of some of the surplus, the burden of the ripple upon the 38th AD would be quite severe. Had the reapportioners reversed the flow by working south to north, they would only have shifted the burden from the 38th AD to the 28th AD.

The linear ripple along the coast was exacerbated by the fact that the 24th AD was overpopulated by an incredible 108,000, which meant that the 38th AD actually faced a potential displacement of over 200,000. Neither the Democrats nor the Republicans could find a way to lessen displacement in that area, and they disagreed about which direction the ripple flow should go. The Republicans wanted the flow to ripple northwards to pull the Democratic incumbent in the 35th AD into the more Republican areas of San Luis Obispo County, and the Democrats wanted the flow to go south to put the 35th into Ventura. Such are the issues that bitter reapportionment struggles are fought over.

Linear ripples can be the most burdensome because deficits and surpluses cannot be dispersed over as many borders. The more districts that border a particular problem seat—because of its over- or underpopulation—the more the burden can be shared. Consider the example shown in Figure 6. *D* can take from *A, E,* or *G.* By taking from two or more seats, the burden can be lessened for any one neighboring seat, and displacement for reapportionment purposes can be dispersed. This is important, since minimizing reapportionment displacement frees up population for strategic displacement. When operating under some constraint as to the maximum allowable displacement, the less population that must be used to cover initial needs and ripple effects, the more that is then available strategically for protecting city and

A 100	B 100	C 150
D 50	E 100	F 100
G 100	H 100	I 100

FIGURE 6   *Dispersing a Ripple*

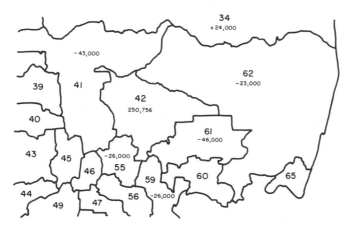

FIGURE 7   *Absorbing Area on Several Borders*

county boundaries, strengthening marginal seats, or avoiding the division of ethnic minorities. Sometimes the restraint of the linear ripple works to the linedrawers' disadvantage by restricting their options in crucial areas.

The point that ripples can be dispersed when districts have multiple borders with other districts is well illustrated by the situation in Los Angeles County just before the 1981 redistricting, when thirty Assembly districts were wholly or partly contained in the county. All but four of these were underpopulated, and two seats had to be collapsed outright. It was decided to collapse the 42nd AD, which meant that 250,756 people had to be absorbed by the surrounding seats. If this had been a linear situation—i.e., had only one district bordered the 42nd—then someone would have had to absorb an enormous displacement (see Fig. 7). However, there were five Assembly districts on the border of the 42nd with initial deficits ranging from 23,000 to 46,000. Collectively, they could absorb 164,000 of the total 250,000 by just taking what they needed, and the further burden of taking the remaining 86,000 could have been dispersed in clumps of 17,000. This would not have been considered a great burden in California, since the rule of thumb was that any amount of displacement less than one-third of the previous district total was not considered excessive. The additional 17,000 added even to the largest initial deficit of 46,000 would still not have violated the one-third displacement rule.

Still, linear ripples have certain advantages. To begin with, it is easier for the reapportioner to predict the impact of proposed changes in a linear situation. Because the flow can go only in one of two directions, the effects of various options are easy to define. Secondly, a linear ripple can be used strategically to force members to make trades that they might otherwise resist. By demonstrating that a trade has to be made because there is a surplus of a certain amount that carries down from the north, one has an irrefutable answer to complaints about displacement. Therefore, the wise reapportioner may arbitrarily define a situation as linear when in fact there are other options. By announcing that a geographical boundary is a constraint on possible options, the legislators' choices can be limited to a manageable level. Sometimes the constraint of the linear situation works to the linedrawers' advantage.

Methods of Containing Ripples

The fact that changes in one part of the state can affect the boundaries of districts in another means that it is potentially costly to make even minor alterations after the initial lines have been drawn. However, given the pluralistic nature of the process, it is almost impossible to avoid last-minute changes. In addition, of course, minimizing ripples requires closer adherence to the simple rules of the incrementalist approach to reapportionment. Therefore, it is useful to find ways of minimizing ripple effects when they are to no one's advantage.

One way of doing this is to divide the state into certain regions and to rule arbitrarily that changes will ripple within those regions only: for example, that there will be six Assembly seats north of San Francisco and Sacramento in northern California, and that none of those seats will spill below that line.[11] Provided that there is enough population to accommodate six seats, all trades among them could be restricted to that area, which would mean that there would be no reason to worry about the effect that a change in any of those seats would have on Los Angeles seats, for instance. Of course, making zones of containment in this way rules out some options and restricts freedom to some degree. The key is to define the zones in a noncontroversial manner so that the options that are foreclosed are not important.

Two methods that are particularly valuable for dealing with strategic

---

11. *Legislature of State of California v. Reinecke*, 10 C.3d 396 (1973).

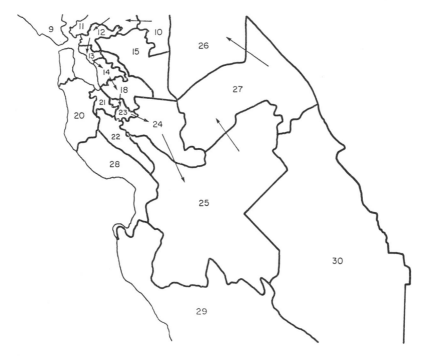

FIGURE 8   *Illustration of Circular Ripple*

displacements are the self-contained ripple and the circular ripple. The self-contained ripple is a compensating trade between two districts that affects no other seats. Trades of this sort—if agreed to by the parties concerned—are easy to absorb. However, such neat trading situations are very rare in the real world, and hence self-contained trades do not usually start from initial or reapportionment population needs as defined earlier. More often, self-contained trades are strategic in nature: i.e., they occur when both seats are at the ideal population and must make some adjustment for reasons other than population shifts.

The circular ripple is a trade between more than two seats that flows around and back to the place of origin so that it does not affect every seat in the state. While initially this may seem implausible, there are real-world examples of this technique. For instance, the arrows in Figure 8 point in a circle between the 24th, 25th, 27th, and 26th ADs and various ADs in Alameda, Contra Costa, and Sacramento counties. In an early version of the Assembly plan, the committee had been unable to keep the 26th AD from spilling over into Stanislaus County, which not only added to its Proposition 6 violations (i.e., an initiative passed in 1978 that required that city and county lines be respected to the extent possible) but which also displeased the incumbent. Towards the

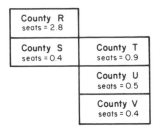

FIGURE 9   *County Lines and Displacement*

end of the negotiations, someone came up with the idea that by diverting one of the Sacramento districts along the delta into Contra Costa—
a large county that was already split several ways—the 26th AD could
be pulled out of Stanislaus County. The problem was how to do this
without changing every district south of the 26th AD.

The solution turned out to be a series of trades, each involving 60,000
people among the six districts in Contra Costa and Alameda, two of the
districts in Santa Clara (including the old 24th), and the 27th and 26th
ADs. By making the trade circle from the 24th to the 27th, the Assembly
avoided having to change the 29th, 30th, and all districts to the south
of them. It also fortuitously linked an Hispanic area in Merced with one
in the Salinas Valley of Monterey County.

A third method of containing ripples is to designate areas of population adjustment that can be sacrificed in order to minimize the splits
of cities and counties. The surpluses and deficits set off by ripples can
make it difficult to hold down the number of city and county splits. Suppose county R has enough population for 2.8 seats, county S below R
has enough for .4 seats, county T below S has enough for .9 seats,
county U below T has enough for .5 seats, and county V below U has
enough for .4 seats. In these circumstances , it seems necessary to split
a large number of counties or cities. County R must take .2 from county
S, which means that S is split between two districts. County T has to
take the residual .2 from county S, so it will have to split .1 off to give to
county U.

However, it is possible to reduce the number of splits by defining
an unincorporated area or a particular city or county as an adjustment
area and accommodating the needs of several seats by multiple divi-
sions of that area. This is illustrative of the principle that if two or three
other cities or counties can be saved from splits by adjustments in another already divided county or city, then there is a definite incentive
to do so.

For example, suppose the alignment of the counties is as shown in
Figure 9. Dividing county S three ways decreased the number of counties that must be split by one. County R picks up .2 of the population

	Seat A	Seat B	Seat C	Seat D
old population	75	75	100	150
new population	90	90	110	110

FIGURE 10 *Using Population Variance to Minimize Displacement*

needed to give it enough for three seats. County T takes .1 from county S to give it enough population for one seat, and the the residual .1 goes to counties U and V to give them one seat together. The trade-off in this case is between splitting S three ways and splitting county T in addition to S.

Another method for minimizing displacement is the strategic use of population variances. The court permits small deviations from the ideal population figure. These permissible deviations tend to be smaller for Congressional districts than for state legislative reapportionments, in which, as will be discussed in Chapter 4, the court has tolerated larger discrepancies from "one man one vote" in order to accommodate other good government considerations. As noted before, if the court put no limit on the size of allowable deviation, then there would be no need for displacement—i.e., there would be no need for reapportionment. By the same reasoning, the larger the allowable deviation, the smaller the displacement has to be. Using the maximum allowable deviation minimizes displacement to the greatest extent possible.

This point can be illustrated very easily by referring back to the previous figure and noting that if there were a permissible deviation of .1— that is, if seats could range between .9 and 1.1 of the ideal population— then both splits could be saved by making use of the maximum allowable deviation. Combining county R with county S would result in a total of 3.2 seats for the two counties. The .2 surplus could be absorbed among three seats without violating the permissible deviation range of .1 by using a distribution of 1.1, 1.1, and 1. County T has enough population for one seat within the permissible range, as do counties U and V combined. By making use of the maximum deviations, all county splits could be avoided.

A further advantage of using allowable deviations is that it minimizes displacement for individual seats. Return for a moment to our previous example of four seats with a distribution as shown in Figure 10. The allowable deviation is 10 percent again, so that seats can range between 90 and 110. Seat A previously took 25 from seat B, and this

TABLE 1   *Displacement Example*

	Plan With Deviations		Plan Without Deviations	
Seat A	Picks Up 25	TD=25	Picks Up 15	TD=15
	Loses 0		Loses 0	
Seat B	Picks Up 50	TD=75	Picks Up 30	TD=45
	Loses 25		Loses 15	
Seat C	Picks Up 50	TD=100	Picks Up 40	TD=70
	Loses 50		Loses 30	
Seat D	Picks Up 0	TD=40	Picks Up 0	TD=40
	Loses 40		Loses 40	

TD = Total Displacement or The Sum of Areas Picked Up and Lost.

meant that seat B had to pick up 50 from seat C. To minimize the disruption caused by reapportionment, seat A could take 15 from seat B rather than 25, giving seat A 90 people. This would decrease the number of new people that are added to seat A as well as the number of people who must be taken out of seat B. Seat B now has 60 people—minus the 15 given to seat A—but would need to pick up only 30 people rather than the 50 people it had to pick up before. This minimizes disruption for it and for seat C, which now starts at 70 rather than at 50. Hence, it must now only take 40 from seat D rather than the 50 it took before, thus lessening the burden for seat D. Seats C and D now have populations of 110. A comparison of the displacements under a plan without deviations and one with deviations demonstrates vividly how population variance can be used to minimize disruption to the system (see Table 1). The major beneficiaries from the population deviation plan are seats B and C. If total displacement is defined as the sum of areas picked up and lost, then the ordering of seats in terms of the amount of total displacement is C, B, D, A. The displacement for seats B and C is reduced by 30 under the plan with population deviations, while there is no reduction for seat D and a reduction of only 10 for seat A.

Once again, it is possible to point to a real-life example. San Francisco County had a population of 677,000 in 1980, but three Assembly seats in it. Since the ideal population was 295,857 and the allowable deviation was plus or minus 2 percent, one of the seats had to be collapsed. However, if each of the remaining two seats took its share of 295,000 people, there would be a residual of 87,000. The seat to the south of them would have had to pick up this remainder as well as an additional 20,000 people from San Mateo County who were in between. A substantial displacement for this seat was thus inevitable, but it could be lessened by almost 12,000 by putting both of the districts wholly contained in San Francisco County at the maximum allowable population of 301,000. This was in fact what the committee did.

It is important to observe that while the use of population variations lessens displacement in the hypothetical example, it does not prevent the violation of the simple rule for fairness in reapportionment. The simple rule was that no seat should have to pick up or lose more than its initial population dictated. The ordering of displacement under the simple rule should be D, A, B, C, since D had a surplus of 50, A and B had deficits of 25, and C had an ideal population. Total displacement should conform as closely as possible to initial surplus or deficit, since it seems fair that seats that are way over or under should change the most and seats that are close to ideal should change the least. However, the ordering of displacement is C, B, D, A, and the ordering of population deviation is D, A, B, C.

Such lack of correspondence between population needs and displacement is a constant problem in reapportionment. The idea that there should be a correspondence is deeply ingrained in the minds of city and county officials, activists, members of the legislature, and the press, and the lack of correspondence is frequently interpreted as *prima facie* evidence of gerrymandering, or of making the process more complicated than it need be, or of politicizing a straightforward technical operation. In fact, there is an inevitable discrepancy between the perspective of fairness held by those individuals whose seats, towns, or counties are being reapportioned and that of those who must do the reapportioning.

The Collapse of Old Seats

A crucial decision in all reapportionments is which seats must be collapsed to make way for new ones. Collapsing seats and creating new ones elsewhere is also, of course, another means of minimizing displacement, since collapsing an old seat solves the problem of many seats in an area being under, and creating a seat solves the problem of many seats in an area being over. Demographic change deter-

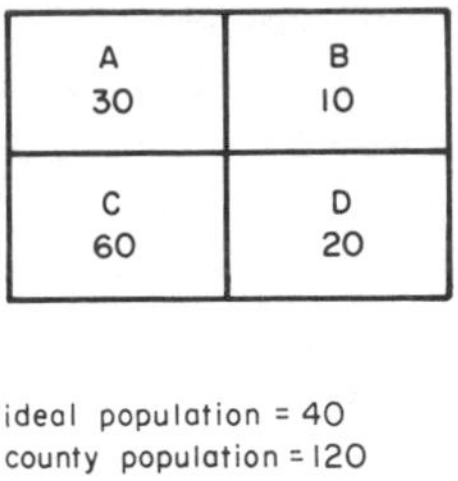

A 30	B 10
C 60	D 20

ideal population = 40
county population = 120

FIGURE 11 *An Example of Seat Collapse*

mines which general regions have seats in excess of their population and must therefore lose representation, but not which seats in those areas to collapse.

To understand better the difficulty of decisions to collapse seats, consider some examples. Imagine a county with enough population for three seats, but with four incumbents and initial populations as shown in Figure 11. Assume further that none of these incumbents either expects to retire at the next election or to run for higher office. Which seat should be collapsed? One possibility is to collapse the seat with the highest population deficit. It could be argued that since Assemblyman *B* has the lowest population, demography dictates that his seat be collapsed: he accounts for the greatest amount of the county deficit and must therefore be sacrificed. Collapsing *C* would be unfair by this principle, since his seat has the highest population and is even in excess of the ideal population. Demography has made him the winner in the reapportionment sweepstakes, and he should be entitled to reap the rewards.

Obviously, this rule has a certain appeal. It allows one to argue that changes are mandated by the impersonal forces of demography, forces that are not controlled by politicians or parties. The reapportioner does not have to take responsibility for the choice of whom to collapse, since the choice is thrust upon him by circumstances beyond his or anyone else's control.

However, there are problems with this rule. To begin with, demographic counts may be inaccurate and biased. Critics of the census have argued that the enumeration procedures adopted by the census systematically undercount minorities and the poor.[12] Those who fear discovery by the authorities, non-English-speaking citizens, those living in back-room apartments, and the like, will be counted more inaccurately than middle-class, English-speaking individuals who live in separate dwellings. The census also designates the occupants of hotels or

---

12. *Conference on Census Undercount* (Washington, D.C.: U.S. Department of Commerce, July 1980).

ships as living in the area in which they happen to have been enumerated, so that the population count may change drastically in short periods of time. At the aggregate level of a general region or area, the biases may be manageable, but they are much more troublesome for an individual seat.

Also, the smaller the population differences between the seats, the more arbitrary and possibly unfair the rule will seem. If there is an error factor in the population count of plus or minus 5 percent, and if the seat that it is proposed to collapse has the highest deficit only by some very small amount, then the rule seems less justifiable. For instance, if one legislator is under by 46,000 and the other by 45,000, then the rule will seem less justifiable than if one is under by 46,000 and the other by 5,000. The former is a difference within the 5 percent error range, while the latter falls well outside that range.

Another possible objection is that the rule does not serve any function or goal of representation. The representative with the smallest deficit or the highest surplus is not necessarily the best legislator, nor the most loved by his constituents, nor the least corrupt, nor the most principled.

Though the highest population deficit rule is certainly a possibility, it is by no means perfect, and it is therefore useful to consider another, such as collapsing the least senior member in the group. This is, of course, a policy that is widely followed in many types of organizations. The usual justifications are that it keeps the most experienced and qualified members in the organization, that it rewards years of service, and that it forces adjustments on those who can respond to adverse circumstances most easily—i.e., the younger and less well-established members. The objections are obvious: that there is no necessary connection between ability and experience, that the object of representation is not to reward long service but to ensure high-quality service, and that it is not obvious that adjustment is less easy for older politicians with higher name identification and wider connections in the political and business worlds.

A third rule, which changes the focus slightly, is that collapses should be dictated by aggregate, and not by individual, justice. *Aggregate*, in this sense, means justice for some group, typically a political party or an ethnic, racial, religious, or occupational group. The most obvious version of this sort of rule is an equal or proportionate sharing of collapses. If four seats are to be collapsed, then two should be Democrats and two should be Republicans. Or, if Democrats outnumber Republicans by a two-to-one margin, then the seats should be collapsed at a two-to-one rate, and the fourth made an open marginal. The collapsed seats could be tied to the creation of new ones, so that if a Democratic seat were collapsed in one area, it would be allowed to reemerge in another. The aggregate approach has much to recommend it, since its logic is at least related to the goals and norms of fair representation. However, a cost is that it ignores crucial individual-level information— this person is a good legislator, or has been very loyal to the leadership, etc.—for the sake of aggregate fairness, and once again reasonable people can disagree about the desirability of this.

A good real-life example of a situation in which a seat had to be collapsed is the Bay Area of northern California. It was noted earlier that San Francisco County in 1980 had a population of 677,000, which was sufficient for two seats with a remainder of 87,000, but had three Assembly incumbents in it, including the present and former Speakers of the Assembly. That made the decision to collapse a seat very much a political decision, in the sense that it affected the partisan balance of the state and involved a value judgment over which reasonable people could disagree. If a seat from one party were collapsed and no compensating seat were created elsewhere in the state, then this would amount to a net shift of two to the other party. Even if a compensating seat were created, many people would regard the trade as unfair, since the exchange of an old seat with an incumbent for a new seat without an incumbent is not equal from an electoral standpoint. The incumbency advantage would be lost with a corresponding rise in the probability of losing a seat. The resolution to this problem did not reside in some mutually agreed-upon rule, but in negotiations and bargaining between the members involved.

It would seem, then, that there is no clear and unassailable rule to apply in these situations. Obviously, it is desirable for there to be a consensus on what particular rule is fair. Short of such consensus, reapportioners may adopt one or another of more "practical" rules, such as "collapse the seat that will cause the least number of defections from the coalition in support of the reapportionment bill." Political solutions such as these will be explored in a later chapter.

Conclusion

Even if the myriad other criteria and values that various participants bring to reapportionment are wholly ignored, inevitable problems of equity arise from the most basic task of trying to make districts equal in size. Since it proves impossible to adhere to the most intuitive principles of justice with respect to displacement, those who judge the equity of a plan from the perspective of their own population needs will feel aggrieved. At the same time, old districts will have to be collapsed to make way for new ones, and this, too, will cause disagree-ments. A computer can be programmed to make such choices, but the criteria it uses will be no less arbitrary than criteria scribbled on a legal pad at some late-night legislative session.

3

Aesthetic Considerations

Most people, if asked, would say that they can tell a gerry-mander when they see one. The term *gerrymander* itself derives from the salamander shape drawn over the map of a weirdly contorted Massachusetts district in 1812. Fingers, slivers, jagged edges, noncontiguous census tracts, and complicated shapes are the images associated with a gerrymander, whereas compact forms such as circles and squares are associated with good government. Consequently, the press and the public tend to measure the worth of a reapportionment plan by its shape. A plan with compact forms is assumed to be in the public interest, and one with noncompact forms is assumed to be in the self-interest of the majority party or of incumbents generally. This is why proposals for reform usually include provisions for compactness. Common Cause, for instance, recommends that "in no case shall the aggregate length of all districts exceed by more than five percent the shortest possible aggregate length of all the districts under any other plan consistent with the population and political subdivision standards."[1]

The popular concern for compactness has several sources. One is the legacy of earlier periods in history when communication and transportation were more difficult. Compactness guaranteed that representatives could meet with their constituents with relative ease and that constituents could easily visit their representatives. This consideration is not as relevant as it once was. Travel over large and sprawling areas is no longer a formidable task. Moreover, the inconvenience of representing a large area can be lessened in fairly simple ways: the represen-

---

1. Common Cause, *Toward a System of "Fair and Effective Representation"* (Washington, D.C.: Common Cause, 1977), p. 51.

tative can have several district offices, he can travel about in a mobile van, or he can delegate much of the day-to-day dealings with constituents to district staff. Furthermore, since a great deal of contact between representatives and their constituents occurs over the phone and by mail, people do not necessarily have to visit the district office at all to get what they want.[2] In any case, whatever additional costs large sprawling districts entail are borne by the representative himself, since it is he who in his quest to establish visibility will have to do the commuting or make the special arrangements—such as renting a plane—to get where he needs to be.

Thus, the historical reason for compact districts—to lessen transportation and communication costs—is less applicable in the modern era; and to the extent that it is, it is less so for constituents than it is for their representatives. Today, the most common argument for compactness is for its indirect value. That is, it is maintained that compactness facilitates the realization of other good government goals. For instance, it is sometimes said that compactness helps preserve communities of interest, whereas sprawling districts often tie together disparate communities of interest. Coastal and desert, urban and rural, and mountain and valley interests, for example, are sometimes mingled to help particular incumbents. Requiring districts to be compact might make it harder for the reapportioner to reach across communities for such purposes. For the same reason, compactness may serve as a preventive against political gerrymandering. Observing compact lines, it is alleged, ensures greater fairness because it make contortions for political advantage more difficult. Compactness may even save cities and counties from being split for political purposes and protect minorities from racial gerrymandering, so the argument goes. In all these ways, then, compactness allegedly encourages compliance with other good government criteria.

Since the argument for the indirect value of aesthetic criteria hinges crucially on the connection between compact shapes and good government principles, it merits further exploration. The strongest case for aesthetic criteria could be made if the connections between shape and other values were necessary—i.e., if compact shapes always produced better political and racial distributions, preserved communities of interest, and promoted the observance of city and county lines. If this were true, then requiring compactness would always make the plan better from the standpoint of good government criteria. If a necessary connection cannot be established, then there should at least be a strong

---

2. Bruce E. Cain, John A. Ferejohn, and Morris P. Fiorina, "Casework Service in Great Britain and the United States" (Social Science Working Paper 359, California Institute of Technology, November 1980).

positive association between compactness and the other criteria; and where there is none, compactness should not conflict with the other criteria. In such a case, while compactness would not always ensure the preservation of good government values, it would usually ensure them and never—or almost never—obstruct them.

A third possibility is that compactness sometimes promotes and sometimes obstructs good government criteria, but this would mean that the compactness requirement would have to be judged on its intrinsic merits, or observed selectively. If compactness were intrinsically good, then its occasional conflict with other good government values could be tolerated. It would simply require judgment as to which is the more important good in a particular case. If compactness had no intrinsic value, then it would have to be applied judiciously: in other words, form compact districts when this promotes good government, but not otherwise. However, this makes compactness almost unnecessary, since it amounts to saying, "observe the other criteria regardless of the shapes that are produced."

The last possibilities are that compactness usually or always conflicts with other good government criteria. Obviously, if either of these were the case, then far from being a desirable criterion, compactness would be highly undesirable unless it had some strong counterbalancing intrinsic value (see Table 2). The case for the indirect value of compactness must therefore be made in terms of the first or second proposition: that there is either a necessarily or usually positive relation between shape and good government criteria.

A Hypothetical Case

One way to explore the logical relation between compactness and good government values is to examine a hypothetical example. Figure 12 shows a hypothetical state with twenty-four inhabitants. We assume that the X individuals belong to one party and that the Y individuals belong to the other. The X individuals with the m subscripts are minorities. The state has regional variations, so the symbol ˆ represents mountains and the left-hand edge of the figure is a coastal area. The dotted lines are county lines, the dashed lines are city lines, and the solid lines are the district boundaries. There are eight seats in the legislature, and the districts must be equally populated with no deviations.

Using the Tabula Rasa approach and starting in the upper left-hand corner, a series of compact districts is drawn from top to bottom. Each of these eight districts will be either square or rectangular with no jag-

TABLE 2   *Possible Connections Between Compact Shapes and Good Government Values*

NECESSARY POSITIVE CONNECTION	If Compactness Always Promotes Good Government Values	Then Direct Value Unnecessary
USUAL POSITIVE CONNECTION	If Compactness Usually Promotes Good Government	Then Direct Value Unnecessary
NO SYSTEMATIC CONNECTION	If Compactness Sometimes Promotes and Sometimes Obstructs	Then Direct Value Necessary
USUAL NEGATIVE CONNECTION	If Compactness Usually Obstructs Good Government Values	Then Direct Value Necessary
NECESSARY NEGATIVE CONNECTION	If Compactness Always Obstructs Good Government Values	Then Direct Value Necessary

ged edges, slivers, or curvy forms. The compactness of the districts is, of course, facilitated in this example by the symmetry of the state shape—drawn as a rectangle—whereas in the real world, states themselves can be oddly shaped. Each of the eight model districts has three people in it, so there is no population deviation (see Figs. 12 and 13).

The symmetry of the shapes in the model plan masks some disturbing features. To begin with, although the Y individuals constitute over one-third of the population (i.e., nine out of twenty-four), they have only one seat. In short, their ratio of seats to population is highly skewed. In addition, the minorities are split so that they cannot control a seat although they have enough people to do so. The city and county lines are in several places violated where they are noncompact. Finally, the coastal areas are linked with the valley and urban areas in several places, making it very hard for them to lobby effectively for their environmental concerns.

1. The Remedy for Partisan Skew

The first problem is how to redress the imbalance between the size of the Y population and the number of seats they control. Given the dispersion of the Y population, compact districts do not accurately reflect

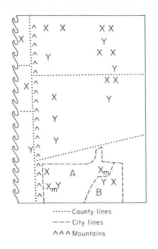

······ County lines
—— City lines
∧∧∧ Mountains

FIGURE 12 *Hypothetical State*

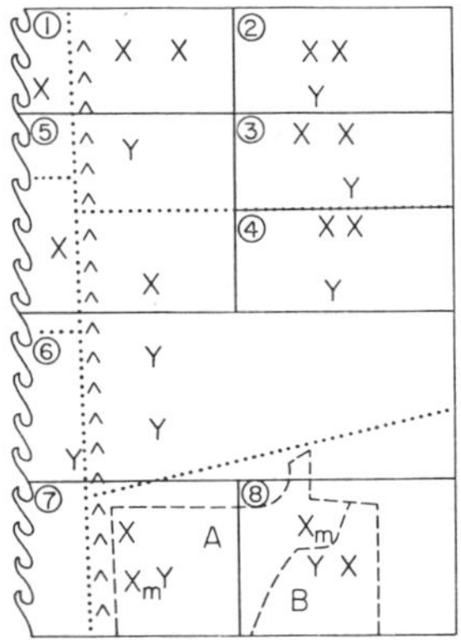

FIGURE 13 *Model Plan with Compact Lines*

their numbers. The kind of partisan skew represented in this example is by no means rare. It is well known that the type of electoral system used in this country is not as fair to dispersed minority parties as is a proportional representation system such as that used in various European democracies, which assigns seats to parties based on their proportion of votes.[3] It is always possible for a minority party to be so dispersed throughout the polity that it comes close to winning several seats but loses them all.[4] In fact, some observers see this as a desirable

---

3. Douglas W. Rae, *The Political Consequences of Electoral Laws* (New Haven: Yale University Press, 1967), pp. 26–39.

4. Imagine, for example, four districts in which party *A* receives 51 percent of the vote and party *B* receives 49 percent. Despite getting 49 percent of the vote, party *B* gets no seats.

feature of single-member, simple-plurality systems. By exaggerating the strength of the majority party, the system ensures a large enough legislative majority to get bills passed.[5] It is a hedge against legislative immobilism.

Though the U.S. electoral system is thus inherently unfair to minorities when they are geographically dispersed, it is apparent that the way the lines are drawn can either increase or lessen the inherent majority bias. The compact option in the simple example exaggerates the strength of the majority party X individuals and the weakness of the minority party Y individuals. Such is the importance of the way lines are drawn that the ability of the minority party to achieve representation hinges crucially on which option is pursued.

For example, the district lines can be adjusted to increase the strength of the minority. In effect, adjusting the district shape compensates for the initial dispersion of the minority party population. The reason the Y individuals have so few seats in Figure 1 is that the Ys in seats 2 and 3 are cut off from each other, as are those in 4 and 5 and those in 7 and 8. In the one seat they hold—seat 6—they are concentrated so that they have more than the simple majority needed to win the seat. To give the Y population control of four seats, the following steps would be necessary:

1. Put the Y from seat 3 with the Y from seat 4.

2. Put the Y from seat 2 with the Y from seat 5.

3. Put the X from seat 5 with the Ys from seat 6.

4. Put the Y from seat 7 with the Y from seat 8.

The shapes that result are by most definitions noncompact, or what is known in the trade as "ugly" (see Fig. 14). The situation has changed from one seat for the Y individuals to four seats by making the Y districts as dispersed as the Y population. This indicates dramatically the potential effect of line drawing upon the partisan distribution of a state. It can change the Y population from a minority position to one of political equality, but not without some attendant costs. First, the district lines still cross county and city lines. Secondly, they violate communities of interest by linking the coastal and noncoastal areas in the new seat 6. The urban areas of cities A and B are linked with nonurban areas in seats 7 and 8. Moreover, the minorities Xm are left unrepresented by the plan, since their population is still divided between seats 7 and 8. Most importantly, however, allowing the Ys to have a fourth seat gives them more seats than they deserve. They only have nine out of twenty-

---

5. Rae, *Political Consequences*, pp. 74–76.

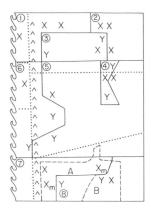

FIGURE 14 *Extreme Partisan Remedy*

four individuals in the entire population, but the new plan gives them 50 percent of the seats. In short, this remedy is excessive.

A more moderate proposal for partisan distribution (although one that still ignores the other criteria) would be the following. Starting once more from the original "aesthetic" reapportionment:

1. Put the *Y* from seat 2 with the *Y* from seat 5 and with the *X* from seat 1 rather than the *X* from seat 3, as in the first revision.

2. Put the remaining *X*s from seat 2 with one *X* from seat 1, and put the remaining *X* from seat 1 with the two *X*s from seat 5.

3. Put the *Y*s from seats 7 and 8 together with an *X* from one of those seats.

This gives the *Y*s three seats out of eight, which is exactly proportionate to their population distribution. The lines are not as "ugly" as in our first revision, although they are by no means as compact as in the original set (see Fig. 15).

2. A Remedy for Communities of Interest

The first observation about shapes, then, is that compact forms are not necessarily fairer in a partisan sense than are noncompact forms. Now, a second characteristic of the American electoral system must be considered: namely, American legislative districts are geographically based, and each representative has exclusive responsibility for one of these districts. By contrast, representatives in a proportional representation system are elected at large or in big multi-member districts. Typically, voters in such a system choose from alternative party lists. The

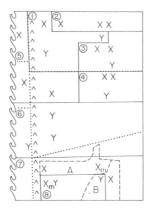

FIGURE 15 *Moderate Partisan Remedy*

number of candidates elected from those lists is meant to be commensurate with the party's share of the vote. No representative in such a system has sole responsibility for representing a particular geographic area. The mandate to represent distinct geographic interests in single-member systems is clearer when the districts are more homogeneous— i.e., when coastal communities are not thrown together with inland industrial areas, when agricultural interests are separated from urban, and so forth. This is the underlying rationale for the idea of preserving communities of interest in reapportionment. While the Supreme Court has not accorded the principle of respect for communities of interest the same standing that it has given to the principle of equal population, the logic of our electoral system makes it desirable to preserve these communities of interest wherever possible.[6]

Here, too, a passion for compactness can be an impediment. Consider our hypothetical state again. The coastal area in it has been very narrowly defined, but there are real-life situations in which one does not have to travel very far inland before encountering attitudes on issues such as the environment that are very different from those held by individuals living along the coast. In the previous example, a seat that was purely coastal—or even mostly coastal—would be very long and narrow in shape, whereas seats that cut across the mountains to take in coastal areas would be more compact but would dilute the voice of the coastal interests.

A second community-of-interest problem in the example is the urban-rural division. There are two cities at the bottom of the state that

6. See *Reynolds v. Sims*, 377 U.S. 533 (1964), which considered the issue of bases for representation other than equal population and dismissed the idea, saying that the only legitimate basis was substantially equal districts.

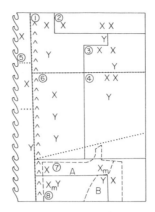

FIGURE 16 *Communities of Interest Respected*

were kept as urban districts in the first plan, but were put together with nonurban areas in the revision that would have given the *Y* population four seats. Mixing urban and rural interests can create a situation in which the more populous urban areas swamp out the less populous rural areas. Preserving urban interests in a manner compatible with the compactness requirement is somewhat easier than preserving rural interests. This is because urban areas, being more densely populated, will need less area to achieve their required populations than will rural districts. Compact and homogeneous rural seats are harder to construct, since by definition there will be fewer people per unit of area. This being the case, the reapportioner who wants to maximize compactness will be sorely tempted to combine urban areas with rural areas, thus reducing the total area needed to construct a seat. But maximizing compactness in this way diminishes homogeneity.[7]

A plan that observes the communities of interest in our model state (see Fig. 16) would do the following:

1.   Unite the coastal *X*s from seat 5 with the coastal *Y* from seat 6.

2.   Keep the two urban seats wholly contained so that they are not tied in with the coastal population.

3. The Remedy for Minority Dilution

The third flaw in the original aesthetically pleasing district plan is that

---

7. The claim before *Baker v. Carr* was that rural interests should be protected by districts that were undersized in rural areas and oversized in urban and suburban areas. The distortions caused by this are outlined in Gordon E. Baker, *The Reapportionment Revolution* (New York: Random House, 1967).

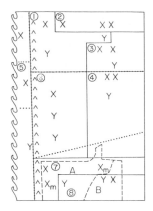

FIGURE 17 *Minorities United*

it divided the minority community in a manner that deprived it of a seat. As with minority parties, so with minority groups: to the extent that support is efficiently concentrated, the minority group will not suffer underrepresentation; to the extent that the minority group is dispersed, it will suffer underrepresentation.

The division of the minority population can be remedied by putting the Xm from seat 8 with the Xm from seat 7. In order to preserve the earlier move to give the Y party proportionate strength in the legislature, this Xm population should be combined with the X individual in seat 7, thereby allowing the Ys to control one of the urban seats (see Fig. 17).

4. The Remedy for City and County Splits

Finally, the quest for compactness is made more difficult when city and county boundaries are not compact themselves. Several states have adopted constitutional amendments that require reapportionment plans to respect city and county lines to the extent possible.[8] One justification for these provisions is a version of the community-of-interest argument: since cities and counties are communities with special concerns, dividing them makes it harder to articulate those concerns. Some observers have also argued that neatly interlocking local, state, and

---

8. California, for example, passed Proposition 6, which adopted from the California Supreme Court's reapportionment criteria in 1975 the following: equality of population; contiguousness of districts; maintenance of city and county boundaries and of the state's basic geographical regions to the extent it could be done consistently with other criteria; and using the decennial census as the basis for reapportionment.

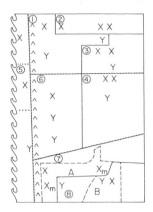

FIGURE 18 *Final Plan*

Congressional lines lessen confusion in the minds of the voters and facilitate cooperation between officials at all levels.[9]

Whatever the merits of constitutional provisions mandating respect for city and county lines, the relevant point is that they will sometimes cause districts to be noncompact. Recall that the dotted lines in the hypothetical state represent county lines and that the dashed lines represent city lines. If county lines are to be respected, new seats 4 and 6 must be wholly contained in one county. The new forms are less compact but more consistent with city and county line criteria. The counties at the top are larger than one district in size, so it is necessary to divide them both to create the surplus seats. But it is possible to preserve the city and county lines in our urban area by drawing two seats that are wholly contained in the county. It is common, however, to find that cities annex in very peculiar—and often politically shady—ways, and this is reflected in the nonpopulated appendage of the hypothetical city line. If there were projected growth in that area, it is quite possible that the city would insist that its projected border be respected even though no one presently lived in the area (see Fig. 18).

A comparison of the original aesthetic plan with all the changes that have been made so far in the interests of good government is striking. Though the new lines are less compact, they better satisfy the other good government criteria. As before, there are still eight seats with three voters in each, but the new lines have given the Y individuals control of three out of the eight seats, which is exactly proportional to their population. The minority group Xm also has gained control of a seat, and the new plan conforms better to county and city lines. Finally, the

---

9. This was one of the criteria adopted by the court masters in California in 1973. See *Legislature of the State of California v. Reinecke*, 10 C.3d 396 (1973), at 412–413.

new lines preserve the distinction between coastal, urban, and rural communities of interest to a greater extent than did the old.

Hypothetical Cases and Real-World Constraints

The hypothetical case just discussed demonstrates that it is fairly easy to construct an example in which compactness conflicts with other good government norms. It is evident that there is no necessary logical relation between compactness and other criteria. Still, it is possible that even though there is no logical relation between the two, there is nonetheless an empirical connection. In other words, there could be a happy coincidence between compact lines and proportional outcomes for minority groups and parties, respect for city and county lines, and the preservation of communities of interest. From the point of view of salvaging the indirect value of compactness as defined earlier, it would not matter much whether the connection were logical or empirical. The relevant consideration is simply that it happens.

In order for this happy coincidence to occur, the following conditions would have to hold:

1.   A fair distribution of partisan support for both parties would have to be compact.

2.   City and county lines would have to be compact.

3.   Minority communities would have to be concentrated.

4.   Communities of interest would have to be compact or divisible into wholly contained compact forms.

The first proposition simply reiterates the point that single-member simple plurality systems will produce especially disproportionate results if the minority party's support is either too concentrated or too dispersed. No doubt, states vary a great deal in this regard, but it seems likely that adherence to a strict compactness requirement would hurt the minority parties in most states, since it would take away a remedy for dealing with wasted strength. In California, for instance, both parties have areas where their strength is too dispersed and other areas where it is too concentrated. The problem is especially acute for the Democrats, who are too highly clustered in urban areas and too dispersed in rural and suburban areas; but to a lesser extent, Republicans are too highly concentrated in suburban areas and too dispersed in urban and certain rural areas. True efficiency for both would require that inner-city areas be annexed to outer-city areas, but that would result in very elongated and noncompact districts.

Consider, for instance, the case of Los Angeles County, where the pattern of partisan division is quite stark (see Fig. 19).The Republican seats ring the periphery of the county, while the Democrats hold the seats in the inner-city area. The question of what constitutes an efficient level of strength will be considered later. For the moment, assume that seats with Democratic registrations of 70 percent or more are inefficiently Democratic and that seats with Republican registrations of greater than 45 percent are inefficiently Republican. Even ignoring respect for communities of interest, for city lines, and for the integrity of minority neighborhoods, it is clear that making some of these seats efficient would require noncompact districts. The Democratic seats in the center of the county—the 48th, 49th, 47th, and 56th—share no common border with Republican seats and are themselves surrounded by safely Democratic seats. Those Democratic seats that do have common boundaries with the Republicans—for example, the 39th, 40th, 43rd, 45th, and 46th—are already so close to an efficient level of strength that trades between them and the seats in the Republican periphery would make the former marginal or worse and the latter efficient without affecting the efficiency of inner Democratic seats such as the 48th. The inefficiency of the California Democratic party is such that if it were to become the minority party, the electoral system would hurt it significantly. It also means that if the Republicans wanted to gerrymander the state in a partisan way, they would be in a better position to do so, given the existing distribution of partisan support.

The second condition for the "happy coincidence" to be achieved is that city and county lines would themselves have to be compact. While this may be true in some states, it is certainly not the case everywhere. In California, for instance, cities and counties have noncompact lines. Recently incorporated Californian cities are particularly good examples of this problem. In his study of municipal incorporation in Los Angeles, Gary Miller found that city lines were determined by a variety of political motives. The city of Industry, for example, incorporated an industrial area so that it would not be annexed to nearby cities attempting to increase their tax bases. The effect is that Industry provides a minimal amount of services, since it has practically no residents. Nearby cities— several of which have sizable poor populations and high service needs—are deprived of a potential industrial tax base. Miller concluded that this pattern of incorporation by rich communities to avoid annexation with—and hence taxation by—poor communities is quite prevalent in Los Angeles.[10]

---

10. Gary Miller, *Cities by Contract: The Politics of Municipal Incorporation* (Cambridge: MIT Press, 1980).

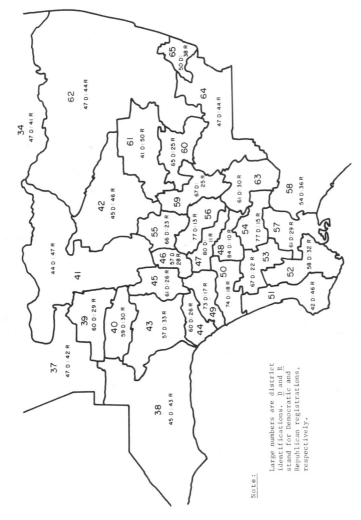

Note:

Large numbers are district identifications. D and R stand for Democratic and Republican registrations, respectively.

FIGURE 19 *Partisan Distribution of Assembly Seats in Los Angeles County*

The point is that these politically motivated incorporations have not been compact or symmetrical. The city of Industry looks like the hull of a boat. The city of Monrovia has a narrow appendage with less than a hundred people in it that is connected to the main body of the city by a drainage ditch. The city of Los Angeles itself is connected to its port area in San Pedro by a narrow corridor that skirts the cities of Carson and Torrance. Pasadena has a stovepipe extension to the north which protrudes up through a reservoir area into unincorporated county land. Commerce, like the city of Industry, is a largely unpopulated industrial area with many jagged sides. The city of Riverside is a mosaic that rivals the most creative efforts of gerrymanderers over the years. This list could be indefinitely extended.

If cities and counties are not always or even usually compact, then it will be harder to make districts look compact. The reapportioner will be forced to choose between straightening out lines at the expense of splitting parts of cities and counties, on the one hand, and preserving the city and county lines at the expense of compactness, on the other. An attempt to preserve compactness would probably necessitate a reevaluation of what constitutes a city or county split. If the separation of even small amounts of territory from a governmental unit is defined as a split, then it will be extemely difficult to improve districts aesthetically. A less strict definition of a split—one that tolerated separation of a certain percentage of population or area—would make the reapportioner's task much simpler.

The third condition for a happy coincidence of aesthetic and other good government criteria is that minority communities should not be dispersed. As noted already, minority communities, like minority parties, cannot afford to be inefficiently distributed under our electoral system. Of the two sorts of maldistribution, a minority is far better off being overly concentrated than overly dispersed. Hence, as long as the minorities in a given state are concentrated geographically, the bias against them will not be too great. If the state has very dispersed minority communities, then the bias will be substantial.

California is an interesting case in this regard, since it has both dispersed and concentrated minority communities. The Black community in California is concentrated in a few areas: south-central Los Angeles, Pasadena, parts of San Francisco, Oakland, and Richmond. The Hispanic community, by contrast, is dispersed both within the urban areas and over the rural areas. The Los Angeles Hispanic community is centered in East L.A., but spills into a number of communities in the East San Gabriel Valley, downtown L.A., and the San Fernando Valley. There are also large concentrations of Latinos in San Diego, parts of

FIGURE 20   *Los Angeles County, 1980*
                              Black Population

Orange County, the Imperial Valley, the Salinas Valley, San Jose, the
Central Valley, and Ventura.[11]

The contrast between the concentration of the Black community and
the dispersion of the Hispanics in California is graphically displayed in
Figures 20 and 21. These maps show the percentage of the population
that is Black or Hispanic by census tract in Los Angeles County. The
lighter color indicates a smaller concentration, and the darker a larger
concentration. The pictorial contrast is sharp. The Black community is
largely confined to south-central Los Angeles and the Pasadena area,
while Hispanics are spread over a large number of communities. There
are many tracts that have a 5–25 percent Hispanic population, but far
fewer tracts with that percentage of Blacks. By contrast, there are many
more tracts that are less than 5 percent or greater than 40 percent Black.

---

11. Specifically, the census figures are as follows:

	Blacks	*Hispanics*	*Total Population*
San Diego Division	91,853	219,181	1,485,749
Los Angeles City	505,191	815,984	2,966,438
Orange County	25,285	286,331	1,937,570
Imperial County	2,310	51,384	92,110
Pasadena	24,594	21,590	119,374
Oakland	159,234	32,491	339,288
Richmond	35,799	7,713	74,676
San Jose	29,157	140,566	636,396
Salinas	1,550	34,694	92,345

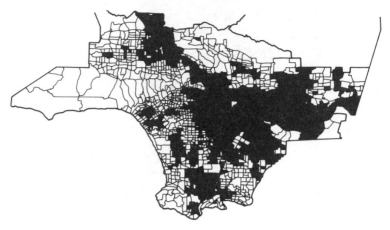

FIGURE 21   *Los Angeles County, 1980*
                             Hispanic Population

Ironically, the greater segregation of the Black community has been
beneficial politically. Since the Black community is not as dispersed as
the Asian or Hispanic communities in California, it was easier for the
California Supreme Court, when it took over the job of reapportionment in 1973 (because the legislature could come to no agreement), to
create seats that were winnable by Black candidates than it was to create
seats that were winnable by Asian or Hispanic candidates. The Hispanics made gains in 1981 because the California legislature had much less
concern for compactness.

The last of the conditions that would have to hold is that communities of interest would have to be compact or at least divisible into compact seats. Obviously, the reapportioner is constrained by the shape of
the terrain he or she has to work with. If valleys, coastal areas, deserts,
and urban areas are compact and symmetrically shaped, that is just
good luck. However, if the community of interest has a sufficiently
large population, it may be possible to divide it into symmetric forms.
Even so, a purely rural seat will always tend to be dispersed in area
because of the low ratio of population to territory. The more homoge-
neously rural the seat is, the more likely that it will be a sprawling
district.

To illustrate this point, Figure 22 shows the percentage of an Assembly seat (requiring 295,857 residents) each county should get, given its
population. Thus, Monterey with its population of 290,444 had 98 percent of the population required for one Assembly district in California.
Only sixteen out of the total fifty-eight counties in California had
enough population in 1980 for at least one seat, and Los Angeles alone
had enough population for twenty-five seats. As a consequence, dis-

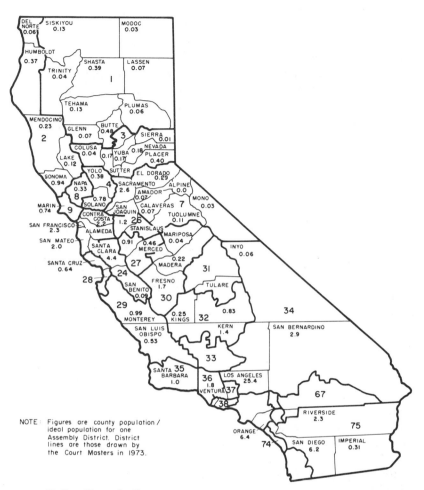

FIGURE 22 *Seat Shares by County*

tricts composed of rural counties can be quite large—for instance, the 1st, 3rd, 7th, 34th, and 75th. The sizes of these rural districts could have been lessened in 1980 by adding to them more population from the urban areas of Sacramento, Los Angeles, San Diego, and Bakersfield, but this would have meant trading off the homogeneity of the rural district for compactness. For instance, the area of the 34th could have been reduced by giving Inyo County to the 31st, the remainder of Kern County to either the 32nd or the 33rd, and then pushing the 34th further into the suburbs of Los Angeles County, but this would have made the seat less rural in character and given a suburban politician a base from which to run.

Summing up, there is not only no necessary relation between aesthetic considerations and other good government criteria, there is no happy empirical coincidence, either. The conditions that would produce such a happy coincidence are very stringent, and the California example shows how in one major state they certainly did not pertain. The conclusion one has to draw is that there is not a great deal to be said for the indirect value of compactness, since there is no reason to expect that it is a useful facilitator of other good government criteria. If there is any reason to retain compactness as a reapportionment guideline, it would have to be for its direct or intrinsic value.

The Intrinsic Value of Compactness Reconsidered

Does compactness per se have any intrinsic value? One possibility—that compact districts lessen transportation and communication costs—has been considered already. It might seem that there are no others. Surely, no one would argue that compact districts produce more conscientious, thoughtful representatives than noncompact districts. However, there is one feature of compactness that is absolutely central to the working of Anglo-American electoral systems, and that is the contribution that compactness makes to stability.

One of the strongest arguments for a geographically based, simple plurality system such as the one in the U.S. is that by preventing the proliferation of small parties, it increases the strength of the winning party. In other words, the fact that the rules discriminate against dispersed minority parties and groups, it can be argued, is an advantage. Anglo-American electoral rules restrict entry by small parties into the legislature because they discriminate against dispersed strength. This keeps right- and left-wing extremist groups out of the legislature. It forces interest groups to articulate their demands through the two major parties rather than form their own splinter parties. It exaggerates the strength of the winning party in the legislature, and so makes large legislative majorities possible. Proportional representation (PR) systems, by contrast, give each group above a certain threshold size its share of seats. This tends to cause the number of parties in the political system to proliferate and to give extreme groups a public forum. Governments in PR systems tend to be coalitional, because no one party has enough seats to form a legislative majority by itself.

Of course, electoral rules are not the only factor that explains two-party stability, but they are a major contributing factor. The effect of intentionally making districts noncompact is to undermine the bias in the rules against dispersed minorities and by so doing to weaken the stabilizing feature of single-member systems. Districts that are intentionally noncompact will concentrate a minority group or party even though their residential patterns are electorally inefficient. By reaching out and uniting individuals of the same party, race, or ethnic group, it is possible to give them representation in the legislature commensurate with their population. This would happen naturally in a PR system; it even happens naturally in a single-member system when the minorities reside in moderately concentrated areas. Without PR rules or a fortuitous geographical distribution, commensurability between voting strength and seats can only occur by some willful effort to make minority strength efficient. In the U.S., we are torn between the demands for representational equity and the nature of the electoral system.

Requiring compactness preserves the nonintentionality between district shape and the efficiency of minority strength. If it so happens that a minority party or group is efficiently distributed, then they will not be discriminated against. If that group or party is not so fortunate, then the rules will be biased against them. Since most minority parties and groups are dispersed inefficiently in at least some part of every state, the stabilizing feature of the single-member system is preserved. The key, however, is that the districts must be compact; and where they are not compact, they must not be shaped to help minority parties or groups. If the districts are weirdly shaped to help minority parties or groups, then they will weaken the system's majority bias.

What this means is that there may be a fundamental tension between aesthetic criteria and two good government goals: fair representation for the minority party and fair representation for minority groups. Those who argue for the importance of compactness must be willing to accept limitations on the achievement of equity for minorities. This may be less of a problem for minority parties than for minority groups. It seems reasonable that minority parties should pay the price of a bias against them in return for two-party stability. However, the bias against minority groups is more troublesome in the light of recent court efforts to ensure that minority communities are not carved up. From the perspective of the white, median voter in this country, compactness is desirable, since it enhances the strength of the majority. From the perspective of the nonwhite population, compactness deprives them of equitable representation for the same reason. For the reapportioner, it presents the first of many conflicts between supposedly consistent good government goals. We will consider other such conflicts next.

4

The Consistency of Good Government Criteria

A major theme of reapportionment reformers is the need to take the politics out of line drawing. The fact that state reapportionments have resulted in bitter partisan struggles and costly lawsuits is often attributed to the participation of legislators and their staff. Legislators, these reformers argue, politicize reapportionment. Because their careers are at stake, they quite naturally use whatever political means they can to ensure that the adopted plan is favorable to them. Disinterested and impartial citizens, on the other hand, can afford to look at redistricting from the perspective of what is best for the whole community. They, unlike legislators, will not try to gain some personal benefit from the plan. Since all reasonable people can agree on the value of good government criteria, there should be little room for bitter controversy.

This vision of a nonpartisan, nonconflictual reapportionment is certainly attractive, but several scholars in recent years have questioned the feasibility of this goal. Robert Dixon urged that "the task of apportionment, awkward and difficult as it may be," should not be given over to nonpartisan commissions. Moreover, he was convinced that attempts to ignore political factors were potentially disastrous. All lines favor one party over the other, no matter what their intent may be. "Politically uninformed districting solely on the basis of symmetry, compactness and population equality, with the aid of computers," he argued, "can only lead to chance goodness or badness, or to a bad plan which is the product of hidden special motives cloaked in the guise of population considerations alone."[1] Another scholar reviewing the ex-perience of various reapportionment commissions has concluded that they are never nonpartisan: "Either by the mode of its selection (com-missioners selected by legislative leaders) or by its history (the inability of nonpartisan commissioners to agree to a plan because of political dif-ferences), every commission has experienced the significant strain of partisan discord."[2] Even the formal criteria of good government reap-portionment have been criticized. Grofman and Scarrow have little faith in the promise that formal criteria will constrain reapportionment to be fair. It is apparent to them that "there are multiple and conflicting criteria." They suggest that the courts "are going to have to face in the 1980's the task of untangling what various sets of criteria really mean and how reapportionment statutes shall be interpreted when statutory provisions include conflicting criteria."[3]

The central issue, then, is whether redistricting is an inherently po-litical question or not. If it is not inherently political, the fact that past reapportionments have been messy struggles is not too disturbing. The task would be to find the right institutional remedy and overcome the forces in the body politic that oppose reform. However, if reapportion-ment is inherently political, then institutional fixes will not cause the politics to disappear, and the question becomes: what kind of institu-tional framework is best suited to resolving these inevitable political conflicts?

An inherently political issue is one that causes disagreements be-tween groups, parties, and interests in society. Governments have the legitimate authority to exercise certain powers, and politics concerns disagreements over how to use those powers. Political disputes are therefore disputes over what is important, who should benefit, and how things should be done. The key to whether reapportionment is a political issue is whether it is true that all reasonable people can agree on what a fair plan is, or whether reapportionment raises questions that various groups, parties, and interests in society will disagree over.

The good government definition of a fair plan is one that meets a set of criteria such as equal population, compactness, contiguousness, re-spect for city and county lines, observing communities of interest, avoiding racial gerrymanders, and creating competitive districts. The notion that reapportionment can be nonpartisan and nonconflictual as-sumes the following condition:

---

1. Robert G. Dixon, *Democratic Representation* (New York: Oxford University Press, 1968), p. 19.

2. Alfred Balitzer, *The Commission Experience* (Claremont: Rose Institute of State and Local Government, October 1979), p. iii.

3. Bernard Grofman and Howard Scarrow, "Current Issues in Reapportionment" (UC–Irvine, School of Social Sciences Working Paper, January 1981), p. 9.

1.   All reasonable good people will agree on the value of these criteria.

Obviously, if people disagree about the value of any of these criteria, then there is a potential conflict. Also, if there are any additional goals beyond those that normally appear on good government lists, then they, too, must enjoy unanimous or near unanimous support.

Conflict can also arise if there are contradictions among the different criteria. The criteria must be mutually consistent, or else people have to decide between two desirable values. Hence:

2.   The criteria should not conflict with one another in a serious way.

If there are inconsistencies between the goals of good government, then conflict can still be avoided so long as there is agreement about the best way to resolve these inconsistencies. In other words, there should be a way to order the goals of good government so that whenever there is a conflict between any two of them, the higher-order value is chosen:

3.   Where there is conflict between values, there is an ordering or weighting of importance that all reasonable good people can agree to.

The question whether reapportionment is inherently political really boils down to whether these three conditions obtain. This is what will be considered in this chapter.

The Value of Good Government Goals

At first glance, the typical sorts of goals that reformers propose for reapportionment seem uncontroversial and worthy. Who could deny the importance of "one man, one vote"? Again, it seems right that counties and cities not be fractured unnecessarily. Similarly, it is understood intuitively that communities of interest should be respected, and that competitive districts are central to the responsiveness of American democracy. Few would publicly admit that they favor lines that discriminate against minorities. It would seem, therefore, that with the exception of compactness—which was considered in the previous chapter—the normal good government criteria for redistricting are generally accepted and so are not "political" as previously defined. However, a closer examination reveals enough problems with each of them to make them "political" after all.

Equal Population Considered

Since *Baker v. Carr* (1962), the most important redistricting criterion has been "one man, one vote." In a series of cases since then, the Supreme Court has raised the question of what constitutes a permissible range of population deviation. Although the Court has never set forth an explicit *de minimis* population deviation, it has indicated in other ways the need for states to make their districts as equal as possible. There are, in fact, two different standards for Congressional and state legislature lines, in the sense that the "one man, one vote" doctrine has been applied more stringently to the former than the latter. In *Wesberry v. Sanders* (1964), the Court maintained that Article 1, Section 2 of the Constitution required that "as nearly as practicable, one man's vote in a Congressional election be worth as much as another's."[4] This line of reasoning was further developed in *Wells v. Rockefeller* (1969) and *Kirkpatrick v. Preisler* (1969), in which the Court argued that "the 'nearly as practicable' standard requires that the State make a good faith effort to achieve precise mathematical equity."[5] Applying this "good faith" doctrine, the Court struck down in *Kirkpatrick v. Preisler* a Missouri Congressional plan with deviations between +3.13 and −2.84 percent, and in *White v. Weiser* it struck down a Texas Congressional plan with deviations between +2.43 and −1.7 percent.[6]

By contrast, the application of the "one man, one vote" principle to state legislatures has been more lenient. In developing the "substantially equal" doctrine in *Reynolds v. Sims* (1964), Justice Warren stated that population deviations were permissible "so long as the divergences from a strict population standard are based on a rational state policy."[7] It seemed at first that the Court would still strongly emphasize the primacy of the equal population requirement when it overturned Florida's state district plans—which had Senate deviations of +15.09 to −10.56 percent and House deviations of +18.28 to −15.27 percent—but then it backed off a strict application of the doctrine in *Mahan v. Howell* (1973) and *Gaffney v. Cummings* (1971).[8] In *Mahan v. Howell*, the Court upheld a Virginia state legislature plan with deviations of 16.4 percent, accepting the state's contention that these deviations were necessary in order to respect the boundaries of political subdivisions. In the Gaffney case, the Court ruled that minor deviations—in this in-

---

4. *Wesberry v. Sanders*, 376 U.S. 1 (1964), at 7–8.
5. *Wells v. Rockefeller*, 394 U.S. 542 (1969); and *Kirkpatrick v. Preisler*, 394 U.S. 526 (1969).
6. *White v. Weiser*, 412 U.S. 783 (1973).
7. *Reynolds v. Sims*, 377 U.S. 533 (1964), at 579.
8. *Mahan v. Howell*, 410 U.S. 315 (1973); and *Gaffney v. Cummings*, 412 U.S. 735 (1971).

stance, 7.83 percent—did not necessarily mean invidious discrimination. This doctrine was reinforced in *Chapman v. Meier* (1975), in which Justice Blackmun wrote: "We have acknowledged that some leeway in the equal population requirement should be afforded States in devising their legislative reapportionment plans. As contrasted to Congressional districting, where population equality appears to be preeminent, if not the sole, criterion, on which to adjudge constitutionality."[9]

Some members of the Supreme Court questioned the Court's pursuit of rigorous population equality. Justice Frankfurter, dissenting in *Baker v. Carr* (1962), stated that "what is actually asked of this court is to choose among competing bases of representation, really, among competing theories of political philosophy."[10] In the same spirit, Justice Harlan observed in *Gray v. Sanders* (1963) that population equality had "never been the universally accepted political philosophy of England, the American colonies or the United States."[11] Foreign scholars, too, seem somewhat baffled by this peculiarly American obsession. One recent book on British government noted: "Individual electoral equality is not the holy grail in the United Kingdom that it has become across the Atlantic; as with the arguments surrounding the simple plurality system, the problem of boundary revisions has been discussed in a spirit which seeks a rough-and-ready fairness rather than an absolute equality imposed by a slide rule."[12]

The issue at hand is whether achieving very small deviations in population is indisputably more important than any other good government goals. If, for example, a town that has been in a district for several decades can be kept there by exceeding the allowable population deviation, is this justifiable? One argument against an obsessive concern with population equality can be made on the basis of a calculation of the value of a single vote. The central idea behind "one man, one vote" is that overpopulated districts dilute the votes of their inhabitants, while underpopulated districts give their inhabitants more influence than they deserve. Political scientists have long observed, however, that the size of the voting population is the most important factor in vote dilution. The value of a vote is the probability that a vote will affect the outcome of a race (which is just $1/n$ where n is the number of voters in the district).[13] Obviously, in large districts such as Congressional

---

9. *Chapman v. Meier*, 420 U.S. 1 (1975), at 23.

10. *Baker v. Carr*, 369 U.S. 186 (1962).

11. *Gray v. Sanders*, 372 U.S. 268 (1963).

12. Max Beloff and Gillian Peele, *The Government of the United Kingdom* (New York: Norton, 1980).

13. Discussions of the value of voting in a rational choice framework can be found in William H. Riker and Peter C. Ordeshook, *An Introduction to Positive Political Theory* (Englewood Cliffs, N.J.: Prentice-Hall, 1966), chap. 3.

TABLE 3   *Value of Vote with Different Deviation Levels*

	Number of Voters Per Congressional District	Value of Vote
+20%	302,959	.00000330
+15%	290,335	.00000344
+10%	277,712	.00000360
+05%	265,089	.00000377
+01%	254,990	.00000392
0	252,466	.00000396
-01%	249,942	.00000400
-05%	239,843	.00000416
-10%	227,220	.00000440
-15%	214,597	.00000465
-20%	201,973	.00000495

seats, the probability that a single vote will determine the outcome is extremely small even if the districts are at their ideal population. For example, the average Congressional seat in California after the 1980 census had 525,968 people in it and contained 252,466 voters, which meant that the value of an individual's vote in the average Congressional campaign was .00000396. It should be immediately apparent that anything short of a massive population deviation would not substantially alter that value. Table 3 shows the effect on the value of an individual's vote with deviations of 1, 5, 10, 15, and 20 percent in both a positive and negative direction. As this table illustrates, these deviations would not significantly increase the voter's ability to affect the outcome of a race. There would have to be deviations of almost 100 percent (making the district ridiculously small) before the value of an individual's vote even reached one percent. Clearly, given the size of Congressional districts, departing from precise equality in the number of voters in each district would not meaningfully dilute or exaggerate the strength of an individual's vote.

In fact, the equal population doctrine does not even guarantee that districts will have equal numbers of voters. Districts drawn on the basis of population will vary greatly in the number of registered voters and even in the number of eligible potential voters. Figure 23 plots the number of seats that fell within various voter deviation ranges for four years: 1962, 1966, 1972, and 1974. The lowest range of voter deviation is the 0–5 percent category. Seats that fell into this range had a number of voters

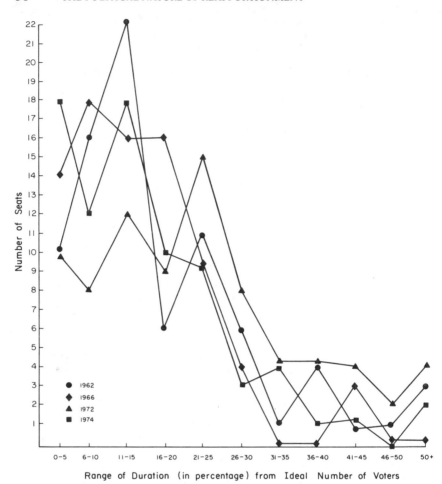

FIGURE 23 *Variations of Voters by Seats in the Assembly*

that was within 5 percent or less of the ideal or average number of voters per Assembly district. Reading the graph, there were ten Assembly seats within 5 percent of the ideal in 1962 and 1972, fourteen such seats in 1966, and eighteen in 1974. The year 1962 is significant, since it follows a 1961 reapportionment that preceded the "one man, one vote" cases. The 1966 districts are important, because they follow the first reapportionment in 1965 after *Reynolds v. Sims*. The 1974 districts follow the court masters' reapportionment in 1973, while the 1972 data show how the districts were distributed before that reapportionment.

The data in this figure reveal several interesting points. One is that reapportionment by population does have an equalizing effect on the number of voters in each district, but the voter deviations are in no way as small as the population deviations. There are, for instance, eight more seats in the 0–5 percent range in 1974 than in 1972, four more in the 6–10 percent range, and six more in the 11–15 percent range. By contrast, there were many more seats in the 21 percent and greater range in 1972 than in 1974. In short, the California Supreme Court narrowed the disparities in the number of voters measurably by its 1973 reapportionment.

The contrast between the 1962 and 1966 data shows the difference between a reapportionment before the "one man, one vote" doctrine of *Reynolds v. Sims* and one after. There is a smaller difference in this comparison. There are four more seats in the 0–5 percent range in 1962 than in 1966, two more in the 6–10 percent range, and five more in the 16–20 percent range. However, there were actually more seats in the 11–15 percent range in 1962 than in 1966, so the difference between the two reapportionments is not as sharp as between 1972 (when there had been no reapportionment since 1965) and 1974. The fact that 1962, 1966, and 1974 all had smaller voter deviations than 1972 indicates that the passage of time between reapportionments creates greater disparities in the number of voters than do differences in the strictness of the population deviation standard applied in the pre– and post–*Baker v. Carr* reapportionments.

Having acknowledged that reapportionment does make some difference, it should be said that the voter deviations that result from redistricting are not nearly as small as the population deviations. The 1974 data are particularly illustrative, since the court masters adopted a standard of 2 percent, which is quite strict for a state legislature. Nonetheless, only 22 percent of the districts fell within a 5 percent voter deviation, and there were two seats that actually deviated from the mean by 50 percent or greater. In fact, the largest district in terms of the number of registered voters was 3.1 times the size of the smallest one. This is still an improvement over 1962, when the number was 6.35, but the simple fact is that population equality is such a crude way of equalizing voters that an obsession with very small population deviations seems rather silly.

Finally, the equal population doctrine of the Supreme Court has produced some interesting corollary principles at the state level. The court masters in California reasoned in 1973 that since percentage population deviations in the state involved greater absolute numbers of individuals, seats in the California legislature should be closer to equality than seats in the legislatures of smaller states. They noted that: "Although a greater percentage variation has been permitted in the reapportionment plan of other states, the population of districts in such states was relatively small. Legislative districts in California are large, so that even a one percent variance in population affects a large number of persons."[14]Actually, the doctrine of minimizing vote dilution would dictate the opposite. The probability of any one individual affecting the outcome of a race is higher in small districts than it is in large ones, and the addition and subtraction of one individual affects the strength of another individual's vote more in small districts, not less. Since deviations are more important in smaller seats, they should be restricted more stringently in states with small districts than in states with large ones in order to be consistent with the doctrine of vote dilution.

Respect for City and County Lines

Some states have explicit constitutional requirements regarding the integrity of city and county boundaries. Voters in California, for instance, adopted Proposition 6 in 1978, which called for the maintenance of city and county boundaries to the extent that this could be done consistently with other criteria. The strongest argument for keeping cities and counties whole is that it preserves their bases of power in a district. Governmental units that are split between one or more districts cannot lobby for their interests as effectively, or so it is argued. The reasoning behind this contention is that if a city or county has less than the population required for one seat, then its share of a seat's population can only decrease if it is not wholly contained in that seat. Hence, a city with the population for .74 of a seat will have the predominant voice in that seat if it is not divided. Dividing the city in half decreases its share to .37 and weakens its hold over the seat. Since cities and counties will have particular concerns that may be antithetical to or at least competitive with those of other cities and counties, a divided governmental unit will be less well represented than a unified one.

A good illustration of this argument is the plea of the mayor of the small California town of Folsom—population 11,000—who testified at the reapportionment hearings in March 1981 that because his community was split between two Assembly districts, the smaller section (constituting 20 percent of the population) got "very little campaigning," and that they rarely saw their representative because, as he put it, "we're in this little corner and it's very small in his district."[15] The Republican Assemblyman who authored Proposition 6, which requires that California redistricting respect city and county lines as much as possible, made a similar argument at another hearing, saying that he

---

14. *Legislature of State of California v. Reinecke*, 10 C.3d 396 (1973), at 411.

15. Testimony of Mayor Stan Gisler of the city of Folsom before the Assembly Elections and Reapportionment Committee (Sacramento, March 27, 1981), pp. 8–9.

represented an area with many small cities and "it's a lot of time to go and meet with city councils and meet with community groups." "So if cities are split," he warned, "you're not going to get the undivided attention of the legislator . . . if that's what you think is important. . . ."[16]

This line of reasoning is intuitively plausible, but if the goal is to maximize the representation of a particular city or county, other factors must be considered. Disagreeing with the author of Proposition 6, another legislator asked why a city is "better off with primary access to one Assemblyman and one State Senator than, say, divided in half, and this applies to any possible number of communities that are less than the average size of the district, and with access to two legislators." "What is the political theory," he asked, "that says we should have our effect limited to the smallest number of representatives?"[17] In fact, several government officials testified that they would prefer to have their city or county divided. A councilman from Torrance, a city that had been split into two Assembly districts by the court masters in 1973, stated: "Our city, the people I represent, have since that time benefited greatly from the wisdom of those who drew the current boundaries. Torrance and the entire South Bay has benefited to the extent that we have two members of the Assembly to work with in solving those problems which can only be dealt with at the statewide level. I am here today asking your honorable body to help the South Bay and the City of Torrance to maintain that dual representation."[18] Another official, from the city of Claremont in Los Angeles County, asked that the committee disregard the county line and tie Claremont with the cities on the western edge of San Bernardino County into one district. She complained that "we are cut apart from the cities of the west end of San Bernardino County where over the past ten years particularly we have developed a common body of interest in a number of areas. . . . In our case, the county boundary is a divisive and counterproductive factor and not a criterion that makes sense." She went on to point out that if it had a representative in common with the cities in San Bernardino County, it might get a bill sponsored that would allow it to put its transportation funds into the West Valley Transit Authority rather than the Los Angeles Rapid Transit District, as it does presently. She claimed that the city tried to do this once before, but the Representative had "other con-

16. Response by Assemblyman Bob Naylor before the Assembly Elections and Reapportionment Committee (East Lost Angeles, February 20, 1981), p. 34.

17. Response by Assemblyman Howard Berman before the Assembly Elections and Reapportionment Committee (East Los Angeles, February 20, 1981), p. 31.

18. Testimony of Mr. Dan Walker, Councilman from Torrance, before the Assembly Elections and Reapportionment Committee (Los Angeles, April 3, 1981), p. 24.

TABLE 4   *Advantages of Single and Multiple Representation*

	Conditions Favoring Multiple Representation	Conditions Favoring Single Representation
Overlap of Interests With Other Units	Compatible	Incompatible
Critical Level of Power	Sufficient	Insufficient
Nature of Interests in Unit	Heterogenous	Homogenous
Value of More Than One Legislative Channel	High	Low

stituents considerably further west who wouldn't be served by that kind of proposal."[19]

In general terms, whether a city or county is made worse or better off by being divided depends upon the trade-off between a potentially lower level of legislative responsiveness and the benefit of having additional channels of representation. In terms of the former, there are two factors to consider, one of which is the compatibility of a city's or county's interests with those of other governmental units in the district. Obviously, to the extent that the interests of various cities and counties in a seat are different or antithetical, it becomes more crucial for each to have the power to influence the representative by itself. This consideration leads to a second, which is whether the governmental unit in question has a population share that is sufficient to force the representative to be attentive to it. A city or county need not have 74 percent of the population to have a critical share of a seat. Much will depend on the political party of the representative, the political composition of the city or county, and its resources—e.g., the number of wealthy contributors in that city or county. Thirty percent of a seat might be sufficient if the representative belongs to the majority party in that city or county or if important contributors live there. See Table 4.

---

19. Testimony of Ms. Eleanor Cohen, Mayor of Claremont, before the Assembly Elections and Reapportionment Committee (East Los Angeles, February 20, 1981), p. 32.

Against the increased risk that a city or county might not have the representative's undivided attention, there is the advantage of having more representatives, which could be valuable for two reasons. First, if the city or county concerned is very heterogeneous, then it may be very hard for one representative to represent all factions well. If a unit is divided between nonwhite and white, rich and poor, rural and urban, or in any of the other ways discussed so far, it may be impossible for one legislator to serve adequately, since the representative may feel the need to avoid taking a definite position on either side, or may choose one side and ignore the other. To the degree that the unit is homogeneous, there is less internal reason for multiple representation.

The other consideration is whether the sorts of issues that the city or county needs to have defended require a coalition or not. It may be that one representative can adequately look out for the interests of a particular governmental unit. On the other hand, having multiple representation adds another vote for legislation the city or county may favor and provides insurance that if one representative is not sufficiently attentive or effective, there is an alternative route. Provided there is a critical level of power to command a representative's attention, it might be better to have two representatives instead of just one.

Preserving Communities of Interest

Although the term *communities of interest* is sometimes distinguished from *geographical regions*, the two can really be combined, since geographical regions are in some sense a kind of community of interest. Other examples of communities of interest are "those common to an urban area, a rural area, an industrial area or an agricultural area, and those common areas in which the people share similar living standards, use the same transportation facilities, and have similar work opportunities, or have access to the same media of communication relevant to the election process."[20] There is no legal standing for this criterion. Indeed, the U.S. Supreme Court was quite disparaging of the idea when it said that "legislators represent people, not trees or acres,"and that they are "elected by voters, not farms or cities or economic interests."[21]

Nonetheless, the press, political scientists, and most especially the public tend to take the idea more seriously. Consider the case of Marin County, whose officials lobbied very hard to prevent it from being

---

20. *Legislature of State of California v. Reinecke* (1973), at 412.
21. *Reynolds v. Sims*, 377 U.S. 533 (1964).

placed in the same district with San Francisco County to the south. Said one county representative:

> We are small towns. . . . We are concerned with small town issues. We are suburban in character, not urban like our respected neighbor across the Bay. While we share many of the same problems in the areas of housing, transportation and crime and other matters, the very nature of these problems in our area is different from San Francisco, and the range of solutions applicable in our area is vastly different. It is essential that our state representatives continue to be responsive to our concerns, and reflect our point of view. This perspective could be lost if state posts were split across the Golden Gate. While emphasis of concerns will shift as one moves north and east from the Golden Gate, it is clear that there is much more in common between the counties to the north and east than there is with San Francisco. The northbay region already has a good track record of working together. We share the common bond of suburban and rural character. Reapportionment from these areas makes much more sense than jumping the Golden Gate Bridge to San Francisco.[22]

The question of the relative merits of preserving communities of interest demonstrates the point that issues of reapportionment often touch upon fundamental issues of representation. The argument that districts should not divide communities of interest is in effect a plea for homogeneous districts. If a legislator represents an area with a single, well-defined interest, then his mandate will be unambiguous. The legislature will be composed of individuals representing clear and distinct interests, and out of the clash of these interests—by compromise and logrolling—will come a common policy. The advantage of homogeneous districts is that their representatives will have no opportunity to play one district interest off against another or to avoid taking a clear and definable stand.

The goal of constructing homogeneous districts through reapportionment is most consistent with the ideal of descriptive representation.[23] According to this ideal, elected officials should defend the unique interests of their own districts and not try to take a broader or more statesmanlike position. If the legislature is truly representative— which it should be if all the interests of society are to have a voice in the government—then it should mirror all the interests of the population. Drawing homogeneous districts makes representatives spokespersons for whichever interest dominates the district, and if the elected officials do their jobs correctly, then the mix of interests in the legislature will

---

22. Testimony of Douglas Binderup, Vice-Mayor of the city of Mill Valley, before the Assembly Election and Reapportionment Committee (Sacramento, March 27, 1981), p. 23.

23. The concept of descriptive or faithful representation is borrowed from Hannah Pitkin, *The Concept of Representation* (Berkeley: University of California Press, 1967).

faithfully duplicate the characteristics and interests of the population. An electorate is well represented in this view when all its interests are articulated by various representatives.

The obvious objection that could be raised is that a system with homogeneous districts encourages its representatives to take an excessively narrow perspective. An alternative theory of representation is that representatives should perform their duties with independent judgment and not be captives of the narrow concerns their particular constituents have. The goal is to construct districts in such a manner as to broaden and moderate the viewpoint of representatives. This second ideal would especially appeal to those who believe that special interests and parochial perspectives contribute to an irrational, uncontrolled public sector. Such persons would not regard communities of interest as sacrosanct, because they cause legislators to become entrapped by the special interests that happen to dominate a district. Indeed, people who hold this second view might even consciously try to mix communities to ensure that the one balances the power of the other.

This second view of representation is the Burkean, and it is commonly associated with the British parliament at various periods in history.[24] The central tenet of this position is that elected officials should be elected for their personal and intellectual qualities and then be given the opportunity to exercise their independent judgment on matters of state. The reasoning behind this ideal is that the representative, if chosen correctly, will be in a better position to assess issues and make choices than his or her constituents. Pure independence of this sort probably does not exist in the United States, but if representatives' districts are sufficiently heterogeneous, they may be able to achieve some measure of independence by playing interests off against one another, or by putting together a unique coalition that coincides with their personal views.

A variant of the Burkean theory is the median preference theory of representation, which can be traced to the Progressive movement. If districts are sufficiently large and heterogeneous, then each representative will have to be responsive to the median position—in normal political parlance, the "average guy in the street"—and cannot afford to be too narrow in perspective. At-large elections, nonpartisan campaigns, and city council governments were Progressive devices to take government out of the hands of ethnic machines and overcome the excessive parochialism of a district-based party system.[25] The best way to force representatives to be responsive to the moderating influence of

24. Ibid., chap. 8.
25. Eugene C. Lee, *The Politics of Nonpartisanship* (Berkeley: University of California Press, 1960).

the median preference is to have legislators run at large, so that the overall majority can vote down any representative who moves too far from the median. In the absence of at-large districts, a similar effect can be achieved by making each district as representative of the whole as possible. Minority voters, to the extent possible, would always be counterbalanced by majority voters. Obviously, the median theory of representation, like the Burkean, is less consistent with preserving communities of interest than the first, or descriptive, theory of representation.

Protecting Racial and Ethnic Communities

Protecting racial and ethnic communities is a special case of protecting communities of interest, made special because of the long history of discrimination against minorities in America and more recent attempts to redress racial inequalities affirmatively. But while plans that deliberately weaken minority communities are now universally condemned, there is a good deal of debate about the extent of protection minorities should receive. The distinction between passive and active corrective measures is crucial. Passive protection prevents the carving up of compact ethnic communities. Active protection—what is called an affirmative action gerrymander—links together dispersed minority communities as much as possible in order to achieve commensurability between the proportion of racial and ethnic minorities in the population and in the legislature.

The Supreme Court has been unclear on whether race should be considered in drawing legislative districts. In *United Jewish Organizations v. Carey* (1977), the Court held that it was not a violation of the Constitution to consider race "in drawing district lines as long as such consideration does not involve a scheme . . . employed as part of a contrivance to segregate; to minimize or cancel out the voting strength of the minority class of interests; or otherwise to impair or burden the opportunity of affected persons to participate in the political process."[26] The Court in that case upheld a plan that divided an Hasidic Jewish community in order to establish nonwhite districts. However, legal scholars point to the contrasting actions in *Gomillon v. Lightfoot* (1960) and *City of Mobile, Alabama, et al. v. Bolden* (1980) as demonstrating that except where there is evidence of racially discriminatory intent, the state is not constitutionally compelled to consider racial factors.[27]

---

26. *United Jewish Organizations v. Carey*, 430 U.S. 144 (1977), at 179.

27. *Gomillon v. Lightfoot*, 364 U.S. 339 (1960); *City of Mobile, Alabama, et al. v. Bolden*, 100 S.Ct. 1490 (1980).

Apart from the legal aspects of considering racial factors, there is considerable unease in the public about the creation of minority seats. The notion that nonwhites can best represent nonwhites and whites can best represent whites has itself been challenged in various quarters. Consider the plea of one newspaper columnist:

> The belief of the various ethnic populations of the state, mostly Black and Hispanic, is that they should have persons of their own ethnic group representing them in direct proportion to their numbers in the overall population. This notion is counter to the idea that this nation is a melting pot where people of all races and nationalities merge into unified people.[28]

No doubt, some significant segment of the white population shares this view that minority representation of minorities is unnecessary and undesirable. Others might ask whether, as with communities of interest generally, it is more desirable for legislators to represent the narrow interests of one group or for them to have to try to take a broader perspective of the common interest? Is it always or even usually the case that a nonwhite can better represent the interests of the nonwhite community than a white representative?

Advocates of strong political parties may also be uneasy about the increasing emphasis on racial and ethnic representation. It manifests a breakdown of trust between minority and nonminority members of the Democratic party when the former feel that the Democratic party, and the political system generally, will only be responsive to them if they have their own representatives. Nonminorities tend to view racial representation as excessively parochial and insensitive to the larger coalition of forces that constitute the Democratic party as a whole. In this way, the issue of racial and ethnic representation causes serious intraparty tensions.

Competitive Districts

Some reform proposals call for a concerted attempt to create more competitive districts through reapportionment. This assumes that reapportionment is in fact significantly related to competitiveness, but there are good reasons to be cautious about accepting such a claim. Various studies have documented the decline of party voting in the United States since 1964. As a consequence of this decline, many seats that were formerly considered safe in terms of the underlying party loyalty are no longer so. The large incumbency advantage that legislators have enjoyed in recent years does not seem to be related to a higher

---

28. Earl G. Waters, *News-Sentinel* (Lodi, Calif.), September 8, 1981.

level of partisanship among the electorate. Quite the contrary, it is occurring at a time when partisanship is waning. There is considerable debate as to what has caused this advantage, but two plausible hypotheses are the incumbents' resource advantages and their higher name recognition, neither of which is affected by reapportionment except in the sense that incumbents can be moved out of areas where they enjoy high name recognition and into areas where they are not known. However, unless reapportionment takes place shortly before the election, the incumbent will still have time to work on his name recognition in the area. Moreover, whatever temporary destabilizing advantage is gained every ten years by the reapportionment process will erode by the time a second set of elections is held under the new lines.

However, even if these problems are ignored, there is still the question of whether it would be desirable to make more seats marginal than would occur by chance. On the one hand, representatives in a highly competitive system would have to be more responsive to shifts in public opinion. Although most people would agree that this is desirable, it is important to realize that it implies a commitment to the descriptive and median theories of representation, rather than to the Burkean theory that some might prefer. Moreover, even if greater responsiveness is held to be a social good, it is not without a cost, since competitive seats have been shown to be more expensive than noncompetitive ones.[29] Unless there is a major reform of campaign spending, increasing the number of competitive seats will increase the cost of elections considerably. Apart from the social waste of added campaign expenses, it would seem that a system with many competitive districts would be to the advantage of wealthier white candidates with greater access to money and the media.

In short, while some number of competitive seats is necessary to permit legislative majorities to change with the political climate, there are definite short-term disadvantages in creating an artificially large number of partisanly balanced seats, and these disadvantages may not be compensated for by any long-term benefits such as a lessening of the incumbency advantage. Once again, fundamental issues of reapportionment are linked to fundamental "political" issues.

The Consistency of Good Government Criteria

Clearly, the first condition necessary for an "apolitical" reapportionment seems not to hold, since reasonable people can and

29. See especially Gary Jacobson, *Money in Congressional Elections* (New Haven: Yale University Press, 1980).

TABLE 5   *Redistricting Values*

	Equal Population	Competitive Seats	Community Of Interest	Minority Protection	City/County Lines
Equal Population	X	1A	1B	1C	1D
Competitive Seats		X	2A	2B	2C
Community of Interest			X	3A	3B
Minority Protection				X	4A
City/County Lines					X

do disagree about the relative merits of good government criteria. In the 1980s, the most salient reapportionment controversy of this type has concerned the protection of minority political strength. However, disputes over the merits of specific good government criteria are not the only sources of potential conflict. Conflict will also occur if people must choose between two competing criteria. In order to avoid such situations, good government criteria must be consistent with one another. Is this always the case?

Table 5 shows an index of situations in which two criteria may conflict with one another. Excluding the aesthetic criteria, which have already been shown to be inconsistent with other good government criteria, each case will be considered separately.

Equal population and competitive seats (1A).

Whether these two criteria conflict is the central issue in reapportionment. Obviously, territory can be added to strengthen or weaken a seat. As discussed earlier, the choice of what kind of territory gets added to a seat is not always under the reapportioner's control. Ripple effects will sometimes force a seat to take undesirable areas. This can mean either that safe seats get safer or that weak seats get weaker. To the extent that the reapportioner can control the territory that a seat must absorb or lose, the effect that it will have on the competitiveness of the seat will depend on two factors: the amount of area that must be absorbed and its partisan nature. Small changes in a seat's population will make very little difference to the competitiveness of the seat. Adding territory that is only marginally stronger than the area the seat already has will also not affect the competitiveness much. Major changes in the competitiveness of the seat involve a substantial number of people and significantly stronger or weaker areas. The reapportioner does not always have it in his power to alter the competitiveness of a seat, but when he does, this can become a hotly contested political issue, since Republicans will want to make Democratic seats competitive, and vice versa.

Equal population and preserving communities of interest (1B).

This tension was felt most strongly at the time of *Baker v. Carr* (1962). Those who lived in rural areas argued that they needed the protection that unequally populated districts provided. Certainly, "one man, one vote" has diminished rural representation—especially in the upper houses of state legislatures—but there is some debate over whether this has greatly influenced policymaking. The tension between rural interests and equal population still persists in California, but has been lessened somewhat by growth patterns in the 1970s. Many of the rural areas in California enjoyed relatively high population growth, whereas the cities experienced relative or even absolute (e.g., San Francisco) decline. In this sense, the equal population doctrine came back to haunt the urban areas in the 1981 reapportionment.

Equal population and respect for city/county lines (1D).

The earlier discussion on ripples pointed out how the equal population requirement can cause multiple city and county splits and how higher population variances can be used to minimize those splits (see Chapter 2).

Equal population and protecting minority political strength (1C).

One consequence of the Supreme Court's stringent population requirements is that they can make it very difficult for small minority communities to obtain representation. In California, the Black and Hispanic communities are sufficiently large to win control of seats in key urban areas, and so their goal of achieving representation in the legislature that is commensurate—or nearly so—with their numbers in the population generally is realistic. However, the Asian community, to take an example of a smaller minority group, could only dominate seats in California if the population requirement were loosened considerably.

Preserving communities of interest and protecting minority political strength (3A).

Some minority groups are primarily restricted to one geographical area. The Black community in California, for instance, is situated in urban areas, and the Portuguese tend to inhabit the rural and agricultural parts of the state. Other California minority groups live in both rural and urban areas, the best example being the Hispanics. Given the dispersion of the Hispanic community, one might be tempted to link the urban Hispanic communities with the rural ones. The California Assembly plan, which put the Hispanics in rural Imperial County with those in urban Chula Vista and National City in San Diego County, was praised by the Hispanic community as a major gain and denounced by white civil leaders as a violation of natural communities of interest. It all depends on which community of interest seems important.

Respecting city/county lines and protecting minority political power (4A).

The contradiction between these two goals arises frequently. Minority communities do not often coincide neatly with existing city and county borders, since they are forced to settle where they can get housing. Some cities in California are heavily populated by minorities—for example, Compton (75 percent Black) and Bell Gardens (79 percent Hispanic). Other cities have pockets of minority population that could be linked together to give them control of a seat—for instance, Pasadena (20 percent Black and 18 percent Hispanic) and Whittier (26 percent Hispanic). When a pocket of minority population from one city exists next to an underpopulated minority seat in another one, there is a strong argument for splitting the first city in order to preserve the ethnic or racial community. Referring to the problem of protecting minorities in Los Angeles, one community worker testified: "Yes, there is a problem. If reapportionment occurs according to jurisdictional lines, such as along the eighty-one incorporated cities in Los Angeles County, the representation of minorities will be well diluted."[30]

Competitive seats and protecting minority political strength (2B).

This is one instance in which two goals almost always contradict one another, because of the historic voting patterns of minorities in this country. The overwhelmingly Democratic bias of the Black and Hispanic communities means that the seats they control will almost

---

30. Testimony of Juanita Dudley, Chairperson of Women on Target, before the Assembly Elections and Reapportionment Committee (Los Angeles, April 3, 1981), p. 23.

always be safely Democratic. Only the addition of a highly registered (i.e., with a high ratio of voters to unit of population) white, Republican suburb to nonwhite urban seats would make such districts competitive; but as noted already, this would likely be struck down as racial gerrymandering.

Competitive seats and preserving communities of interest (2A).

There is no strong contradiction between these two goals, but there are occasions when they are not compatible. The best example of this phenomenon is the urban-suburban division in which the suburbs tend to be predominantly safe Republican areas and the inner-city areas tend to be predominantly safe Democratic. Los Angeles is a particularly graphic case in point, since all of the areas in the center of the county are Democratic, while the cities on the periphery tend to be Republican. There are similarly stark contrasts between the inner-city and suburban areas of Santa Clara, San Francisco, and Oakland. To the extent that urban seats are kept out of suburban areas, and vice versa, their electoral safety will be preserved.

Preserving communities of interest and respecting city/county lines (3B).

Conflicts of this type arise when cities and counties encompass disparate areas. Los Angeles is again a good illustration. In addition to its urban and suburban areas, it also possesses a region of high desert to the north (i.e., Palmdale and Lancaster). Many residents in this desert area quite rightly feel that they have more in common with rural Kern County than with the rest of L.A., but they do not have enough population for a seat in either Congress or the state legislature by themselves. For instance, a representative from the Antelope Board of Trade, headquartered in Lancaster, asked that the region that includes the desert communities of Los Angeles, Kern, and San Bernardino counties be kept together because the "life style in the upper desert is fairly common throughout that area and it's quite different than you have here in the urban part of the Los Angeles Basin, including the San Fernando valley, Burbank and the Glendale area."[31] Preserving the Los Angeles County border required either attaching Palmdale and Lancaster residents to an urban or suburban seat to the south or uniting the desert communities and breaking the county line to put them in a seat with Kern and San Bernardino counties.

---

31. Testimony of John Huerta, MALDEF, before the Assembly Elections and Reapportionment Committee (East Los Angeles, February 20, 1981), p. 21.

Competitive seats and respecting city and county lines (2C).

To the extent that the governmental units in question are racially, ethnically, or economically homogeneous, they will tend to be also more politically homogeneous and less competitive for that reason. Respecting the boundaries of homogeneous cities and communities will therefore lessen the competitiveness of the seats that they belong to. On the other hand, if these governmental entities are heterogeneous or are small enough so that different types of homogeneous communities can be put together into the same seats, then there will be no contradiction between the two goals.

In summary, this brief discussion demonstrates how the various formalist criteria often conflict with one another. This means that choices must be made either on a case-by-case basis or by following some general rule. The general rule would have to take the form of some ordering of the criteria from most to least important, so that when a conflict arose between any two criteria, the higher-ordered one would be chosen. If, instead, the inconsistencies are resolved on an ad hoc, case-by-case basis, those who felt aggrieved by the decision would want to know why a criterion was favored in one instance but not in another. The first method would solve that problem, but the question is whether there is an ordering that all or most individuals would consider fair.

The Ordering of Good Government Criteria

Can there be a fair ordering of good government criteria—that is, one about which there will be no "political disagreements"? The application of any reapportionment plan always produces winners and losers. Some cities will be split and others will not. Minority groups will do well in some areas, poorly in others. Some incumbents will be pleased, but others will not. And so on. The winners will think the plan fair, and the losers will just as predictably think it unfair. If there is to be any hope of achieving a consensus on fairness, it must occur before any one participant knows what the outcome will be. In Rawlsian terms, people must agree on what is fair "behind a veil of ignorance."[32] So put, the question is whether anyone has reason to expect that an ordering of the criteria would be unfair generally, not whether a specific plan adversely affected it or not. Normally, this kind of Rawlsian condition is nearly impossible to achieve, but the complications of reapportionment are so great—due to ripple effects—that most participants

---

32. John Rawls, *A Theory of Justice* (Cambridge: Harvard University Press, 1971).

do in fact start from a position of ignorance with respect to how the plan will affect them personally.

Is there an ordering under these conditions that all groups could consider fair? The answer is no, and for the same reason that the first condition does not hold. That is, people will inevitably disagree about the value of individual criteria and will therefore not be able to agree on how to rank or weight them. To conclude that the preservation of city or county lines should be ordered as more important than the protection of minority political strength depends on a prior consensus that it is more important for cities and counties to be able to lobby effectively for their interests than for some minority candidates to be elected.[33] Or, to take another example, ranking competitive seats ahead of respect for communities of interest would necessitate agreement that responsiveness is more important than homogeneous districts.

Clearly, all of the criteria are controversial in this sense. Removing the Rawlsian veil makes them even more so. Minorities value the protection of their communities most highly. City and county officials—many of whom hope to run for higher office and do not want to see their power base eroded—will rank the preservation of city and county lines most highly. Rural interests will argue for the importance of respecting communities of interest. Groups with concentrated populations will be more disposed towards compactness than those with dispersed populations. Those with money and access to the media will favor competitive seats. In short, even if the effects of a specific plan are hidden behind a Rawlsian veil, people will disagree about the importance of criteria, thus making a noncontroversial, apolitical ranking of these criteria impossible.

Fairness as Seats-Votes Ratio

Although good government criteria evidently cannot eliminate conflict over reapportionment, it has been argued that there is an approach that at least assures political fairness, even if it does not eliminate the inevitable conflicts between different reapportionment values. The central idea of this method is to define a standard of fair-

33. The Rose Institute completed a survey of 523 California city and county officials out of 1,200 officials in the initial sample. It found that 75 percent felt that their cities and counties would receive better attention "if they were not unnecessarily divided in the 1981 reapportionments." However, the report did not consider such issues as whether the officials were planning to run for higher office (and therefore would want to keep their political base united) or whether there might be some response bias in the mailbacks. See "Major Survey Reveals Need to Preserve City and County Boundaries" (Rose Institute press release), March 30, 1981.

ness for sharing seats that is based on a neutral ratio of seats held by a given party to the votes it received.[34] The basis of this measure is that the representation of parties in the legislature should be approximately proportional to their strength among the electorate. Since the U.S. system is not based on proportional representation, the ratio between seats and votes will not typically be exact. Assuming a normal distribution of political strength, it will instead look like the S-shaped curve. This approach to fairness amounts to claiming that the fairest plan is the one that most closely approximates the ideal S-shaped curve.

One problem that various people have pointed out is that the measure will be influenced by biases in the residential patterns of the state. If there are enclaves of homogeneous support for one or the other party, then it will be necessary to distinguish between partisan inefficiency caused by residential segregation and that caused by redistricting per se.[35] One proposal to solve this problem is to generate as many plans as possible, and then take the one that is closest to the ideal S-shaped curve.[36] How far the best plan is from the ideal of proportionality will then depend only on inherent factors and not political gerrymandering.

Another problem with this notion of fairness is that it is not based on the population standard of reapportionment. Lines are drawn on the basis of population, not citizenship, registration, or participation in the electoral process. There is no reason to expect that a standard of political fairness based on the ratio of seats to votes will correspond well with redistricting by population. It was observed earlier that redistricting reduces the disparities in the voting population—vote dilution—somewhat, but that the range of voters per district after redistricting is still quite large. Better-educated, higher-income, English-speaking, and older individuals are more likely to participate in elections than are the poor and minorities, with the result that seats with equal populations will not necessarily have equal numbers of voters in them. There

34. See especially Richard Niemi and John Deegan, Jr., "Competition, Responsiveness and the Swing Ratio," *American Political Science Review*, 72 (December 1979), 1304–1323; and Edward Tufte, "The Relationship Between Seats and Votes in Two-Party Systems," *American Political Science Review*, 67 (1973), 540–554.

35. P. J. Taylor and R. J. Johnston, *Geography of Elections* (Harmondsworth, England: Penguin Books, 1979); and John K. Wildgren and Richard L. Engstrom, "Spatial Distribution of Partisan Support and the Seats/Votes Relationship," *Legislative Studies Quarterly*, 5:3 (August 1980), 423–435.

36. Charles Backstrom, Leonard Robins, and Scott Eller, "Issues in Gerrymandering: An Exploratory Measure of Portion Gerrymandering Applied to Minnesota," *Minnesota Law Review*, 62 (1978), 1121–1159; and Wildgren and Engstrom, "Spatial Distribution," p. 433. A more elaborate model is presented in Guillermo Owen and Bernard Grofman, "A New Approach to the Seats-Votes Swing Relationship" (School of Social Sciences, UC–Irvine, September 1981).

TABLE 6   *Equity and Number of Voters*

	VOTERS	OUTCOME	POPULATION	PARTY
A	60,000	83%–17%	200,000	Blue
B	50,000	80%–20%	200,000	Blue
C	110,000	81%–19%	200,000	Red

were seven seats in the California Assembly, for instance, in which 35 percent or less of the population were registered to vote in 1980; and in all those instances, the minority population was greater than 50 percent of the district population. Low minority participation can be attributed to differences in the mean levels of education and income in these neighborhoods, the number of noncitizens living in the area, the number of individuals under the voting age, and the transiency of the population in the region. The relevant point is that two seats can be equally inefficient from a partisan standpoint, but because one has a higher number of voters in it, the aggregate measure of seat fairness will show a higher bias against one party.

This point is easy to demonstrate. Assume that districts *A*, *B*, and *C* all have equal populations but unequal numbers of voters. Further assume that *A* and *B* belong to one party and *C* belongs to another. The outcome from the last election shows that the partisan strength of both parties is inefficiently distributed (see Table 6). The Blues have a two-to-one seat advantage. The margin in seat *A* is 83 percent for the winner to 17 percent for the loser (50,000 to 10,000); for seat *B* it is 80 percent to 20 percent (40,000 to 10,000); and for seat *C* it is 82 percent to 18 percent (90,000 to 20,000). The total votes cast for the Blues is 110,000 and for the Reds is 110,000. In other words, both parties receive the same number of votes even though one party has two safe seats and the other has only one safe seat. The seats-votes ratio is biased in favor of the Blues, and for that reason seems unfair.

Thus, the proportional standard of fairness in seat allocation is not only biased by residential segregation, but is further exacerbated by the Supreme Court's requirement that minority communities be protected from division. Of course, this only amounts to saying that the range of alternative plans will be additionally restricted to those that protect minority communities. The procedure of generating as many plans as possible and picking the one that comes closest to proportionality could still go forward, but would be altered in this crucial way. However, one suspects that by the time residential patterns and minority protection are accounted for, there is not much variation left. The small changes in partisan strength brought about by reapportionment pale by comparison with residential and differential participation factors. Short of abandoning the idea of geographically based districts or moving to reapportionment by registered voters instead of population, the proportional norm of fairness cannot be met very well.

Conclusion

The claim that a nonpartisan, noncontroversial reapportionment process is possible rests on the assumption that reapportionment is not a political question per se. However, this assumption is incorrect. By influencing who gets elected and by whom, redistricting can affect policies—or to use the classic Lasswellian definition of politics, who gets what, how, and why. In this sense, reapportionment is a political question, and as such, it may be best treated in a political manner. At least, this is the logic of a legislative reapportionment.

PART TWO

The Political Reapportionment
Examined

5

A Tale of One Reapportionment

Reapportionment for the California Assembly began when its long and bitter Speakership struggle finally ended in November 1980. For months, two rival factions of the Democratic party had fought an intense battle between themselves to gain control of the Speakership. On one side, there were those who supported the incumbent Speaker, Leo McCarthy, a liberal legislator from San Francisco. The opposing faction backed Howard Berman, a liberal legislator from the West Side of Los Angeles. The vote in the caucus had been deadlocked for some time when a Black Democratic legislator from San Francisco, Willie Brown, stepped forward and announced his candidacy. Brown had run for the Speakership once before in 1974 against McCarthy and had lost. The stalemate between the McCarthy and Berman forces gave Brown the second chance that he had been waiting six years for. Among those who switched to the "compromise candidate" and secured his election was an Hispanic legislator from East Los Angeles, Richard Alatorre, who had been pledged to Berman up to that point. Since Alatorre's vote was pivotal, Brown rewarded Alatorre with the assignment of chairing the Elections and Reapportionment Committee.

Because of the unusual coalition of forces that brought Brown to power, there was a great deal of initial speculation as to how the Speaker and Alatorre would conduct this reapportionment. Brown was elected with a bare plurality of the 48-member Democratic caucus and with the votes of twenty-eight members of the Republican caucus. Some Assemblymen thought that a deal had been struck between Brown and the leader of the minority caucus, Carol Hallett, and that Brown would take care of the Republicans during reapportionment.

There was also considerable speculation in the press that Alatorre was interested in reapportionment because he wanted to draw a Congressional seat for himself. But despite the rumors and speculations, no one knew for sure what the plan was, and this caused considerable anxiety in Democratic circles.

There was a great deal of pressure on the Assembly to draw partisan lines, partly because Brown had been elected Speaker by a coalition of Democrats and Republicans. Some people inside Democratic circles simply wanted to see Brown prove himself to the party faithful. Had he sold out to the Republicans, or would he remain true to his liberal Democratic roots? Alatorre, the Chairman of the Reapportionment Committee, was also suspect to party hard-liners, partly because he had joined the same unholy alliance, but also because he was an Hispanic, and Hispanics seemed to be saying that their interests would take priority over party concerns in the 'eighties. Certainly, the California Republicans were hoping as much.

The Speakership fight, however, was not the only source of partisan pressure on the Assembly. By the late spring, the results in states reapportioning early—Indiana, Colorado, and Washington—had become known, and they were alarming. Democrats observed that the controlling Republican parties in those states had made the most of their power and had devastated the Democratic Congressional delegations where they had the votes. In Indiana, for instance, the Republican plan had protected five Republican incumbents and had placed three Democratic Congressmen into one district. The Washington state legislature—also controlled by Republicans—had passed a bill that endangered two Democratic Congressional incumbents, Tom Foley and Mike Lowry. In Colorado, the Republican plan assured a 5-to-1 margin for their party and carved up Democratic strongholds in several counties. Although the latter two plans were both vetoed by the Governors of the states involved, certain factions of the California Democratic party felt that California needed to retaliate. As one journalist saw it: "When the Republicans opened up with Washington, Colorado and Indiana-type blitzkriegs, they inevitably stirred the Democrats to reply in kind, and in states like California, those replies in kind are shredding Republican hopes. Redistricting never had a chance to be a GOP treasure trove; party leaders should have anticipated recrimination."[1]

Memos and letters came to the Assembly from other states, the Democratic National Committee, and key political figures, urging the Democrats in the Assembly to keep the national Republican strategy in mind when they drew their lines. Even before the experiences of other states were known, the hard-liners in the Democratic party had urged a plan

---

1. "How the GOP Got Mugged," *The Sacramento Union*, October 1, 1981.

that protected the party's interests. A resolution passed at the California Democratic Party convention in January 1981 noted that the Republicans had only 33 percent of the state's registered voters, but 42 percent of the Senate and 40 percent of the Assembly seats. Therefore, it asked that if the Republicans were going to pick up any new seats allotted to California, the Democrats should "compensate by drawing boundaries in such a way that the Democratic party nets a number equal to the new seats in other areas." Secondly, it recommended that the boundaries "provide for the election of a Democrat to every seat held by a Democratic legislator whether he retires or not." Where there had to be collapses, it urged that the legislators "draw boundaries in such a manner as to 'collapse' or destroy districts which have Republican incumbents and reject the practice of destroying Democratic seats where the Democratic incumbent plans to retire."[2] This resolution passed by voice vote without debate.

Technical Considerations

Alatorre's first task was to develop the technical capacity to undertake reapportionment, since preparations in the Assembly had been delayed by the prolonged Speakership battle. The 1970 reapportionment had introduced computer technology into the California redistricting process, and the continuing evolution of computers in the middle and late 'seventies had upped the technical ante for all participants in the 1980 reapportionment. It was clear that the committee would need a computerized data file in order to have the capacity to analyze alternative district proposals rapidly, but it would be a formidable task to build such a file from scratch nine months before the deadline for a redistricting bill. The census and political data would have to be merged into a common file, but since there was no exact correspondence between the precinct units of the political data and the tract or block units of the census data, the merger process would be tedious and difficult. With tens of thousands of tracts, blocks, and precincts involved, and with the need for a very high standard of accuracy, the data set would have to be checked and rechecked many times to eliminate inevitable human errors.

Alatorre's options were (1) to build his own information, (2) to share data with the State Senate—whose members would have primary responsibility for drawing their own lines and would share the responsibility for the Congressional lines with the Assembly—or (3) to

2. Bruce D. Pettit, "The Pettit Report," February 16, 1981.

purchase data from the Rose Institute, a self-proclaimed "nonpartisan" research center. Some Assemblymen initially felt that the best way to make up for lost time was to pursue the third option of buying the data from the Rose Institute, but that alternative was soon ruled out, as the ties of the Institute to the Republican party, which had become a state-wide controversy, made many suspicious of its work product. As one powerful Sacramento aide put it: "Given the paranoia that exists in pol-itics, it's inconceivable that the Democrats will ever rely on Republican data."[3] The second option therefore seemed more appealing, and it was agreed that the Senate, Assembly, and Congressional delegations would all share the Senate's data base.

There were, however, some troubling aspects to this arrangement. Because both the Speaker of the Assembly and the President Pro Tem-pere of the Senate had just been elected to their offices, they were both insecure about their positions within their own caucuses and with each other. This exacerbated an existing tension between the two houses, a tension built on natural interhouse rivalries and intraparty fears that Willie Brown had sold out to the Republicans in order to win the Speak-ership. As long as the Senate controlled the data, it was in a position to threaten to withhold the data to get what it wanted. It could dictate the schedule of the legislation and prevent the Assembly from introducing its bill earlier than the Senate. It could even potentially use the data to veto the Congressional lines, which would have to be jointly decided by the two houses. No one maintained that these were high-probability events, but they were not impossible, and the Speaker and the Chair-man of the Reapportionment Committee did not want to be vulnerable in this way.

Things were not made any easier by the Senate staff's modus oper-andi, which was highly secretive and cautious. The Assembly found that it was very hard during the first few months to get any information from them about their data set or their intentions generally. Phone calls from the Assembly were typically not answered, and the rare conver-sations that did occur between the staff were largely uninformative. The cloak and dagger style of the Senate was epitomized by its staff director, who informed the Assembly staff on several occasions that he held his most important discussions in restaurants because they were harder to bug, and who once advised them to board up the air vents in their offices so that their conversations could not be overheard. Some amount of secrecy and discretion could be justified on the grounds that it helped keep rumors under control and gave the leadership an advan-tage in bargaining with their anxious members. Nonetheless, it was ob-vious to many observers that the preservation of secrecy had been car-

---

3. "Democrats Get Slow Start on Redistricting," *Los Angeles Times*, March 8, 1981.

ried too far in the Senate, especially when it impeded cooperation with the other house of the legislature.

When the Assembly finally discovered that the Senate's data set had not yet been constructed, and that it would have to be sent to a contractor, the Assembly offered to pay the contractor's costs so that it could in effect become the owner of the data set. For its own part, the Senate wanted to hold down costs by making the Assembly pay for the data construction so that it could claim after reapportionment that it had actually spent less in 1981 than ten years before.

The agreement reached was that the contractor would process the political data into machine-readable form, and that the Senate and Assembly staffs would themselves undertake the arduous task of merging the census with the political data. The Senate intended to build a version-1 data set, which meant that all the political data would be reported at the census tract level (a census unit ranging in size from a few thousand to ten thousand people). The Assembly felt that it needed greater precision and opted for a version-2 data set that would give political and census data at the precinct level (a political unit of a few hundred to a few thousand people). The reasoning was that since the Senate districts were twice the size of the Assembly districts, they would not need the level of precision the Assembly needed. To stay within a 2 percent population deviation and achieve the various goals that the Assembly leadership wanted to achieve would require splitting tracts later, and it seemed sensible to create a data base from the start that could do this. There was even talk that the two houses might trade data sets so that both would have the complementary benefits of the different approaches, but this never occurred.

Since reapportionment happens every ten years, there is little experience in data construction of this sort. Many of the contractors who were trying to sell their services were new to this type of data construction and made wild, obviously unattainable promises. Moreover, the established firms tended to be identified with a particular party or a faction in a party, and could not be trusted for that reason. This led the California legislature, on the advice of the Senate, to contract with a relatively inexperienced group at Sonoma State University, a decision it would later regret.

A contract was drawn up after weeks of negotiation, and deadlines were finally established. The legislature expected to get its data in six weeks, but when the due date arrived, the data were not ready. The job had turned out to be too large for the contractor. They had bitten off more than they could chew, which was understandable, but it left the Assembly in a difficult position. The Assembly staff had nearly finished preparing the census data for merger, but now it had no political data to merge it to.

The situation, perhaps, would not have been so difficult had it not been complicated by political considerations. The legislature had to pass its budget in June, or else the state would have no money to pay its bills. In previous years, the budget had been delayed past the deadline, but Brown had vowed that this year the trains would run on time. It was for him a symbolic gesture of the professionalism he intended to foster as Speaker. The vote on the budget, however, required a two-thirds margin, and many Democrats feared that the Republicans would hold up the budget until they got specific concessions from the Speaker on reapportionment. The prudent strategy seemed to be to pass a reapportionment bill before the budget so that the Republicans could not hold the one bill hostage in order to get their way on the other. The reasoning was impeccable, but it was predicated upon the idea that lines could be drawn by June. If all went smoothly, the committee staff thought they would be able to meet this schedule, and they assured Brown and Alatorre that they would be ready. This violated two fundamental principles. The first is never to promise anything one is not sure he can deliver, and the other is that in reapportionment nothing ever goes as smoothly as planned.

The failure of the contractor to provide the data on time meant that the reapportionment staff could not make good on their promise, and that the strategy of passing a reapportionment bill before the budget could not be implemented. The Democrats had to hold their breath throughout the budget negotiations, hoping that the Republicans would not play their trump card at this highly vulnerable moment in time. Surprisingly, they did not, and the budget passed both houses. However, this episode did irreparable damage to relations between the Speaker and the committee staff. Their failure to deliver had put the Speaker in a vulnerable position and had undermined his confidence in their ability to fulfill their promises, putting enormous pressure on them and on Alatorre throughout the summer.

Rumors circulated that Brown had lost faith in Alatorre's operation, and that he was negotiating with the Berman faction to turn the job over to Michael Berman, Howard Berman's brother and the chief consultant in 1973. In the meantime, the political data started to trickle in from the contractor, but not at a rate that would enable the committee to finish reapportionment before the end of session. It was too late to turn to another contractor, and the Rose Institute was still ruled out because of its Republican ties. The people at Sonoma were working very hard, but they resisted any attempts to share the task with the Elections and Reapportionment staff. It had become a matter of pride to them to complete their job, and they did not seem to understand the larger political implications of the problem. This was not surprising, since they were technicians and not political activists, but it meant that the progress of reapportionment was being dictated by a few programmers in Rohnert Park.

Threats and promises seemed to have no effect on the contractor's pace. There was only one option left, and that was to take over as much of the operation as possible, even though the staff had no experience in these matters. The committee secured copies of the raw data and proceeded to process the political data itself. Meeting the end-of-summer schedule would be difficult, given all the technical setbacks the Assembly had had to face. To compensate, the staff had to work in three shifts, twenty-four hours a day.

The Republican Strategy

While data construction dominated the technical side of reapportionment, there were key political decisions that still had to be made by the Speaker. Most importantly, he had to fill out the rest of the Elections and Reapportionment Committee, and he did so by following a pattern he had set with other committees, which was to select members of the losing as well as the winning faction of the Speakership fight. In particular, he placed his chief rival for the Speakership, Howard Berman, on the committee. This was especially significant, since Berman had initiated the challenge against the previous Speaker, Leo McCarthy, because he had felt that McCarthy's people were not taking adequate steps to prepare for reapportionment.

As the negotiations wore on, Berman would play a major role in helping unite the Democratic caucus behind the reapportionment bill. Initially, however, there was a great deal of suspicion between the Brown and Berman factions. Brown had been elected with a bare plurality of Democratic caucus support and with the votes of the Republicans, who viewed him as the lesser of two evils. In the first stages of reapportionment, most of the decisions were not made by the Elections and Reapportionment Committee, where Berman and his followers would be privy to crucial information, but by the Speaker in consultation with Richard Alatorre and an inner circle of important legislators. Later, as the suspicions wore away, the inner circle came to include a key Berman supporter, Richard Robinson, and then Berman himself.

Meanwhile, the Republicans were developing their own capacity to draw lines. The Speakership settlement had given them entitlement to half of the reapportionment funds, and they used this money to purchase their own computer and the Rose Institute data. This meant that unlike previous years, when the minority party had had little information about the likely effect of the lines the majority party was offering them, the Republicans were able to judge for themselves how they would be affected by proposed plans, and were even able to generate their own plans. At this stage, the Republicans were quite confident that reapportionment would work to their advantage. They had helped put the Speaker into office and believed that he would reward them for this. Their confidence was further bolstered by the landslide Reagan victory, which seemed to indicate that the tide of public opinion was shifting away from the Democrats. Reapportionment, they thought, would almost certainly have to reflect this, especially since the new census figures showed that two of the highest-growth areas in the state were Orange and San Diego counties, both of which were predominantly Republican. Moreover, the heart of the Berman faction—the losing side of the Speakership fight—was in West Los Angeles, where there had been relatively little growth since 1970. As a consequence, the six Berman seats on the West Side were collectively under by 175,000 people, and the simplest solution to some observers seemed to be to collapse one of the West Side Jewish seats. Such a move would have been predictably unpopular with the Berman faction, and so it seemed that the Democratic party was headed for yet another collision course. If so, then demographic forces would further cement the alliance that had elected Brown in the first place.

The Republican sanguineness about reapportionment was nowhere better expressed than in a memo from the Republican reapportionment consultant that was circulated among the legislators in the Republican caucus and "leaked" to the press in July 1981. It began with the assertion that "it is not possible for the Assembly Democrats to draw 49 better seats than the 49 they have at the moment." "This is because," he explained, "the 49 current Democratic Assemblymen represent slightly less than 47 seats worth of population. To find 49 seats they must absorb more than two full seats worth of Republican voting population." The memo went on to point out that although the Republicans received 49 percent of all votes cast in Assembly races, they only won 40 percent of the seats. The explanation for this, the consultant argued, was that whereas twenty of the thirty-one Republican districts were overpopulated, only sixteen of the forty-nine Democratic districts were. Moreover, the Republicans had gained registration in fifty-four of the Assembly seats between 1978 and 1980, while the Democrats had lost registration in all the seats in the same period, "suggesting a pattern that could result in our winning a majority of the two-party Assembly vote in 1982." Any attempt by the Democrats to gerrymander the state in a partisan way would (1) place incumbent Democrats in more marginal seats, (2) divide minority communities, (3) split many cities and counties, and (4) so anger the Republicans that they would undertake a well-financed referendum. The consultant concluded that the Democrats would have to pursue a "minimum change plan" that "generally saves all incumbents and maintains the status quo as far as individual members are concerned."[4]

Were all the Republicans really as confident that things would go their way as their consultant was? It is difficult to say for sure, since some of their actions were not consistent with optimism. After all, they had backed Brown for Speaker because they had feared that reapportionment in the hands of Howard Berman's brother, Michael, would have done them great harm. If the demography was as disadvantageous to the Democrats as the Republican consultant told them, then what did they have to fear from the Bermans? Would it not have been more to the Republicans' benefit to have the Democrats try a partisan gerrymander and overextend themselves?

They might also have been made uneasy by the curious lack of communication at the technical level between the Democratic and Republican staffs, and by their difficulty in obtaining information about Alatorre's specific intentions. There were no discussions in the period leading up to the negotiations between the reapportionment consultants of the two parties, and no bipartisan talks at any level about the broad reapportionment issues that would eventually cause the coalition to dissolve. Moreover, the Assembly Republicans were constantly fighting with the Democrats over access to supposedly public data, which surely was a sign that things might not go their way. Nonetheless, they remained confident at the time of the memo in July.

Perhaps this was because if all else failed, they still had two political strategies they could fall back on. One was to support the California Hispanics in their campaign to prevent the Democratic party from carving up their communities in order to save Democratic incumbents. Forcing the Democrats to respect minority communities would strengthen surrounding Republican seats and weaken nonminority Democratic seats. In the words of the minority leader, Carol Hallett: "I feel that there is no way short of outrageous gerrymandering that the minorities in California—the Blacks and the Browns—can be ignored, and that will benefit the Republicans. In San Jose, for example, there is an honest Chicano district that will be impossible to dissect. As a result, that is going to make districts around it somewhat more Republican."[5]

The other political weapon in the Republican arsenal was the tactic of delay. Either by preventing the passage of a bill in 1981, or by qualifying a referendum against the bill (and thereby staying the implementation of the new lines), the Republicans knew that they could postpone

4. Memo to the Republican leadership from consultant Tony Quinn, entitled "Realities of Reapportionment," July 2, 1981.

5. "Hallett: 'GOP Safe Under New Districts,' " *Sacramento Bee*, March 26, 1981.

reapportionment until 1982, by which time they hoped to control the Governorship and/or the state Senate. This line of thinking came to light when a memo from Senator H. L. Richardson was discovered in a copying machine in the Capitol. Among other things, the memo said: "It would be beneficial to us if reapportionment did not go into effect until the 1984 election. We could have a Republican Governor and a majority of the senate by then so that we could write a more equitable reapportionment plan."[6]

The Hispanic Lobby

There were many other people aside from the Republicans who were interested in how the lines would be drawn, including the incumbents themselves. Alatorre held meetings with all of the Assemblymen individually to get their perceptions of their districts and to hear their suggestions. Throughout the next few months, they continued to send their proposals to the committee, where they were duly noted and analyzed. At hearings throughout the state, groups and individual citizens were given the opportunity to express their views about how the lines should be drawn in their areas. Alatorre also got advice from campaign experts in the party and received several specific regional plans from groups outside the legislature such as the Hispanic Californios for Fair Representation.

The role of the Hispanics in the Assembly reapportionment was substantial. In the period between the 1970 and the 1980 census, the Hispanic community in California had grown 92 percent, from 2.37 million to 4.54 million. By 1981, they constituted at least 20 percent of the state by official count, and perhaps more if official counts are indeed underestimates of the true number, as the Hispanic community maintained.

Hispanic leaders were determined to prevent a repetition of what happened to them in reapportionment last time. Their complaint against the court masters' reapportionment was specific in some cases—such as the division of the Hispanic neighborhoods into three Assembly seats in San Jose—but it was mostly general and, to some extent, hard to define. As one community leader explained, the court did not "go as far as one should have in maximizing Hispanic voter potential." The effect of gerrymandering, he observed, was "devastating to our community," and it meant "that concerns that are unique to the Hispanic community, like obtaining municipal services in Spanish, are not met." Not giving Hispanics a significant voice in their districts also

---

6. "Reapportionment Delay Supported," *Los Angeles Times*, February 4, 1981.

caused them to "become apathetic about the political process," making them feel "that their vote won't count because it is diluted."[7] However, without the data and resources to examine specific options, it was difficult to suggest better alternatives to the status quo. What kind of plan would actually maximize Hispanic voting potential? What ought to be the definition of an Hispanic seat? Was it reasonable to think that the Hispanic community could ever achieve parity between its legislative representation and its proportion of the population? These were difficult questions that would require much information and detailed analysis.

The chance to acquire that expertise was offered to the Hispanic community by the Rose Institute, a reapportionment research institute at Claremont Men's College. The Rose Institute, founded by two consultants to the Assembly Republican reapportionment committee in 1970, had announced that it would make its data available to minority groups throughout the state in order to allow them the opportunity to build their own "ideal" districts and compare those with what the legislature offered them. As a way of publicizing this service and bringing attention to its role in reapportionment, the institute sponsored a conference in January 1981 for members of the Hispanic community who were interested in these issues. The conference drew Hispanic community leaders from all over the state, and from that meeting emerged a coalition called the Californios for Fair Representation. The idea was that by bringing all the regional groups together and using the Rose Institute's information, the Hispanic community would be able to mount a coordinated statewide campaign to get the legislature to draw lines favorable to Hispanics. The coalition would be partly funded at the local level by each regional group and partly funded at the state level by grants from such organizations as Security Pacific Bank. In addition, much of the coordination costs (phone bills, xeroxing, etc.) would be underwritten by MALDEF, the Mexican-American Legal Defense Fund.

The alliance with the Rose Institute had made the Hispanics a formidable lobby, but it also raised questions in the minds of many Hispanic and non-Hispanic Democrats about the coalition's motives. Its announced priorities were (1) to protect Hispanic incumbents, (2) to create new districts for Hispanics, and, for the sake of political realism, (3) to disrupt as few incumbents as possible. Those outside the coalition were uneasy about the corporate financing that both the Californios and the Rose Institute had received, and questioned whether Hispanics were best served by a list of priorities that placed Hispanic represen-

---

7. Testimony of John Huerta before the Assembly Committee on Elections and Reapportionment (East Los Angeles, February 20, 1981), p. 20.

tation ahead of the interests of the Democratic party. After all, the Democratic party, not the Republicans, had been the force behind the social and economic legislation that disadvantaged Hispanics had benefited from. Moreover, the Republican leader in the Assembly had made her party's strategy clear with respect to minority representation: they would champion Hispanic seats as a means of weakening non-Hispanic Democratic incumbents and strengthening Republican incumbents. An alliance with the Rose Institute seemed to many Democrats to be playing into the hands of the Republicans. With an Hispanic legislator heading the Elections and Reapportionment Committee, it seemed that the leverage of the Hispanic lobby would be great, and that non-Hispanic Democratic incumbents would be threatened.

The Californios, on the other hand, were not so sure that having Alatorre in the position of Chairman guaranteed that they would have their way. While Alatorre had publicly committed himself to protecting Hispanic interests and had long been a spokesman for their causes, it was not clear to the Californios' leaders that he would be willing and able to stand up to the resistance that the non-Hispanic Democratic legislators would offer. Also, the Californios, like others, were unsure what Speaker Brown's influence over the process would be, and his commitment to their goals was suspect, to say the least, since he had been quoted in the newspapers as having said, "You cannot, and I don't think the House will support, dismembering any incumbent just to achieve a racial minority district."[8] On the subject of drawing lines for the Hispanic community, he said, "They're fine people, but if they're not registered to vote, they can't help you very much." Comparing the loyalty of the Black community to that of the Hispanics, he said: "If you draw Black lines, you're drawing a Black seat. If you draw Chicano lines, you're drawing a Chicano seat—maybe."[9]

The problem the Californios faced, therefore, was how to put pressure on Alatorre and the Speaker to resist placating Democratic incumbents at the expense of Hispanic interests. In practice, if not in principle, they were divided between two possible strategies. One idea was to dramatize Hispanic demands as much as possible and keep the pressure on through constant media attention. This view naturally attracted the more flamboyant members of the organization, including many of those who were ultimately arrested for a sit-in in the Speaker's office.

The other group argued for a lower profile, fearing that excessive media attention would backfire by creating an adverse public image

---

8. "Latinos May Get Little in Redistricting," *Los Angeles Times*, April 30, 1981.
9. Ibid.

and scaring the non-Hispanic Democratic incumbents. It would be better, they thought, to work quietly with Alatorre, Brown, and the incumbents themselves to get the desired changes. If too much attention were directed towards the intentions of the Californios, the incumbents might grow fearful of a potential primary challenge by Hispanic candidates. In fact, they argued, this happened in Los Angeles when the statements of an ambitious, would-be Hispanic candidate, Richard Hernandez, frightened one Assemblyman away from some of the more Hispanic communities in the East San Gabriel Valley. It was better, they maintained, to pursue a less threatening strategy with the legislators and keep the pressure on Alatorre by convincing him that he would have a lot to lose if he did not fulfill his commitments to the Hispanic community.

Of the regions that were particularly important to the Californios, the largest and most important was Los Angeles, where there were three Hispanic Assemblymen in a county that was 27 percent Hispanic in population. There was no question that the Hispanic incumbents would be well taken care of because of Alatorre's position. The thorny issue was whether a new Hispanic seat could be created. There were several seats with Black and Anglo incumbents that could be made more Hispanic, but that would require the incumbents' approval, and none of them were enthusiastic about the idea. Tampering with the Black seats would have been particularly dangerous, since relations between the Black and Hispanic communities in the city of Los Angeles were already far from amicable.

The best opportunity seemed to be to collapse a seat in which there was a retirement or a universally unpopular incumbent, and the Californios met with Brown to discuss this possibility. When the Californios asked Brown to name the seats that could be collapsed, he gave them two names—a Democrat and a Republican—who were not key members of the coalition that brought him to power. The Californios adopted his suggestions and worked on proposals that collapsed these individuals. Several months later, when they met with Brown, the rift in the bipartisan alliance had occurred. The Hispanics had tried to make their proposals consistent with political realities, but those realities had changed, and not being inside the process, they had been unaware that this was happening. The reunification of the Democratic caucus was unfortunate for them in another sense. The most promising scenario for constructing an open, Hispanic seat in Los Angeles involved collapsing one of the Jewish, pro-Berman seats (because the incumbent had announced that he would run for Congress) and then shifting the other seats east to make room for the new Chicano district. Losing the support of the Republicans, however, made it dangerous for Alatorre and Brown to alienate the Democrats in Los Angeles, especially the Berman faction, since they would need all the Democratic votes they could get to pass a bill.

Alatorre was in a difficult position. Since the most visible part of the Californios' coalition was headquartered in Los Angeles, it was important for them to make some tangible gain in Los Angeles County. However, Alatorre could not fulfill his commitment to the Hispanics in Los Angeles and still hold the support of his Democratic colleagues. His only hope was to so exceed the Californios' expectations in other areas that they would forgive his inability to deliver for them in Los Angeles. The committee staff began to look at less publicized areas of Hispanic concentration to see what the possibilities might be and discovered that there were indeed other areas with potential. These areas had the additional advantage of having Republican incumbents, so that creating Hispanic seats there meant that Alatorre could in effect turn the Republican strategy on its head. Uniting Hispanic communities under Republican incumbents would "test" the sincerity of the Republican commitment to minority representation.

At the hearings, several Hispanic leaders from Ventura County had asked that their community be united. Under the masters' plan, the Hispanic communities of Fillmore, Piru, and a portion of Santa Paula had been divided from those in Oxnard and Ventura. In an earlier version of the plan, the committee had been forced by the coastal ripple to move the Democratic Assembly district that lay to the north in Santa Barbara down into the city of Ventura, which perpetuated the split of the Hispanic community and did not please the incumbent. The idea of bringing the seat further down into Ventura to unite the Hispanic communities of Santa Barbara and Ventura counties seemed a good way to avoid the previous situation. Also it arguably strengthened the seat for the Democrats. The consequence of this move was to push one of the other Republican seats into the rural areas of Santa Barbara, Ventura, and Los Angeles counties, which, because it took in a condor reservation, became known as the "condor" seat. The Democrats maintained that the "condor" district made the protection of a minority seat possible by taking the residual area, and that it had a common, rural community of interest. The Republicans complained that although it was not the largest district in the state, a missile fired from one end of the district would not reach the other. As for the incumbent, she was so furious with the proposed district that she told Alatorre to stick his map "where the sun doesn't shine" and stormed out of his office.

Alatorre and his staff also found that they could unite the Hispanics in the Salinas Valley, which was in the Republican caucus leader's district, with Hispanics in the southern part of an overpopulated Democratic district in Santa Clara, creating the "John Steinbeck" district.

While the removal of the Salinas area gave the minority leader, Carol Hallett, a safer seat, it infuriated her to lose almost 100,000 people from her old district and the financial support of the growers in the valley. The Democrats also came up with a district in the Central Valley that united Hispanic towns in Kern and Tulare counties in an area around Cesar Chavez's residence, and this, too, greatly displeased the Republican incumbent. When the dust had settled and a final tally was taken, Alatorre and his staff had managed to increase the number of districts with a minimum of 30 percent Hispanics from ten to sixteen. This exceeded even the number of minority seats the Rose Institute had created, the reason for this discrepancy being that by a curious coincidence none of the minority seats created by the Republicans and the Rose Institute would have adversely affected Republican incumbents. The Republicans, who had counted on being able to go into court with the support of the minorities, were faced with a situation in which the minorities enthusiastically approved of the Democratic plan, and in which several of their own incumbents were greatly inconvenienced by displacement, or partisanly weakened, because of the establishment of minority districts. This further aggravated the Republicans.

However, Alatorre could not ignore Hispanic demands in Democratic areas, especially San Jose and San Diego. The San Jose hearings had revealed considerable disagreement between a liberal Democratic Assemblyman in the area, John Vasconcellos, and the Californios. The position of the Californios was that the three-way split of the San Jose community imposed by the California Supreme Court in 1973 had to end, and that all three non-Hispanic incumbents would have to contribute their fair share. At one point in the hearing, a spokesman for the Californios stated that the area had not been as "effectively and consistently" represented as it might have been if the community had not been divided. He went on to say: "While we appreciate the efforts of our incumbent as they relate to particular issues, it presents something of a different point of view if we had a Hispanic or Chicano legislator to articulate our concerns." Vasconcellos responded angrily: "I take some issue with . . . whether you have been consistently and effectively represented. I am not going to sit here and say that I've not managed to do that."[10] Vasconcellos was really expressing the sentiments of many liberal Democratic incumbents who had some difficulty appreciating the Hispanic point of view on this issue.

The Californios had no trouble with one of the three San Jose Democratic incumbents, since he was planning on running for the State Senate and was amenable to whatever changes the Hispanics wanted, so

---

10. Exchange between Pedro Carillo and Assemblyman John Vasconcellos at the Elections and Reapportionment Committee hearing in San Jose, March 13, 1981, pp. 14–16.

long as the other two Democrats in the area were pleased. The Californios therefore focused their attention on the other two, and had a series of meetings with them. In their initial meeting, Vasconcellos agreed in principle with the idea of a minority district, but he balked at accepting the specific plan the Californios came up with, and hired a consultant to draw up an alternative plan for him. The alternative plan would have divided the Hispanics into two districts of approximately 24 percent Hispanic population each, but this was clearly unacceptable to the Californios, who wanted a district that was 32 percent Hispanic. Vasconcellos's expressed concern was that if his good friend and neighboring legislator, Dominic Cortese, did not get enough of the Hispanic areas, he would have a very weak district. A Memorial Day meeting involving all the parties was particularly acrimonious. Cortese, for instance, threatened to vote more conservatively if he did not get a more liberal seat. The situation deteriorated further when the Californios, in an effort to force Cortese to keep some of the areas in the southern part of his seat, sent a letter to the constituents there warning them that Cortese was planning to abandon them and urging them to write to him in protest.

It was clear that Alatorre and Brown would have to bite the bullet on this issue. Siding with the Democratic incumbents would ensure two votes for the bill, but risk a lawsuit from the Hispanics. Siding with the Californios would prevent the lawsuit, but endanger the support of the incumbents. They took the latter course.

Alatorre and Brown were faced with a similar situation in San Diego, where the 1973 reapportionment had divided the Hispanics into two districts. One of these seats had a Chicano legislator, and the Californios proposed that he be given more of the Hispanic community. They also proposed that there should be an international border district that would stretch across the width of the Mexican line. They hoped this would create a spokesperson for border issues in Sacramento. However, such a border district would have to assume a very narrow form along certain parts in order to keep it within the permissible population range and still cover the entire width of the state's border to the south. This district would also unite the Hispanics that lived in the rural communities along the border with those in the urban areas of National City and Chula Vista in San Diego County. The incumbent who would be most affected by this proposal, Waddie Deddeh, was not planning to run for reelection, but he retained an interest in keeping the district as it was constituted for the sake of a successor and the local communities that he had formed close ties with over the years. Alatorre and Brown were confronted with a now all too familiar gamble. Once again, they chose to risk losing the incumbent's vote, only this time they lost. Deddeh voted against the plan and became one of its harshest critics.

The Breakdown of the Bipartisan Coalition

Starting in March, there was a series of meetings that included the Speaker, Alatorre, and the inner circle, in which various options were discussed. The level of choice at this stage was not which street particular district lines should follow, but the large or "big ticket items" such as where to collapse and where to create new seats, and which counties and cities would have to be divided. Numerous options were examined until finally, in a crucial meeting in July, the major parameters of the plan were established, and work began on producing maps of the new lines and the attendant political and census statistics.

The bargaining with legislators began in the first week in August. Each member of the Assembly was invited to an interview with Richard Alatorre to discuss his proposed district. A map of the member's lines was placed on an easel, and he or she was given a printout of the data describing the proposed districts. Some of the interviews went very quickly, especially in the cases of those who thought they had been given a good deal and wanted to get out of the room before the committee changed its mind, and of those who wanted to study their lines further before giving Alatorre a commitment. The Republicans were always accompanied by a consultant and usually turned their materials directly over to him. They had already agreed that their votes on reapportionment would be governed by the unit rule, and so none of them, including those who were obviously ecstatic about their new lines, were allowed to say whether or not they would vote for the bill.

Negotiations with most of the Democratic members took several meetings and required some alterations in the original plan, but were generally easy. Negotiations with the Republicans stalled very early on the question of which seats should be collapsed and where new seats should be placed. Alatorre stated many times that he hoped to get Republican support for the bill, but he had also made it clear in several interviews that he had an obligation to his fellow Democrats not to sell them out. On the face of it, this might not have seemed alarming to the Republicans, since few in their caucus, or in Sacramento, thought that Alatorre was anything but a figurehead for the Speaker. Upon election to the legislature, Alatorre had risen in the ranks quickly under former Speaker Moretti; but as is the custom in California politics, when he backed Brown in his first and unsuccessful attempt at the Speakership in 1974, Alatorre was banished to the anonymity of the back benches by the then victor, Leo McCarthy. Relegated to lowly positions on meaningless committees, Alatorre acquired a reputation for being bright but unambitious and ineffectual. The fact that he was also an Hispanic only confirmed Republican suspicions about his ability. A favorite Republican joke, which one Republican legislator tastelessly repeated to him, was that Alatorre was planning to draw district lines with spray paint. He simply couldn't be taken seriously.

When Alatorre switched his allegiance from Berman to Brown, people forgot that he had paid so dearly for his loyalty to Brown, and assumed that this was an act of sheer opportunism. It appeared that Brown had cleverly placed Alatorre in the Chairmanship of Elections and Reapportionment as an appeasement to the anxious California Hispanic community. But why did Alatorre accept? Being the Chairman of the Reapportionment Committee was hardly the best assignment in the legislature, and being the pivotal vote in the Speakership struggle, he surely could have had any committee he wanted. In several ways, however, Alatorre was perfectly suited to the job. To begin with, he was not afraid of alienating anybody. Not being one who frequented the Sacramento bars at night, Alatorre had only a handful of close ties with other legislators in both parties, which meant that he could make the hard decisions without letting personal, clubby considerations get in the way. Also, he wanted to show his fellow legislators and the press that he could handle complicated legislative tasks, and that all he had needed over the years was a chance to prove himself. He was in a position to do something of major significance for the Hispanic community, and this, he made clear, was important to him. His priorities were, first, to take care of Hispanic needs and constitutional requirements; second, to protect Democratic incumbents; and third, to win over as many Republicans as possible.

A common postmortem among California Republicans was that the Assembly Democrats never intended to court Republican support, but there is not a lot of evidence for that view. Brown spoke frequently in the press of "reapportionment to protect incumbents," and was smart enough to leave his options open. His goal was to get passed on time a bill that did not threaten his power base, and if that had meant working with the Republicans, he probably would have done so. Alatorre himself did not see the committee's initial plan as one that closed the door on Republican cooperation. It came in a bit high in terms of the burden of displacement, but it preserved the 49-to-31 split in the Assembly and was negotiable on several key points. Why, then, did a bipartisan coalition not form?

The answer is that, two weeks into the August negotiations, it became apparent, first to Alatorre and then to Brown, that the Republicans would not back down from their initial demands concerning displacement and collapses, and that the only hope of getting a bill by the September deadline was to secure the votes of the Berman faction of the Democratic caucus. The decision was not made, as some would have it, from the start—although in retrospect one could see the possibility of things turning out that way—but was instead made during the period in which districts were being shown to the Republican legislators. In fact, the shift was so abrupt that the lines for certain Republican districts were changed just hours before their interviews. Up to that point, the Republicans could have altered the course of events dramatically, but from that point on, they were misled into believing that the Democrats might still do business with them. Although there were several high-level meetings during the last weeks in August, these were diversionary in nature and intended only to buy time for the Democrats to get their coalition together.

The major points of contention concerned how much displacement Republican incumbents should suffer, and most importantly, which seats should be collapsed in areas where there were more seats than the population warranted. As to the latter question, everyone agreed that the former Speaker of the Assembly Leo McCarthy should have his seat collapsed. He had declared for statewide office, and any attempt to keep his seat would have greatly disrupted many seats in San Francisco, San Mateo, and Santa Clara counties. There was also little disagreement over the creation of a new compensating seat in Sacramento County, although the Republican plan made that seat suspiciously marginal. Presumably, had things gotten far enough along, that would have been negotiable. There was also a bipartisan consensus that there would be two new safely Republican seats in southern California, and Alatorre on several occasions suggested that the Republicans could dictate where they wanted those lines.

The problems came in two areas, one that was potentially negotiable and another that was not. The potentially negotiable one was a seat in Alameda County, the fifteenth, which had been a safely Democratic seat until the incumbent, Floyd Mori, was caught by an investigative reporter using his state-owned car for a ski trip in Utah. The hawks in the Democratic party believed that the seat belonged to the Democrats, and that the Republican incumbent would not be there but for his predecessor's indiscretion. On the other hand, it had lost four points in Democratic registration since 1974, and none of the changes that reapportionment could bring could possibly make that seat any stronger. There was a consensus that if the negotiations with the Republicans got serious, this would be the place to make concessions.

Agreement was far less likely in the other troublesome area, Los Angeles County. Two seats had to be collapsed, and there were three broad options. The first was to collapse two pro-Berman Democrats. However, that would infuriate the Berman faction and essentially close off the possibility of winning their votes. The second one was to collapse an inner-city minority seat, but this would bring a certain court challenge and was not consistent with the Brown-Alatorre commitment to help minorities. Finally, two Republicans could be collapsed in the suburban ring around the inner city. If no Republicans were collapsed in the north, then the burden could have been shared equally: the two Democratic collapses in northern California for the two Republican collapses in southern California.

If such an obvious agreement was possible, why did the two parties not arrive at it? One reason was that the Republicans maintained a very inflexible bottom line: they would not tolerate the collapse of any of their incumbents and felt that the burden should fall exclusively on the Democrats. At first glance, it might seem odd that a minority party should try to dictate terms to the majority party when the majority party had the votes to pass a bill without the minority, but one must recall the Republican perception of the world. They had helped get the Speaker elected, and felt that they were entitled to more than the usual consideration given to minority parties in reapportionment. Secondly, Reagan had won impressively in California, and it seemed to the Republicans that a major realignment was in the works. This and the belief that they had not, to date, gotten their fair share of seats in the Assembly made it seem right that they should keep all their incumbents and pick up two seats in addition in southern California. Thirdly, the Republicans in the Assembly were constrained by the positions of Republicans in the Senate and Congressional caucus. Cutting a separate deal with the Assembly Democrats would have been viewed as treachery by Republicans outside the Assembly. Lastly, why not play hard, since the worst that could happen would be that they would have to dip into their ample party funds to finance a referendum? If they could portray the Democrats as unfair, it might even be an issue that would win them some votes in 1982. In the meantime, the qualification of a referendum against a reapportionment bill would stay the implementation of the new lines until the voters got a chance to vote on the measure. If the referendum passed, and if the 1982 elections went well—and there was every reason in their minds to think so—then so much the better, since they would have control of the Governorship and at least the Senate, and then they would be in an even better position to defend themselves. In short, the Republicans had nothing to lose by being inflexible, and they made the most of their opportunity.

A second cause of the failure to negotiate was the interference of various secondary issues. Most annoyingly, the Assembly staff had not paid sufficient attention to where the Republican incumbents lived, and unintentionally drew a half-dozen of them out of their districts. A certain amount of this would have been beneficial to the process, since it is always better in a bargaining situation to come in high so that there is something to give up in the negotiations. However, so many slips only served to poison the bargaining atmosphere and confirm the Republican suspicion that the Democrats had no intention of dealing sincerely with them. Alatorre tried to explain to the Republicans that these mistakes were unintentional, but in each instance, the Republican leader, Carol Hallett, went immediately to the press to proclaim the evilness of the Democratic plan.

Another problem was that the Republicans had a number of disagreements with the Democrats over what the former perceived to be the unnecessary displacement forced upon them by the Democrats. The Republicans were particularly incensed by the so-called "condor" district, by the displacement of the 34th district out of Los Angeles County, and by the creation of a Republican Hispanic seat in the valley. It may be, although one will never know for sure, that these issues could have been resolved, but they were not disputes about collapses, since in all instances the Republicans' homes were included in the district and they all remained conservative seats. These displacements were caused by a conscious Democratic strategy to create Hispanic seats in both liberal Democratic and conservative Republican areas, a tactic that caught the Republicans totally off guard. These issues further muddied the picture and made serious discussion of the collapses impossible.

Reaction to the Bill

Not all of the Democratic legislators were pleased with the course of events, either. Aside from those who had particular gripes about their own districts, there were others who doubted the wisdom of trying to pass a reapportionment bill without Republican approval. Assuming that the bill passed both houses of the legislature and got the governor's signature, the Republicans could still obstruct the implementation of the plan by a referendum drive. This meant that the agony and uncertainty of reapportionment could be prolonged for years to come, and that the Democratic incumbents might have to face election in areas that they had voted to give away. Most did not relish the prospect.

When the time had come for the final bill preparation and the vote itself, there was still some uncertainty about how many Democratic votes the bill would get. Some of the Democratic incumbents wanted changes right up until the last moment and threatened to defect to get what they wanted. Thus, it was only when the vote finally closed that anyone could breathe a sigh of relief.

On September 10, 1981, the California State Assembly passed its reapportionment bill, AB 300, by a vote of 44–31. On the same day, it also approved the reapportionment plans of the State Senate and the Congressional delegation. The reaction to these bills from the Republican party was extremely hostile, and the dispute that ensued over the next few months repeated an all too familiar pattern of partisan bickering over district lines. After the 1970 census, California reapportionment had taken three years and a court intervention to resolve. Republican anguish was particularly strong in 1981 because they had had high expectations for reapportionment. They had firmly believed that since they had helped Willie Brown assume the Speakership, he would protect them during reapportionment. Instead, they complained, he allowed a united Democratic caucus to pass a bill that the Republican leadership vehemently opposed. Bob Naylor, the key Republican legislator on the Elections and Reapportionment Committee, expressed the Republican sense of betrayal when he told the newspapers that reapportionment "is the closest we come in this country to lining people up against the wall with a firing squad. At least the Ayatollah only does that to his enemies. This plan does that to the Speaker's friends."[11]

Many of the newspapers and electronic media in California were also disturbed by the plan, although for different reasons than the Republicans. The Republicans had wanted a plan that would take care of their incumbents, and their unhappiness with AB 300 stemmed from their disagreement with the Democrats over which incumbents should be collapsed to make room for two new seats in Orange and San Diego counties. Unlike the Republicans, the media wanted to see fewer, not more, incumbents protected. Said one paper: "It was evident once more that the controlling, incumbent lawmakers have put their own best interests above those of the people, but that is to be expected."[12] Said another: "Their plans—predictably—protect incumbents and party, and push bothersome foes into political oblivion."[13]

The newspapers were also much offended by the shapes of the proposed districts. One columnist complained that "the fresh reapportionment maps look like Rorschach ink blots, which look like anything you like . . . a nutcracker, or a faceless crab, depending on your aptitude for Rorschach testing."[14] Another was even less complimentary: "Rather than appearing on the map as plans drawn with a sensible regard for order in mind, the pro-Democratic reapportionment districts look like a jigsaw puzzle prepared by a capricious monkey."[15] Compactness was

---

11. "Legislature Approves Reapportionment Plan," *Sacramento Union*, September 16, 1981.

12. Fred Kline, "So Let the Computer Do It," *San Diego Daily Transcript*, September 22, 1981.

13. "Cut and Dried Redistricting," *Modesto Bee*, September 10, 1981.

14. "All About Ink Blots," *Sacramento Bee*, September 10, 1981.

15. "The Reapportionment Mess," *Chico Enterprise Record*, September 22, 1981.

equated with a logical and fair reapportionment plan. Districts that "slither through the state like snakes, over hill, over dale, across deserts and into suburbs" could only have one intent: to "pull in votes to protect the self-interest of some legislator."[16] Many people seemed to feel the way the *San Jose Mercury* reported these Republican activists reacted upon seeing the Democratic lines:

> "Blatantly unique," said one.
> "Ridiculous," said another.
> "I couldn't believe it," said a third.
> "Somebody must be smoking wild root," said Clark Bradley, a veteran Republican politician. . . .[17]

Others attacked the plans—the Congressional one, in particular—for violating natural communities of interest. Walter Zelman of Common Cause told the *San Francisco Examiner* that "the public is getting districts that don't make any sense, that jump all over the place. They are not getting districts that would reflect the people's interests and communities."[18] Several counties were especially upset that they were split into multiple parts or linked in a district with new areas with which they felt they had little in common. One Santa Barbara paper, for instance, protested the treatment of its county, arguing that "none of this makes any sense where the common interests and hopes of voters are concerned. It is a weird, phooey-to-people gerrymander aimed at sewing up our thin coastal strip for the Democrats."[19]

There were a few voices of praise for the new lines, most notably from the Hispanics. John Huerta of the Mexican-American Legal Defense and Education Fund said that he was "shocked, favorably, by the plan." "For the first time in the history of the California Legislature," said Huerta, "Hispanics have made gains from an Assembly reapportionment plan."[20] Said another, succinctly: "We ended up with what we asked for."[21]

---

16. "Protecting Incumbents," *Fresno Bee*, September 9, 1981.

17. "District Without Senator Startles Both Parties," *San Jose Mercury*, September 13, 1981.

18. Walter Zelman, "Change the Remap System, Common Cause Counsels GOP," quoted in the *San Francisco Examiner*, September 18, 1981.

19. "Jigsaw at Work," *Santa Barbara News Press*, August 28, 1981.

20. John Huerta, "Assembly District Reapportionment Plan Released," quoted in the *San Diego Union*, September 15, 1981.

21. Manuel Pema, "Hispanics Back New Assembly Map," *Santa Ana Register*, September 10, 1981.

6

What Legislators Want

In Chapter 4, it was argued that reapportionment can only be a political process—that is, there is no single good plan that all reasonable people can agree on. There are only the differing perspectives of the individual participants. Decisions are not made by consensus, but by building a coalition that is large enough to win. The best plan is not an ideal "best." Whereas the nonpartisan plan is drawn without regard for its consequences on partisan races, the political plan consciously weighs the political impact of various alternatives. The nonpartisan plan claims to satisfy the public interest, while the political plan claims to please its supporters only.

A legislative reapportionment is a form of political reapportionment in which the individual legislators vote on their district lines. The plan that gets put into effect is the one that gets the requisite number of votes in the legislature. In this sense, a legislative reapportionment is fashioned out of the preferences of individual members of the legislature. Ultimately, enough of them have to be persuaded to vote for the plan to obtain a majority, and often—but not always—this means their districts will reflect their preferences.

Curiously, little has been written about the process of legislative redistricting.[1] The popular image is of a group of politicians meeting in a smoke-filled back room to decide whom to punish and whom to reward. However accurate this image may have been of past reapportionments, reapportionment in the 'eighties has become more technical

---

1. Exceptions are Leroy Hardy, "Considering the Gerrymander," *Pepperdine Law Review*, 4:2 (1977), 243–284; and Malcolm E. Jewell, ed., *The Politics of Reapportionment* (New York: Atherton, 1962).

and complex. The introduction of computers and political data, the increasing sophistication of census materials, and the Supreme Court's demand for population equality have increased the technical demands of redistricting. Some states have passed constitutional guidelines that have added to the requirements that plans must meet. Moreover, interest groups have now gone through reapportionment several times and have gained more sophistication in their understanding of the process. They know how to lobby to get what they want, and the threat of a lawsuit and court intervention has given them a credible weapon against the legislature. Political conditions have also changed. Party loyalty has decreased so much among voters and legislators alike that it can no longer be taken for granted.

If the image of politicians in the smoke-filled room is an outmoded simplification, what is the correct image? What do legislators want from reapportionment, and how do they get it? How do personality and situational factors figure in the bargaining? What are the strategies available to individual legislators and to the leadership? This and the next three chapters will consider these questions at least as far as the 1981 reapportionment in California goes. It cannot be said for certain that the California experience is typical of all legislative reapportionments, but it is probable that much of what is said here applies to other states as well. This chapter will begin with actual cases and conclude with a discussion of the principles they illustrate.

Case 1: The "Give Me What I Need Only" Syndrome

The first case concerns a senior legislator who had been through several reapportionments in the past and who believed—whether rightly or wrongly is immaterial—that he had been treated unfairly by previous committees. He recalled losing favorable areas and being forced to take less favorable areas, and this memory made him very suspicious of the current reapportionment. Not surprisingly, discussions with him about changes in his district tended to be difficult and unpleasant.

His district had traditionally been very safe, but in recent years the registration level had dropped significantly and his position had become less secure, which, of course, only increased his anxiety about the process. He needed to pick up 15,000 people to bring his district up to the ideal population, and he had very specific ideas about the sort of people who were acceptable to him. One option for him was to add a nearby minority neighborhood, but he opposed this idea because he had recently had a falling out with members of that community over the hiring of a consultant to his committee. He also opposed picking up areas with large concentrations of young, college-age people, since he had found it hard to communicate with them in recent years. As much as possible, he wanted his constituents to be like him in age, attitudes, and racial characteristics.

The area where his seat was located had to make some major adjustments because of ripple effects from the north. The committee staff did not have a great deal of trouble giving him the territory that he said was most acceptable, but the plan called for him to take more than his initial deficit demanded and to give up some strong areas to a weaker district. Instead of a displacement of 15,000, he would face a displacement of 36,000. Some disagreement over this proposal was anticipated, but his reaction still caught Alatorre and his staff by surprise.

Arriving for a meeting to discuss his new lines with Alatorre, he sat down directly in front of his district map and intensely surveyed his lines. After a few moments, he got up and announced that there was "nothing to say" about the proposal. He began to storm out of the room and would have left had Alatorre not insisted that he stay and explain why he was upset. He explained that he would find no plan acceptable that required him to pick up more people than he needed and that took some of his best areas away from him. Alatorre pointed out that he only lost a point in registration and that adding extra population was dictated by changes elsewhere in the plan. However, he steadfastly resisted the suggestion that he might have to take more than his deficit and in return surrender some of the best areas that he currently represented—no matter how important the reasons seemed to be. Simply stated, his position was that since he needed only 15,000, he should not be expected to pick up any more than that. The Chairman in turn maintained that no one district could be considered in isolation from the state, and that while his district needed only 15,000 people to get to the ideal number, it had to adjust to overpopulation or underpopulation in the surrounding seats.

This legislator proved to be extremely unyielding in the negotiations, and as the time for presenting the bill drew closer, Speaker Brown and Alatorre had to decide whether to give in to his demands or write his vote off. They ultimately chose to hold one last meeting with him along with his neighboring legislators, hoping to make clear to him that he was boxed in by the needs of his neighboring legislators, and that any change he wanted would have to be negotiated with them. He in turn presented a proposal at this meeting that called for a complicated series of trades among the three seats on his border. The keys to his plan, however, were a trade with his neighbor to the north—which would have pushed the neighbor into the minority areas and him into the areas the neighbor left behind—and the return of areas that the committee had planned to take away from him. This would have given him voters that he felt more comfortable with and lessened his displacement. The problem was that the neighboring legislator lived in one of those areas he wanted to take. If this neighbor could be assured of selling his house, he was willing to be accommodating and give the area up. However, without this assurance, there was no guarantee that he could establish residence in the new district boundaries in time to file for the 1982 elections, which would mean that this person would be ineligible to run again. The senior legislator's plan was thwarted, and as it became clear that he would not relent, the meeting was terminated and his vote was written off. Predictably, he voted against the plan.

Case 2: "His County's Keeper"

The second case concerns a freshman legislator who had never been through reapportionment before. Unlike the first legislator, he had no residual suspicions about the committee and its motives, but he did have rather idealistic notions about how reapportionment ought to work and the ability of individual legislators to influence the outcome. Consequently, he made the mistake upon appointment to the Elections and Reapportionment Committee of pledging to his constituents that he would protect the interests of his home county. This set him up to bear the brunt of whatever criticisms people in the county would have about the plan. Having never been through a reapportionment before, he had no reason to believe that he would not be able to make good on his promises, and there was no way he could have anticipated the controversy the final legislative plan would produce.

His district was safely Democratic by any definition of the word *safe*. Short of a drastic alteration in the status quo, he himself was not seriously threatened by any change the committee contemplated. While his personal interests were not at stake, he nonetheless had strong views about what small changes could be made in his district and how other districts in the county should look. Several seats to the south needed to pick up population, and the committee naturally looked for areas that could be taken out of his seat to assist them. This legislator was willing to move east to pick up the 40,000 he needed, but he would have had to move even further east to accommodate the seats below him. He opposed that idea because the eastern and western ends of the county had historically been in different seats and had their own separate organizations. An extensive intrusion into the eastern part of the county would be resented by the activists and media there. Another option would have been to move north to pick up area in a neighboring county, but he resisted that idea because there was no natural community of interest between the two counties. Again, he claimed, his presence would be resented.

This legislator also had strong views about which areas in his present seat he would be willing to surrender to other districts. Several of the smaller, wealthier, and white communities were important to his fundraising efforts, and the urban ethnic areas had always been in the seat. Also, it was important to him that the number of seats in the county be no greater than the amount dictated by population. People in his county did not want to be put together in legislative seats with people from neighboring counties.

Faced with this tight set of constraints, Alatorre and his staff came up with a proposal that would actually have strengthened his already secure seat by moving him east. However, as a result of population needs in other seats, his displacement was one of the largest in the state under this plan. In addition to the 40,000 he had to pick up, Alatorre proposed that he take an additional 50,000 new people and surrender an equivalent amount to other seats. He was not pleased with the committee's proposal, and in the period between its presentation to him and the day the reapportionment bill reached the floor, he had numerous meetings with other legislators in the area to explore alternatives. The consensus that emerged from that group was that the committee should place the burden of displacement on an open seat to the south and not on this legislator's seat. Alatorre and his staff resisted that idea, pointing out that it turned a competitive Republican seat into a safe Republican seat.

The negotiations failed to resolve the issue, and the legislator informed the committee that he would wait to see the public reaction before deciding whether to vote for the plan or not. The public presentation of the plan was not well received in his county, either by the media or by local party leaders. This seemed to confirm his resolve to vote against the plan, and in the Democratic caucus he refused to commit his support. He indicated to the party leadership that he could not support a plan that was so unfavorably received in his county. In the short period between the caucus meeting and the final vote, it appeared that the committee would not get his vote, but several of his closest advisors continually worked at convincing him that a vote against the plan would not be in his best interests. The stakes were potentially high. As a freshman who refused to support the plan, he faced the prospect of being relegated to powerless positions on unimportant committees. In the end, these negative considerations proved to be too great and he supported the bill.

Case 3: "Hedging Your Bets"

The third legislator had had a distinguished career in the Assembly and was considering various statewide races he might enter. At the time of the initial reapportionment negotiations, he was still unsure about which race he would enter, or for that matter, whether he would run at all. Much depended on who entered which races, how the polls looked, and how much money he could raise. It was possible that if things did not go well, he might not have an Assembly seat to fall back upon.

His Assembly seat was a safe one. There was no question that he would hold it again if he ran in it. However, the preliminary demographic data from the census bureau indicated that the area where his seat was located had not grown as fast as other areas in the state, and that as a consequence his district and the others surrounding it were well under the ideal population. It was clear to most observers that the simplest solution would be to collapse one of the seats in that area and make up the population deficits of the others with the population of the collapsed seat. To try to preserve all the seats would cause them all to be dislocated massively. It seemed that everyone in the Assembly, including this legislator, understood this. He did not even schedule himself for one of the regular interviews with the committee.

Several months later, the Chairman of the committee received a note from this legislator indicating that he would like to come in to discuss his Assembly seat. Although he did not say so, it was apparent that things had not gone as well as he had hoped in his bid for statewide office. Recently released polls indicated that his prospects were not good. He needed to hedge his bets: by keeping the Assembly option open, he would have an office to fall back to if his statewide prospects continued to deteriorate.

Alatorre and his staff reacted to his note with dismay. Plans were already well along, and to accommodate this desire to retain an Assembly option would have meant starting over. The inertia of reapportionment planning worked against a major change at such a late point in time. More importantly, however, preserving his option would have greatly inconvenienced the legislators in surrounding seats, many of whom had been his close political allies in the past. It was clear that the best way to handle this problem was to bring together all the legislators who would be most affected by his requests and let him try to persuade them to make the necessary accommodations.

The legislators from the surrounding seats arrived at the meeting first, and it was clear from their remarks that they were no more enthusiastic about his plan than Alatorre was. When the legislator arrived and the meeting began, he explained that he would like to keep open the option of running for the Assembly until he was more certain of what his statewide plans would be. The member from the district that would have been most drastically affected said nothing, but one of the others who seemed more sympathetic to this legislator's request began to suggest ways to avoid collapsing a seat in that area. Most of his suggestions called for extremely grotesque districts that would have sprawled across county and city lines in a number of directions. Alatorre quickly made it clear that a plan of this sort would not be acceptable, and he pointed out that keeping all of the seats and collapsing none would have rippling effects on all of the seats in the larger region, displacing many and substantially weakening a few members of his own party. Relations between this legislator and Alatorre were not good to begin with, and it was clear that he was quite annoyed with the Chairman's position. He announced that he was "unhappy with the way this discussion is going" and left the meeting to appeal to the Speaker. A few days later, the papers carried his formal intention to leave the Assembly.

Case 4: "Nickel and Diming"

The fourth case concerns a freshman from an urban area. He was very careful and scrupulous in his management style, traits which probably suited him well in the business he owned before he entered the Assembly. Members of his staff liked to tell stories of how their boss would assign a task to one of them and then oversee it so closely that he in effect did the job himself. His election had been close, and he quite rightly felt that while his prospects for reelection were good, they were by no means certain. An added complication was that the normal indices of political strength, registration figures, were less valuable in his area because of the high level of disloyalty—i.e., voters crossing over and voting for candidates in the other party. Constrained by such uncertainties, he had every reason to feel uneasy about reapportionment.

The best option from his standpoint was blocked by the hard facts of demography. The surrounding areas of highest partisan strength were already in a Democratic seat, and the incumbent—who was both more senior and more powerful—was unwilling to give these areas up. The committee staff was forced to look elsewhere and managed to find some census tracts that could be added to give the Assemblyman an ideal population without weakening his registration even a point. He said nothing when the committee's plan was unveiled to him, and took his map back to study with his staff. Later that afternoon, the Chairman received a phone call from him complaining that while the area that was proposed for him had good registration, the disloyalty was so high that even Cranston did not carry some of those precincts. He requested that the staff provide him with data on another set of precincts in a different location. The committee staff complied, and after several days of negotiations, the lines seemed to be set again. He pledged his vote for the plan, and the committee staff shifted its focus elsewhere.

The next day, he called back and questioned the committee's political data. It seems that he had called the county registrar, and that office had given him different data from those that the committee had given him. A check of his figures revealed that he had miscopied one, and that he was using the registration precinct and not the voting precinct data. In California, voters register in registration precincts, which are then aggregated into larger voting precincts on election day. Moreover, the county clerk's data came from the recently released post-purge figures, which were not available at the time the committee had assembled its data. After several discussions, these discrepancies were straightened out.

Once again, he renewed his commitment, and the committee resumed its work on other problems. Soon thereafter, he called with another precinct change. The committee pointed out that small changes—on the order of several precincts—would not significantly affect the political composition of his district. The law of large numbers renders marginal changes meaningless. Still, he insisted that the changes be made, and the committee obliged, partly to be helpful and partly because every vote counts until you know that you have enough. Even after this change, he continued to make requests. He wanted to change one precinct because it would make his district look more symmetric, another because it had his favorite country and western bar in it, and so on. Some of the requests were granted and some were denied, but it seemed that they would never end and that his commitment would remain uncertain unless the committee complied with each and every request. His scrutiny was so intense that he arrived at the office the night before the bill went to the floor to personally proofread the legal description of his district. At one point that evening, he became convinced that the committee had made an unauthorized change in his district, and angrily demanded that the bill be corrected. After checking the data file, the staff pointed out to him that the blocks and tracts he objected to were ones that he had personally approved, and that he had been mistaken. Upon rechecking his materials, he conceded that he had been wrong and approved the bill as printed. The next day, he voted for the bill.

Case 5: "There's No Place Like Home"

The fifth case concerns a legislator whose seat lies outside the major metropolitan areas of California. His previous election had not been close, but many in the party perceived the district to be marginal nonetheless. He had a good name in the area, and as long as he ran for the seat, he could expect to run ahead of registration comfortably. Another, weaker candidate, on the other hand, could easily lose the seat.

At his initial interview with the committee, he made it clear that it was very important that the lines be drawn so as to include the house that he had recently purchased. He was not prepared to move in order to keep his seat. This presented the committee with a problem. His seat was overpopulated and needed to shed areas that were currently in its boundaries, and his house was located in a Republican stronghold that the committee would have liked to have taken out of the seat and given to his Republican neighbor. This option, however, was ruled out by his unwillingness to move. Alatorre attempted by various methods to persuade him to change his mind, but with no success. The party activists and campaign strategists were particularly annoyed with his domiciliary attachment, feeling quite rightly that the good of the party was being sacrificed for one individual's convenience.

It appeared that the committee would have to resign itself to either losing his vote or giving in to his demand. After some thought, the staff formulated a plan that would keep the house in the district, but would not in any way weaken the seat politically. When the plan was shown to the legislator, he told Alatorre that he did not like the proposal because it would look like an obvious gerrymander designed to keep his house in the district. This, he felt, would be more harmful to him than dropping a few points in registration to make his district look more compact. Somewhat exasperated, Alatorre invited him to present his own plan, which it turned out kept his house in the district by retaining more of the surrounding Republican neighborhood. Since the area he wanted to retain was highly Republican and the areas he proposed to discard in order to get rid of his population surplus were some of his most Democratic precincts, the effect was to make his district even more competitive than it already was.

The leadership was once again faced with the prospect of accepting the member's proposal in spite of its doubts or losing his vote. Although his plan was extremely unpopular within Democratic party circles, they had to accept it, and he voted for the bill.

Case 6: "Constraint from the Top"

This is the case of a tough-minded and respected member of the legislature who had served several terms and had held key committee chairmanships. Since his previous race had been very close, whether he held his seat in the next election could be determined by reapportionment. As the seat was presently constituted, it had a favorable mixture of white working-class and wealthy suburban towns, but if it were pushed further south, it would pick up more of the affluent communities and become harder to hold. If it moved north, it could pick up more of the white working-class areas and get a couple of registration points stronger. This would hardly make it a safe seat, but it was easily his best alternative.

However, his fate was not in his own hands, since much depended on what the leadership wanted to do with that area. If no seat were collapsed, then his district would be pushed south, and if one were collapsed above him, then he would be pulled north by a considerable amount. Either way, his seat would suffer a great deal of displacement. While his interests were very much at stake, he maintained a low profile during the negotiations, choosing to lobby quietly for his cause.

Since the leadership, as well as a large number of the Assemblymen themselves, felt that pushing his seat to the south would be disastrous for all concerned, there was a consensus that he should be moved north into the safer, working-class areas. His initial deficit was approximately 40,000, but the plan called for him to absorb closer to 90,000, which was perilously close to the one-third displacement rule the committee had tried to observe. After some consideration, he notified the Chairman that he would support the plan.

Shortly thereafter, the committee staff discovered that it had made a mistake in the maps that it had given him, omitting an area in the southern part of his present district that he needed in order to have the proper population. The committee staff was somewhat hesitant to bring this matter up, since reopening negotiations gives the legislator an opportunity to change his mind. However, there was no real choice in the matter, since it was better to risk the danger of his second thoughts than to incur his wrath at a later point when he discovered that there was more to his district than he had been told. Considering the circumstances and the committee's vulnerability at that point, the second round of negotiations went reasonably well. The legislator secured an apology from the committee staff and suggested a substitution of area for the one the committee proposed to add. Once again, he agreed to support the plan, and Alatorre and his staff breathed a collective sigh of relief.

As the negotiations drew to a close, the committee received a phone call from the consultant to one of the neighboring legislators who wanted to make some last-minute changes, and since this person was extremely powerful, there was no question that the changes would have to be made. The essence of them was that our legislator's district picked up some less desirable precincts and lost a point in registration from what he had agreed to. The committee staff carried out these changes on the assumption that he would be informed about them by the leadership. Somehow, communication broke down, and he did not find out that his lines had been changed until the day the bill was to be voted on. The legislator was understandably furious at the committee staff when he found out what happened, and, while the bill was being debated on the floor, he summoned the chief technical consultant to a room in the back of the Chambers. Since the legislator was a tough, burly ex-Marine, the consultant was understandably apprehensive about this confrontation, and entered the room uneasily. The legislator demanded an explanation, and became angrier at what he heard. At that point, the consultant cared less for the potential vote loss than for his own personal safety, but then the Speaker arrived. Brown listened to the legislator's angry denunciations, and then, turning to the consultant, asked, "What is my registration under this plan?" The consultant told him that it was 58 percent, and the Speaker responded, "You mean, you bastard, that you dropped my registration five points?" Since both the Speaker and the consultant knew that the Speaker's registration had not been over 60 percent for some time, and had actually risen in reapportionment by a point, the consultant knew that the Speaker was up to something, and, playing along, he answered, "It was the best that we could do." Turning to the angry legislator, Brown then asked, "How much did you drop him by?" To which the consultant responded, "We didn't drop his registration, we raised it by three points." Brown then said, "Wait a minute, you're complaining about getting three points in registration when this bastard dropped me five points." At that point, the legislator calmed down considerably, and after further discussion of the great injustice perpetrated by the committee staff upon the Speaker, the Speaker and the legislator walked out of the room arm in arm commiserating over the Speaker's plight. The consultant beat a hasty retreat from the room, and the committee received the legislator's support a few hours later.

Case 7: "On Being Vigilant"

This Assemblyman was a friend of the committee chairman and had a great deal of influence in the leadership circle. His district contained a mixture of ethnic neighborhoods and was in no particular danger of being lost. At his interview, he suggested that he would be willing to give up some Black areas on the corner of his seat to help out the surrounding severely underpopulated minority districts. The committee took his suggestion quite literally and presented him with a plan that did exactly what he recommended. His initial reaction was quite favorable, and when he indicated that he would vote for the plan, the committee proceeded to negotiate the lines of the surrounding districts on the assumption that he would vote for the plan.

As the bill reached its final stages of preparation, his consultant came to the committee office and requested that some of the Black neighborhoods that had been taken out of his district be restored to the seat, and that some of the Hispanic areas be taken out. This presented a very serious problem, since all the surrounding districts had been negotiated on the assumption that the committee's agreement with him stood. Any attempt to change things at such a late date would have caused great disruption in the committee's plans. Thus, he was told that the committee could accommodate him only if he negotiated the agreement with the other legislators himself, and if all the trades were self-contained so that there would be no rippling throughout the county. He agreed to this and went to the other legislators to ask them to trade with him. However, they were not willing to do so, and he was stuck with the committee's plan.

Basic Principles Concerning Legislative Preferences

It is possible to make some generalizations from these cases about the reapportionment process. The most important is that the perspective of the committee—especially that of its consultants and the party strategists—is often different from that of the legislators. In particular, legislators tend to have a much narrower view of the plan. What matters to legislators most is how a reapportionment plan affects them at that moment in time: will this plan hurt them or help them?

There is nothing unreasonable or irrational about this. They should be concerned about how the plan affects them, since reapportionment can determine the strength of their seats, the number and quality of challengers they will face, and even the kind of grass-roots organizations they will have to work with. The reapportioner can have the luxury of looking at the long-term consequences of a proposal, but the reapportioned can only afford to look as far as the next election.

A corollary to this principle is that if the legislator does not look after his own interests, no one else will. Legislators will sometimes profess to care about the interests of other seats, but they will not generally sacrifice their interests to help out another. Hence, the most effective participants in reapportionment prepare themselves thoroughly and stay on top of all the leadership's plans. It is important for them to know when what is vital to their interests is affected and to move quickly when they are going to be adversely affected. Trusting others for protection can be disastrous. As in most pluralistic processes, the law of least resistance applies. If hard choices have to be made, those who are least attentive and most compliant will bear the burden.

A third principle is that reapportionment is heavily influenced by uncertainty and motivated by risk aversion. Members do not know for certain what they are getting when new territory is added to their district. The political data may indicate that the new voters are friendly, but it may turn out that they are hostile. Every new precinct contains a potential challenger with unknown sources of strength. Consequently, much of what legislators do during reapportionment can be explained as risk aversion. Wanting to hold on to a seat even though a legislator is planning to run for higher office is risk aversion. Insisting on a one-third displacement rule is risk aversion. Wanting to have districts made safer is risk aversion. The cumulative effect of risk-averse strategies is an enormous amount of inertia in reapportionment. Most members want the least amount of disruption possible to their districts and view departures from that rule with a great deal of suspicion.

A participant in New York reapportionment during the 'sixties nicely described the reluctance of legislators to enter reapportionment in the following manner:

> The typical legislator suffers from the long proceedings: the need to guard himself against too much tampering with his own boundaries; the need to lose thousands of known constituents and acquire thousands more who are completely unknown; the need to reorganize associational ties of many kinds with churches, union locals, businessmen, clubs and the like; the necessary struggle with other legislators with whom he had hitherto been at peace; the need to read new newspapers; perhaps a change in his home address; the possibility of increased risk of losing his seat; the need to shuffle his staff around to accommodate new interests

and drop old ones; the need to reconsider his factional alignments in the legislature; the need to familiarize himself with new units of government, new school districts and all their legislative needs.[2]

The popular myth is that legislators enter reapportionment with the joyous expectation of securing their careers for a decade. In fact, most simply want to come out of reapportionment as relatively unscathed as they possibly can.

Finally, it is interesting, and a little ironic, to find that legislators sometimes find themselves in the position of defending good government principles against the wishes of party leaders. To be sure, the motive behind defending some formalist principle is typically self-interest, but the important consideration is that it does happen. The legislator who defends city and county boundaries may actually be protecting his reputation with local officials, or trying to block a plan that would displace him substantially. The legislator who did not want to move from his house knowingly made his seat more competitive. Even the legislator who complained about his displacement was preserving district continuity. It is not the case that the self-interests of legislators always conflict with good government principles, just as it is also not the case that they always coincide. There are enough of these principles, and they conflict so frequently, that one can almost always find a good government reason to defend any decision that is made.

Reversing the Downsian Model

To some extent, the preferences that legislators have about their districts are idiosyncratic. It would be hard, and of little consequence, to theorize about when and why someone would want to have his mother-in-law or an amusement park or a shopping center in his district. It is enough to say that some legislators will insist on odd things, and that district lines will sometimes reflect these requests. More generally, however, the process can be characterized as the reversal of the normal Downsian electoral model.[3] In the usual case, voters compare candidates on the positions they defend and the actions they have taken, and vote for the one that is closest to their own interests. In reapportionment, the reverse is true. The candidates compare voters and choose the ones that are closest to them, subject to a strong displacement constraint. Just as the voters must try to synthesize the

2. Alfred De Grazia, *Apportionment and Representative Government* (New York: Praeger, 1963), p. 146.

3. Anthony Downs, *An Economic Theory of Democracy* (New York: Harper and Row, 1957).

many positions the candidates take into one overall assessment, so the legislator must try to characterize potential constituents in terms of their overall political disposition, ethnic composition, and electoral behavior. The incumbent's instinct to want voters who are like himself is a self-preserving one. The more they are like him, the more likely they will vote for him. If he is a liberal, he will be apprehensive about acquiring conservative voters, and vice versa.

The analogy of reapportionment to the Downsian model applies also to the problem of uncertainty. Voters will often have difficulty figuring out where candidates stand on various issues and must resort to crude rules of thumb such as which party the candidate belongs to or what other leading figures in the candidate's party are saying. Similarly, the candidate will often be uncertain about the voters being added to his district, particularly when they live in areas that the incumbent is totally unfamiliar with. Incumbents will therefore have to resort to rules of thumb such as the registration of the area or the general ethnic and economic makeup of the community.

The analogy can be extended further. Voters are less affected by a few disagreements with a particular candidate if the candidate agrees with them on most other issues, or has done so for a considerable period in the past. In the same way, incumbents will tolerate the addition of a small number of incompatible voters if the incumbents are very close to, and hence very secure with, most of the remaining voters in their district. On the other hand, a marginal district is one in which the ideological or ethnic differences between the incumbent and the electorate are greater, and so the addition of more incompatible voters is more threatening.

In the voter model, the candidates shift their positions to increase their electoral chances. In the reapportionment model, the positions of the voters and the candidates do not change; rather, the incumbents choose their voters so as to increase their chances of winning. Nonetheless, the basic idea is the same in both models, which is that by diminishing the differences between the candidate and the voters, the rational voter's utility increases, and the probability of voting for the candidate increases as well. The irony of making incumbents safer is that it does so by giving voters representatives who are more like themselves, which is curious to consider, given the generally negative connotations of a gerrymander.

Conclusion

The concerns of legislators with respect to redistricting are various and in some instances very idiosyncratic. However, their behavior can generally be described as risk-averse and cautious. Politics is a career for most legislators, and the professionalization of the office has encouraged them to think of politics as a full-time, lifelong vocation. They react to the various threats that reapportionment poses in much the same way that those in other professions would react to threats to their job security. The changes brought about by redistricting bring out the politician's enormous fear of the unknown. Those who are less content with the status quo or who consider themselves to be invulnerable will be more willing to take risks, but those who fall between these two extremes in the spectrum will fear the effects of change much more.

7

Bargaining and Legislative Reapportionment

The heart of legislative reapportionment is the trade of territory among legislators. This can mean either that legislators themselves engage in bilateral negotiations, or that the committee staff and political leaders impose what amounts to a trade between two members. Either way, seats that are below the ideal population gain new areas, and seats that are above it lose some of their old ones. The problem for the legislator with the underpopulated district is to add population in such a manner as to minimize dislocation (i.e., displacement as defined earlier) and to improve, or at least maintain, his partisan strength. The legislator with the overpopulated district wants to lose as little old territory as possible while at the same time maintaining or increasing the level of partisan support. The role of the reapportioners—which in California means the Speaker of the Assembly, the President of the Senate, the Elections and Reapportionment Committee Chairmen, and other top-ranking legislators—is to direct legislative trades to make them conform more closely to the leadership's overall partisan, bipartisan, or affirmative action goals.

Some trades make both of the legislators better off and are therefore easy to consummate. Others make one or both of the legislators worse off and require the application of influence and power from the reapportioning party's leadership. This chapter will consider the kinds of situations in which the incentives of the legislators who are trading are compatible, and the kinds of situations in which they are not.

TABLE 7   *Typology of Seats*

	Underpopulated	Overpopulated
Marginal Seat	TYPE I "The Needy"	TYPE III "The Cautious"
Safe Seat	TYPE II "The Martyrs"	TYPE IV "The Big Spenders"

A Typology of Bargaining Positions

The cases discussed in the previous chapter demonstrate that legislators have many things to consider when they decide how they want their districts to be changed. However, two factors stand out as most important. One is the partisan strength of the seat. Obviously, those in highly marginal seats will want to improve their position as much as possible, whereas those in safe seats will want to preserve an adequate level of strength. The other crucial consideration is the amount of displacement the seat must absorb. As discussed earlier, all legislators will want to minimize the number of new people they must absorb, since new people introduce uncertainty and require more initial work. Those legislators with higher initial deficits or surpluses will have to expect greater displacement than those who are closer to having the ideal population. On an individual basis, concern for a successor, the location of key fund-raisers, public opinion in the county, and personality will matter, but *ceteris paribus*, the difficulty of trades should vary systematically with partisan strength and displacement problems.

Table 7 shows four typical kinds of bargaining positions. The first type is "the needy." These are holders of seats that are both underpopulated and vulnerable from a partisan point of view. They have to pick up new areas, but they must be very careful not to add too many hostile voters. This usually means that they will be very discriminating in their choices and will rule out many simple alternatives as unacceptable because of their adverse partisan effects. When Type I seats are clustered (where *cluster* is defined as a set of seats with common boundaries), a particularly difficult problem arises. Type I seats that belong to the same party will oppose surrendering their good territory to each other and will want to give their bad territory away, but will find no neighbor who is willing to accept it. When the Type I seats belong to different parties, trades may be possible from a partisan perspective, but still can cause substantial displacement problems, since the seat that surrenders territory adds a ripple change to its initial population deficit.

The second type of seat is one that is underpopulated but partisanly strong. Legislators holding such seats can be called "martyrs," since they are often in the position of having to suffer a slight loss in partisanship in order to get to the ideal population. A cluster of "martyrs" raises issues of displacement and equity. Since they are all underpopulated, unless the trades are handled carefully some will have to absorb more displacement than others. Some may also experience larger losses in partisan strength than the others, and the committee will have to spend a great deal of time assuring them that the exchanges are equitable. Provided they can agree on what is a fair level of sacrifice, Type II cases are not as difficult to handle as Type I.

The third category is the overpopulated and weak seat, or simply "the cautious." The Type III seat is slightly better off than the Type I, since legislators generally know what they already have in their own districts better than what their neighboring legislators have. This gives the legislators who have to lose some of their own territory an advantage over those who have to pick up someone else's area, since they are in a better position to know what can be done to strengthen their seats. Nonetheless, the situations of I and III are not all that dissimilar, since in both cases the areas that must be discarded or acquired have to be chosen with care if the incumbent's position is to be maintained. When two or more Type III seats border one another, this can cause displacement problems unless there is a new or open seat in the region that can absorb everyone's excess territory. Provided that a Type III legislator is willing to take more displacement, it is advantageous to be surrounded by Type III seats from the other party: they will be glad to get rid of some of the excess, and it can be useful to shore up the position of another seat. This is less likely to be the case when the surrounding Type III seats belong to the same party.

The last of the four types is the overpopulated and safe seat. Holders of such seats have the most enviable position, in the sense that they are less vulnerable to partisan changes and also have the slight informational advantage of losing territory they are familiar with rather than picking up areas that belong to another seat. When a cluster of Type IV seats from the same party occurs, the party usually has an opportunity to create a new seat in a given area, just as a cluster of Type I seats from the same party usually means that the party loses a seat in that area. A cluster of Type IV seats from different parties will result in a marginal seat unless one of the parties can persuade its legislators to give up substantial amounts of good area to the open seat. Such altruism is rare.

A state can be described as a distribution of these seat types that must trade with one another. Some trades will be Pareto improvements—in which at least one of the traders is made better off, and neither is made worse off—but many others will not be. Of those that are not strictly Pareto improvements, some are nonetheless complementary. This is because safe seats can afford to be made a little worse off so long as they stay above a certain reservation level of safety. Complementarity so defined is a kind of modified Pareto rule. Complementary trades should occur more naturally than noncomplementary ones, since there is a stronger incentive to trade. For the same reason, there should be less need for leadership intervention in those cases.

Using this modified definition, it is possible to identify complementary and noncomplementary conditions with respect to partisanship and displacement. Beginning with strength of partisanship, two seats in the same party will be complementary (1) when one is strong and the other is weak (if the strong seat can give up some of its best territory but still remain safe), or (2) when both are strong (since each can remain safe although giving up good areas). However, they will be noncomplementary when both are weak, because neither can make the other stronger without weakening itself. All trades between seats from the opposite party will be partisanly complementary, since each will improve by giving the other its weakest areas. In terms of demographic needs, seats will be complementary when one seat is over and the other is under, since, *ceteris paribus*, this minimizes displacement for both. When both the partisanship and the demographic needs are complementary, the incentive to trade should be strongest. When neither partisanship nor the demographic needs of the seats are complementary, then the incentive to trade should be weak. Obviously, when the seats are complementary in one sense but not the other, the incentive is mixed, and much will depend on how the legislators value potential electoral strength versus displacement.

These expectations are expressed in Table 8. *C*, *NC*, and *M* stand for complementary, noncomplementary, and mixed, respectively. The rows of the table represent the different combinations of types, and the columns represent whether the seats are in the same or different parties. Rather than going through each of the cases in excruciating detail, the predictions can be summarized as follows:

I. The two noncomplementary conditions occur when two seats from the same party are marginal, and both either need to lose population or to gain it. Their population needs do not mesh, and neither can help the other without suffering itself.

II. Seats from the same party are strongly complementary when one is strong and over and the other is weak and under, or when one is weak and over and the other is strong and under.

TABLE 8   *Complementarity of Trades Between Seat Types*

	Same Party	Opposite Party
I, II Marg, Under Safe, Under	M	M
I, III Marg, Under Marg, Over	M	C
I, IV Marg, Under Safe, Over	C	C
II, III Safe, Under Marg, Over	C	C
II, IV Safe, Under Safe, Over	M	C
III, IV Marg, Over Safe, Over	M	M
I, I Weak, Under Weak, Under	NC	M
II, II Safe, Under Safe, Under	M	M
III, III Marg, Over Marg, Over	NC	M
IV, IV Safe, Over Safe, Over	M	M

III.   Since seats from opposite parties always have complementary partisan needs, they are strongly complementary when their population needs are also complementary.

IV.   In all other cases, the incentives are mixed.

Several observations are worthy of note. It is ironic that the only conditions of pure noncomplementarity occur between seats in the same party. This may explain why some of the bitterest controversies during reapportionment stem from the competing claims of legislators from the same party. The absence of a pure noncomplementary situation between seats in opposite parties may also help to explain why the bipartisan gerrymander occurs as frequently as it does.

This is not to say that a bipartisan gerrymander is inevitable, as shall be discussed in greater detail later. First of all, six of the ten conditions

TABLE 9   *Classification of Assembly Seats by Types*

	All	Democratic	Republican
TYPE I Marg,Under	14	12	2
TYPE II Safe,Under	30	21	9
TYPE III Marg,Over	24	15	9
TYPE IV Safe,Over	12	1	11

have mixed incentives, and this means that bipartisan gerrymanders can break down over the issue of displacement (which occurs when demographic needs are not compatible). Also, if a legislator from one seat decides that he does not want to trade with another legislator because he wants the other legislator's seat to be weaker, then the complementarity breaks down. This amounts to saying that complementarity demands that a legislator look only at whether the trade makes him better or worse off: he cannot refuse a trade because it makes another seat better off per se. Partisanship enters the reapportionment process when legislators from one party either refuse to strengthen themselves or decide to weaken themselves in order to weaken their opponents. In other words, partisanship occurs when legislators do not regard their self-interest exclusively and are willing to sacrifice their self-interests to adversely affect the interests of others.

In the 1981 California Assembly reapportionment, there were numerous examples of all four types of seats in this classification scheme and of almost all of the twenty possible types of trades. Specifically, the breakdown for seat types appears in Table 9. The figures of 60 percent Democratic and 40 percent Republican registration are used as measures of safety, although any flat categorization of this sort will, of course, necessarily be inaccurate in certain cases. There are a few safe Democratic seats with less than 60 percent registration, and some that have over 60 percent registration and are not very safe at all. The same is true of the Republican classification. However, the criteria are generally applicable, and where they are not, it does not change the overall picture greatly: namely, that the Democrats had more seats in the underpopulated categories than the Republicans. Conversely, the Republicans had by far the largest concentration of safe, overpopulated (i.e., Type IV) seats. The Democratic underpopulated, weak seats (i.e., Type I) were scattered widely across the state, with the exceptions of two pairs of adjoining seats, one pair in Los Angeles County and the other in San Diego County. In both instances, as the model suggests, the negotiations were long and laborious, involving numerous iterations until the final compromise was accepted. The Democratic underpopulated but safe seats (i.e., Type II) were mostly concentrated in Los Angeles and San Francisco, and the issues in these trades were primarily displacement and ethnicity. The overpopulated and marginal seats for both parties were mostly situated in non-urban areas, since the census figures indicated considerable growth in some of the valley and mountainous counties. The Republican Type IV seats were concentrated in Orange and San Diego counties.

It is also possible to look at the distribution of territorial trades that occurred in the 1981 Assembly reapportionment, omitting trivial exchanges of blocks and partial census tracts that were necessary to mend city splits or ease the precincting burden for the county clerks. A trade can only count once, so that if X takes some territory from Y, and Y takes some from X, it counts as one trade even if it occurred in steps or discretely over time. The breakdown of trades so defined appears in Table 10. As noted before, the two pure noncomplementary conditions are I, I and III, III, and as predicted, negotiations were in fact difficult in these situations. For instance, both of the two I, I trades were lengthy. Of the six III, III trades, four were between Democrats, and of those, two involved one legislator who was so displeased with the plan in the end that he did not vote for the bill. In the case of one of the other III, III trades, differences were settled amicably between friends without the committee's intervention (one of the legislators took a drop in strength to help his friend), and the other never became a problem because one of the incumbents decided to run for higher office. In addition to those already mentioned, the most laborious trades involved three I, III situations and one I, II. The I, III were instances where both seats needed to strengthen themselves, and so the complementarity of population was not really very helpful: getting the overpopulated seat's worst areas would have only further weakened the underpopulated seat. In two of those cases, the committee lost a vote in the negotiations. The I, II difficulty was largely caused by a particular incumbent's fear that he could only move into certain very specific types of areas, and might have been avoided with a different incumbent. In summary, there is some evidence in the Assembly's experience that the partisan and demographic situations of seats have an important impact on the process of negotiations. Once again, it should be said that this does not mean that other, more idiosyncratic factors do not matter: only

TABLE 10 *Breakdown of Trades in Assembly Reapportionment*

	Same Party	Opposite Party
I,II Marg,Under Safe,Under	7	8
I,III Marg,Under Marg,Over	8	3
I,IV Marg,Under Safe,Over	1	6
II,III Safe,Under Marg,Over	4	4
II,IV Safe,Under Safe,Over	0	4
III,IV Marg,Over Safe,Over	3	8
I,I Marg,Under Marg,Under	2	0
II,II Safe,Under Safe,Under	18	7
III,III Marg,Over Marg,Over	6	8
IV,IV Safe,Over Safe,Over	7	0

that partisan and demographic factors play a major role in determining the obstacles of negotiation.

Trades with Intervention

For many reasons, legislators will either refuse to trade or will make the wrong kind of trade from the perspective of the overall plan. It is the job of the committee chairman and the legislative leadership to persuade, or to force, recalcitrant members of the legislature to accept the plan. Persuasion means getting the legislators to change their opinions about the options that are presented to them. This can be called facilitating a trade by influence. However, it is not always possible to change a legislator's mind, and in those cases the leadership must resort to force and threats. Imposing a trade by power is defined as a situation in which the legislator is never persuaded that the plan is in his or her best interests, but votes for it for fear of the consequences of opposing the leadership. To be sure, the distinction between power and influence is not always so clear in real life, since fear of the consequences of voting against the bill may be a major factor in determining legislative preferences. Still, it is possible to distinguish between those who must be dragged kicking and screaming into support for the bill and those who vote for the plan with happiness in their hearts.

The simplest method of influence is to persuade legislators that a plan is actually in their best interests and that their contrary preferences are based on misinformation. This is typically a staff task, since it involves analyzing alternative possible moves and showing the political consequences of each. If legislators can be brought to see that areas they think are weak are in fact strong, or conversely, that areas they think are strong are in fact weak, they will sometimes change their opinions.

One example of this procedure is the case of a freshman legislator who had been a county supervisor prior to his election to the legislature. He felt that he knew the areas he had represented as a supervisor pretty well. When the committee proposal called for him to lose some territory in the southern part of his present seat and to move north into some ethnic areas, he was initially very hesitant, since it did not raise his registration to a level he deemed acceptable. Based on his knowledge of the county, he felt that his registration would improve more if he took some areas on his western border and regained some of the territory to the south that the committee had removed. The committee staff did an analysis of every precinct on his borders and demonstrated that the northern precincts were stronger and that what kept his registration from getting any higher was his reluctance to give up more of his precincts to the south. The committee even brought in one of its staff who knew the area very well to give a neighborhood-by-neighborhood description of the legislator's district. In the end, the weight of the committee's evidence persuaded him that he had been given the best areas available to him, and he voted for the bill.

Sometimes, instead of needing more information, legislators paradoxically need less. Sometimes, that is, trades can only take place if the relevant information is withheld from them. This sort of situation occurs when the attitudes of the legislators and the leadership towards goals or risks do not agree. For instance, the leadership may think that a certain level of partisanship constitutes a safe seat, while the legislator, being more risk-averse, may want a greater margin of safety. Or the legislator may think that partisan considerations come first, whereas the leadership may need to fulfill some commitment it has to minorities. Whatever the reason, there may be times when certain facts should not be emphasized to the legislator.

Consider the case of a legislator from an urban seat that on paper had strong registration but had been won in the previous election by only a slender margin. His seat had to pick up additional population as well as lose some of its strong ethnic areas to surrounding ethnic seats. A projection of the 1980 race into the new seat indicated that the legislator would have lost it if it had had the new lines, but the committee concluded that with the advantage of a couple of years as an incumbent and with a more favorable electoral climate than 1980, the incumbent legislator should be able to hold on to the seat in 1982. Normally, these projections would have been incorporated in the information legislators were given by the committee, but the committee chairman decided that no good would be served by including the projections on this occasion. Unfortunately, just before the meeting with this legislator, a diligent staff member spotted the omission and unwittingly included the projection in the seat's packet. This change was not noticed until the committee chairman opened the packet and started to recite various facts and figures to the legislator. As his eyes hit the projection sheet, he realized that a mistake had been made, and without missing a step, he pulled the offending piece of information from the packet and handed it to a consultant. This legislator later voted for the plan with some minor alterations.

Persuasion sometimes means giving unambiguous and unwavering signals about what can and cannot be negotiated. The leaders have to be able to say no to certain demands if they hope to maintain their goals, and being able to say no without losing a lot of votes requires that some ground rules be established: for example, that there will be no splitting of ethnic communities or gratuitous division of cities. In order to maintain these rules, there should be very few, if any, exceptions to them, and those exceptions should either be justifiable or else kept secret. Giving clear and unambiguous signals is particularly important in the last stages of negotiation, when nickel and dime demands such as those outlined in the previous chapter seem to abound. The pressure on the leadership to cave in is enormous because it will always seem that saying no increases the probability of losing a vote and hence the bill. However, the costs of caving in are even greater, since negotiations can quickly unravel as legislators see that others have been able to extract last-minute gains.

For instance, one of the most prolonged negotiations involved a legislator whose seat abutted a growing Hispanic section of the city. Leaders of the Hispanic community had initially proposed that this legislator's district pick up nearly all of that community, making it a 40 percent ethnic seat. Understandably, the incumbent felt threatened by a proposal to transform his district so radically, and he countered with a plan that would have divided the Hispanics between two Assembly seats. After many weeks of negotiation, the Hispanics changed their position to 30 percent, and it was Alatorre's job to sell the idea to the incumbent. All proposals that would have lowered the Hispanics below 30 percent were ruled unacceptable by the chairman. The incumbent appealed to the Speaker, but to no avail. The rule that there would be no division of ethnic communities under a Black Speaker and an Hispanic Elections and Reapportionment Chairman was upheld. Faced with the strength of this ground rule, the incumbent accepted the plan and voted for the bill.

A final instrument of persuasion is peer group opinion. While it is not as strong as one might hope, there are occasional indications that legislators feel constrained by an implicit sense of fairness. For instance, the words *rape* and *being a pig* often enter legislative reapportionment discussions. *Rape* in this context means the use of political muscle to take unfair advantage of another (to get his or her best areas), and *being a pig* means taking more good territory than one needs or failing to surrender good territory to those who need it more. If the other legislators think that a legislator is being piglike and selfish, he runs a higher risk that they will coalesce against him and that he will be cut out of the final deal. This really follows from the principle of least resistance, in that if a legislator is being unreasonably obstinate, others may write him off as too expensive to deal with (i.e., it costs more to win his support than to lose it), and they may form their coalition with those who are less resistant. The skillful bargainer has to have some sense of when he has stepped over the line between reasonable and unreasonable demands.

Peer group pressure figured in the 1981 California reapportionment in several instances. One example involved a legislator who, upon seeing his lines, told Alatorre that the plan for him was too conservative and that he needed a more drastic alteration in his district lines. A week later, he submitted to the committee a farcical proposal for a rambling, contorted district that linked all the areas he thought he might want by a network of narrow corridors. The committee chairman and staff reacted with horror at the idea that they might have to present such a district to the public, and told the incumbent that they found it preposterous. As word of his proposal got around, he discovered that other legislators also felt the plan was ridiculous, and he seemed to become more self-conscious, and perhaps even embarrassed, by the idea. Later, he negotiated a more moderate settlement.

When persuasion fails, the application of power sometimes becomes necessary. As stated before, this means getting legislators to vote for the bill by inducements that are unrelated to reapportionment. Positive inducements include such things as a chairmanship of a key committee or money for the next campaign. A negative inducement can mean withdrawing such rewards or withholding them in the future. Recall, for instance, the earlier case of a freshman legislator who had to weigh the cost of losing promotions by voting against the bill versus the cost of adverse county opinion if he voted for it. The pressures are even stronger for senior legislators who already hold key committee chairs.

An example of an occasion when side payments (in the game theoretic sense of the word) became necessary is the case of a "broken promise" which involved a legislator who had negotiated a set of lines with the committee very early on in the process. On the whole, this person was pleased with what had been negotiated and was not anxious to make any changes. Towards the final hour, several of the neighboring legislators, who had not committed their support for the bill because they felt they had given up too much, made their votes contingent on the restoration of some of their lost territory. These changes left the first legislator with only part of what had been bargained for, and so this person was understandably disturbed about last-minute changes in something that had already been agreed to. The decision to go ahead with these alterations angered this legislator, and it was up to the Speaker to make things right. While the exact details of their meeting were never revealed, promises were apparently made, and this person's support for the plan was restored.

The greatest weapon, however, that the leadership has is the threat of excluding a recalcitrant member from the coalition. If a legislator is not one of those whose vote is counted on, he is less likely to get what he wants from reapportionment. William Riker, in his *Theory of Coalitions*, proposed that there is an optimal size for coalitions, which he termed the minimum winning coalition.[1] His idea was simply that as coalitions get large, they must make more concessions, with the result that there is less benefit for all the members of the coalition to share. To the extent that the leadership of any coalition can be certain of how the voting will go, its coalition should be just large enough to win and no larger. To the extent that it is uncertain about the support of its members, it must add more members to it to ensure that it has enough to win. The trade-off between the number of concessions and the certainty of winning is very apparent in reapportionment. Since there are few instances of pure complementarity in reapportionment, the leadership must expend time and resources building its coalition by encouraging trades. For the same reason, the concessions made to one legislator often come at the expense of another in terms of displacement or partisan strength. It is easier to try to please the least number that is

1. William Riker, *Theory of Coalitions* (New Haven: Yale University Press, 1962).

necessary in order to get a bill passed and to write off the other votes as the price to be paid for political support. The problem, as Riker aptly explained in his study, is that if the leaders of the coalition are unsure of their support, they will not know how many votes they need to court in order to have enough to win. Of course, the uncertainty works both ways: since the members cannot be sure that they will be needed, their leverage is somewhat diminished as well. The last person to join a co-alition should have enormous leverage, and indeed there was ample evidence of this in the Speakership fight that preceded reapportion-ment. In that case, however, the commitments were well known, whereas in the case of reapportionment the commitments were not well known until a straw vote was taken in caucus, and by then the bill was in preparation. In this instance, the asymmetry of information about the size of the coalition worked to the committee's advantage.

What Makes Legislators Effective Bargainers?

One cannot fail to notice during the reapportionment process that some members of the legislature are more effective than others in getting what they want. That is not to say that the most skillful bargainers necessarily got the best deals, since demographic factors and the intent of the leadership play a major role in determining what a legislator gets. However, it does mean that given an approximately equal starting point in the negotiation process, some of the legislators will be more effective than others in improving on that initial position. Why is this so?

There are several things that make an incumbent an effective bar-gainer. One is that he or she will usually have developed some outside expertise and knowledge of the area concerned. All legislators have some notion of what their districts are like, but many lack information about surrounding areas and other seats. They may know little or noth-ing about the registration, loyalty, or ethnic makeup of neighborhoods that are outside the border of their existing districts. The reapportion-ment committee collects as much information about these areas as it can and uses this data to try to make its case as to why the legislator should move in one or the other direction. Legislators who do their homework, come up with specific proposals, and comment in knowledgeable ways about proposed changes enjoy several advantages.

To begin with, it will be harder for the reapportioner to mislead the legislator. Sometimes areas will be favorable in one dimension but not in another: the registration may be adequate, but the loyalty might be low; the ethnic makeup may be such as to encourage a challenge from an ethnic candidate; or there may be ambitious would-be candidates lurking in the city councils of the areas the committee proposes to add to the district. A legislator who is informed about such things has a much stronger position to bargain from and keeps the reapportioners honest.

Secondly, being prepared early in the process minimizes the chance that the legislator's preferences will be squeezed by the last-minute pressures of bill preparation. If the legislator postpones his judgment while others make theirs, the inertia of completed deals will grow. Consider the situation of legislator X who is surrounded on four sides by Q, R, S, and T. If Q, R, S, and T have already negotiated their lines among themselves with the approval of the leadership, then it will be harder for X to make any subsequent changes. His options will be closed off, and if the leadership does not need his vote, it will probably resist undoing other commitments for the sake of one member. Preparation and making preferences known early in the process are important ways of keeping the negotiations open.

A third factor that influences the bargaining effectiveness of the legislator is his clout. This can take many forms. It can mean power in the sense of being able to get the leadership to change its position for fear of the consequences of a particular legislator not being happy. Such power can come from the legislator's ability to raise money for the party, or from his control over a crucial block of votes that are needed in order to get a bill passed, or from his being in the fortuitous position of being the last vote needed in order to get the bill passed. The last case, as was noted before, is a tricky business, since a miscalculation can mean that the legislator is left out in the cold completely and gets none of what he wants.

Personality can also determine a legislator's effectiveness. Perseverance is a particularly useful attribute in bargaining of this sort. If a legislator is firm in negotiations—but not totally inflexible—people will follow the path of least resistance and try to find someone else to make the concession. If someone has to take bad territory and the candidates are an obstinate legislator and an easygoing one, then the reapportioner will naturally turn to the one who is more flexible. A legislator's persistence can be a strong deterrent. His opponents must calculate not only the immediate cost in time and resources of opposing him at the moment, but also the cost over time of guarding against his retaliation in the future. In short, a legislator can be successful if he can get his opponents to think that it is not worthwhile to oppose him. Possessing this kind of personality gives him a veto power over matters that intimately concern him and can be quite useful in the reapportionment process.

Conclusion

It is possible to characterize the bargaining process by the demographic and partisan needs of various seats and by the complementarity of the needs of neighboring seats. The length of time and probability of success will vary with the compatibility of bordering seats. The leadership has various methods of facilitating trades and will employ these when negotiations stall. Ultimately, the strongest incentive for a legislator to come to some agreement with the leadership is the threat of being left out and getting none of the things he or she wants.

8

The Staff and Data of Reapportionment

One of the most important tasks of reapportionment is to assess the political impact of various trades. This is necessary no matter whether the ultimate purpose is a bipartisan, partisan, or affirmative action plan. Since all reapportionments will necessarily affect the partisan balance of a state, district lines cannot be neutral even if the line drawers are impartial themselves. The reapportioner is faced with two choices: either the plan can be drawn without regard for political statistics, or it can be drawn by closely monitoring its political impact. A plan drawn without political statistics is not necessarily one without political design.[1] Almost every political operative in a state has intuitions and ideas about how the state can be carved up for this or that purpose. What is at stake is whether these intuitions are informed by data. A plan that tries to be neutral in its outcome, or fair in some agreed-upon sense to all the participants, has to be able to justify its final product— to show that it has been neutral or fair. Political data are for this reason a requisite feature of reapportionment.

The crucial role of political data in the reapportionment exercise

---

1. Common Cause recommends that lines be drawn without the use of "the political affiliations of registered voters, previous election results, or other demographic information for the purpose of favoring any political party, incumbent legislator, or other person or group." In *Toward a System of "Fair and Effective Representation"* (Washington, D.C.: Common Cause, 1977), p. 30. Robert Dixon was scornful of this position, saying that "Politically uninformed districting solely on the basis of symmetry, compactness and population equality, with the aid of computers, can only lead to chance goodness or badness or to a bad plan which is the product of hidden special motives cloaked in the guise of population considerations alone." Robert G. Dixon, Jr., *Democratic Representation and Reapportionment in Law and Politics* (New York: Oxford University Press, 1968), p. 19.

raises a number of issues. One might think that the increasing sophistication of computers and data development would give incumbents an enormously powerful tool for their self-protection. The capacity to know the ethnic or partisan breakdown of a neighborhood at the block level should greatly diminish the incumbent's uncertainty. Is this the case, however? What sorts of data are most persuasive to legislators? How accurate is the information given to them, and does it really answer the sorts of questions that concern most legislators?

Institutional and Quantitative Approaches Compared

Political data can take many forms. The qualitative sort is the data of the political operative, the kind obtained from walking a district or working on many campaigns in a particular area. One veteran of several reapportionments, for instance, recalls that he designed a district in 1970 by sending an assistant out to the neighborhoods to call back information from corner phone booths about the kinds of cars parked in the streets, the ethnic makeup of the kids playing in the neighborhoods, the type of housing stock, the existence of trailer parks, and the amount of new construction in the area. Allegedly, the Burton Congressional plan was built with similar information:

> Meanwhile Burton, Hardy and Berman had thrown out an intelligence-gathering net to collect the information they couldn't get from the senate computers. Burton made hundreds of telephone calls to a network of sources—an old friend from the Young Democrats here, a local politician's aid there—asking what the trends were, where best to draw the lines. Hardy actually traveled to Pasadena and San Diego and cruised neighborhoods that had to be split, looking at the makes and models of cars on the streets, trying to divine the socioeconomic character and the political mood. Later, Burton would be able to divert a boundary line a little bit this way or that—to take in a Jewish condominium complex, or a clump of black voters, or a block of student housing.[2]

This approach has several advantages. To begin with, it is far cheaper than building a large computerized data set and takes less effort. Moreover, qualitative data generated from the detailed knowledge of local political operatives can in some instances give the reapportioner a better feel for the areas in question. A computerized file will contain only standardized information such as registration figures, the percent of Hispanics, age breakdown by tract, and the like. The operative can re-

2. Rian Malan, "The Boss," *California*, November 1981, p. 164.

call the history of a seat and the idiosyncratic characteristics of neighborhoods—things that would not show up on census or registration
forms. One might ask, therefore, whether the introduction of computerized data has been an improvement?

The main advantage of computerized data is its objectivity. With
qualitative data, there is no guarantee that the observations and intuitions of any two political operatives will agree. For instance, when the
Assembly reapportionment committee first began to examine where it
would place its new Hispanic seats, it received contrary opinions about
whether there were enough Hispanics in the Salinas Valley in Monterey
County to create what was later to become known as the "John Steinbeck" seat. Since disagreement over options will occur even when all
parties agree to the facts, arguments over the data can only make matters worse. Of course, this is true also, though to a lesser extent, of
quantitative data, even though there is only one official census tape and
one official voting return for each county, because keypunching errors
are possible and methodological assumptions differ about how to
merge census and political data. Even so, it is still an order of magni-
tude easier to get people to agree about "hard data" than about "soft
data."

Consider one kind of problem that arises when reapportioners rely
on qualitative data. Assume that a Democratic committee draws for a
Republican party legislator a district that it claims is safely Republican,
according to its sources. Even if the two parties could agree on the
meaning of the word *safe*, it would be possible for a Republican political
operative to convince the Republican legislator that the seat was not as
strong as the Democratically controlled committee said it was. To resolve this dispute, it would be necessary to arrive at some consensus as
to what the actual level of registration really was or what the outcome
of past political races had been. In addition, in order to satisfy the U.S.
Supreme Court that the districts unarguably adhered to the principle
of "one man, one vote," it would be necessary to show that the population of the tracts adds up to a number that is within an allowable deviation from the ideal and that, where applicable, the percentage of minorities had not been lessened significantly. Both of these tasks would
require "hard data."

Once committed to providing objective data, the enormous size of a
data set for a large state such as California requires that the data be entered into a computer. It is possible to draw lines in a large state without
the aid of a computer, but there are several drawbacks. First, trying to
work by hand with tract data—let alone smaller units such as precincts
or blocks—is a time-consuming operation. Secondly, it is not possible
to carry out continuous negotiations this way, since last-minute
changes would be deadly. There would be no way that large areas could

TABLE 11   *Sample of Short Printout Provided to Members*

1980 General Election Percent voting for:			Assembly District 44 —————Demographics———————	
———————President———————		125,583	Total Population	291,995
Carter	(Dem)	43.24%	White	82.20%
Reagan	(Rep)	42.59%	Black	6.10%
Anderson	(Ind)	10.32%	Asian	5.23%
——————U.S. Senate——————		122,006	Hispanic	12.73%
Cranston	(Dem)	64.87%	—————Registration———————	
Gann	(Rep)	29.72%	Total Registration	175,160
———————Congress————————		117,935	Democratic Reg	57.75%
	(Dem)	60.58%	Republican Reg	30.10%
	(Rep)	35.56%	Declines to State Reg	9.66%
—————State Senate——————		16,259	Turnout	137,500
	(Dem)	44.60%	Democratic Turnout	57.64%
	(Rep)	51.12%	Republican Turnout	32.14%
———Attorney General————			————————Issues——————————	
Burke	(Dem)	51.18%	Proposition 4	37.03%
Deukmejian	(Rep)	45.36%	Proposition 10	54.77%
——Lieutenant Governor——				
Dymally	(Dem)	49.12%		
Curb	(Rep)	44.35%		

be redrawn quickly. Consequently, working without a computerized data base restricts the freedom to negotiate. Negotiations have to be closed well in advance of the deadline, and the plan must be constantly defended against the urge to make last-minute changes or incorporate second thoughts. This requires consummate political skill and sufficient nerve not to cave in under the pressure. By permitting constant adjustments, the computer makes the negotiations more open and flexible.

Ways of Assessing Partisan Effects

However soft and hard data are balanced, the basic task is to measure the impact of various plans on the relative strength of the two parties in order to advise legislators on the desirability of adding new or losing old areas. One straightforward method of doing this is to look at the results of different races in new areas and conclude from the tendency of those races whether the area is safe, marginal, or hopeless in its partisanship. Table 11 shows the short-form printout of the kind that was provided to legislators when the committee made changes in their districts, giving them the results of several races as well as the registration, the number of voters, demographic information, and a list of the precincts in their district. The software was set up so that as the lines were changed on a graphics terminal, the data would appear on another screen and then could be printed out to give the legislator a copy.

Legislators can look at how they ran in various parts of their districts in order to decide which parts of their current districts are good or bad for them. But it is not as easy to assess how they would do in new areas, since they have no track record to go on. One commonly used technique is to look at how other candidates have done in this new area and project on that basis what it means for them. For example, if a legislator knows that he typically ran ahead of Jerry Brown and that Jerry Brown did very well in the proposed area, then he can assume that he will do well also. If he ran behind Jerry Brown and Brown did well, he has to figure how much on average he ran behind him, and what that would mean for his prospects in the area. Clearly, the calculations quickly become very complex.

The Assembly committee developed a method for making these projections in a formalized statistical manner and presented this data to members in the form of what were called "expected vote models."[3] The idea behind these models was to use data from statewide races to predict how individual Assembly, Senate, and Congressional candidates would do in their new districts. In any given year, there are statewide races and district-specific races. Obviously, every precinct in the state will have reported votes for the statewide races, but this will not be true for the district-specific races. Candidate A will know how he ran in his old district, but he cannot know how he would have run in new areas. Correlating the votes that the district candidates received with those of statewide candidates tells whether the district candidates did well in the same areas as the statewide candidates, or vice versa. On the assumption that the relationship between the district candidates' votes and the statewide candidates' votes would be the same in the new district as it was in the old district, what the district candidates would have won in their new districts can be projected by using the estimated statistical relation. Since information regarding the performance of several statewide candidates was available, the information of several such statistical relations could be combined by multiple regression.

In order to test the accuracy of the projection and to demonstrate its value to the legislators, the staff compared its model's prediction of what would have happened in the old districts with the actual results. Table 12 is an example of the projections the staff provided members, using Assembly Districts 39–64 (i.e., Los Angeles County) for illustra-

---

3. The normal way of computing what a candidate for a particular legislative seat would get in his new district is simply to add the votes in that new area received by the previous candidate of the same party. Thus, the Assemblyman's expected vote in the new district is his vote last time in the old areas he retained plus what the Assembly candidate in his party received in the last election in the new areas. This is obviously less than satisfactory, since the previous candidate may have been weak or in some way different from the incumbent Assemblyman. Computing the expected vote model in the manner described gives an estimate that is more directly applicable to the Assemblyman in question.

TABLE 12　*Projections for Some Los Angeles Districts*

ASSEMBLY RACE	OLD ACTUAL 1980		NEW PREDICTED	
	Incumbent	Opponent	Incumbent	Opponent
39th	38,081	34,500	41,832	36,365
40th	56,447	25,678	60,382	37,106
42nd	Collapsed	--------	--------	--------
43rd	74,710	37,848	78,151	41,346
44th	67,677	26,287	71,463	30,553
45th	61,208	26,440	59,944	21,177
46th	35,454	15,153	29,625	13,387
47th	37,071	6,299	37,497	4,720
48th	39,660	8,194	45,611	9,601
49th	Unopposed	--------	--------	--------
50th	51,598	15,061	59,302	18,487
51st	82,876	20,139	86,089	26,551
52nd	Collapsed	--------	--------	--------
54th	40,294	10,101	50,467	18,383
55th	33,819	14,400	38,392	14,295
56th	24,848	4,017	25,174	4,507
57th	41,417	23,782	43,623	22,911
59th	Unopposed	--------	--------	--------
60th	35,542	14,358	38,007	16,975
61st	67,645	21,225	79,743	26,156
62nd	72,862	28,998	61,823	30,198
63rd	56,636	23,736	61,824	23,809
64th	74,267	27,183	63,944	25,916

tive purposes. The "old actual" column shows the actual result of the 1980 Assembly race for each district in the "Assembly Race" column. The "new predicted" column shows the projected outcome of the 1980 race in the new district lines. This can be called a "counterfactual" use of regression, since it predicts what would have happened in the past under new conditions (i.e., different district lines), and not what will necessarily happen in the future.

Some legislators found this projection helpful, and others ignored it completely. The skepticism of the latter was not unfounded. While the fit between the statewide and district races is very close, the projections are subject to several important qualifications. To begin with, they assume that the legislator attains the same level of name recognition in the areas he is acquiring that he had in the areas he is losing. However, the fact that he ran ahead of Jerry Brown in his own district does not necessarily mean that he would do so in his new area; he may have done well because of his long service to the seat or because of the name recognition that he managed to build up over the years. More fundamentally, it is hard to correlate the legislator's ability to run in an area with that of other candidates who may be running on different issues or who have idiosyncratic campaign styles that are better suited to the new area. If the legislator's old seat had no areas like the new ones, then the model would not have crucial information and may mispredict. Finally, the model only tells the legislator how he would have done in 1980, not what will happen in the future. A change in national or state-wide political and economic conditions could make a substantial difference. The 1980 election was a better baseline election for Democrats than for Republicans for this reason. When most legislators calculate their chances, they like to take a worst-case approach, because that tells them what is the worst that could happen to them if they go into a particular district. An election in which the party did unusually well nationally could be deceiving to an individual legislator; hence, 1980 was more useful to the Democrats than to the Republicans. Jimmy Carter's legacy was not all bad.

While looking at other races is a useful approach in several respects, it does not answer the question of whether a seat is fundamentally Democratic or Republican. The most common way that the political operative and the legislator get at this is by looking at registration figures. Registration figures are not biased by candidate, election, and issue-specific factors. They are easy to work with and appealing as a measure of partisan strength. Typically, rules of thumb develop about the safety of seats with registrations of certain amounts. For instance, 60 percent is popularly held to be a safe Democratic seat, 55 percent is winnable, 50 percent is marginal, and below that is almost impossible to win. These rules of thumb become so universally accepted that they affect the decisions of all sorts of political actors. The opposing party will base its targeting decision on the level of registration. Challengers and potential candidates will assess their prospects by studying registration figures. These figures will even influence the decisions of contributors.

For the most part, there appears to be some empirical truth behind these standard rules of thumb. A comparison of party registration figures with the percentage of seats each party held at various registration levels reveals that the Assembly Democrats held all seats above 58 percent in Democratic registration in 1980, and the Republicans held all seats above 39 percent in Republican registration. Grouping the other registration figures, the Democrats held eight out of eleven seats in the 55–57 percent category (73%), twelve out of eighteen in the 50–54 percent category (67%), two out of fourteen in the 45–49 percent category (14%), and none of the ten seats below 45 percent. The Republicans show a similarly regular pattern. They held four of twelve seats in the 36–38 percent category (33%), seven of twenty in the 30–35 percent category (35%), and none of the twenty-seven seats below 30 percent Republican registration. (See Table 13.)

Attaining certain benchmark levels of registration even assumes an importance over and beyond what it indicates about latent partisan strength. Many candidates and activists believe that being below a desired level of registration by as little as one-tenth of a percent can affect

TABLE 13 *Probability of Holding Seats at Various Levels of Registration*

PROBABILITY OF DEMOCRATS HOLDING THEIR SEATS AT DIFFERENT
LEVELS OF DEMOCRATIC REGISTRATION

Percent Democratic Registration	1980	1978	1976	1974	Combined 1974-80
61% and Above	100% (19/19)	96% (26/27)	94% (32/34)	93% (25/27)	95% (102/107)
58%-60%	100% (8/8)	78% (7/9)	75% (6/8)	80% (12/15)	83% (33/40)
55%-57%	73% (8/11)	62% (8/13)	75% (9/12)	86% (6/7)	72% (31/43)
50%-54%	67% (12/18)	50% (8/16)	64% (7/11)	85% (11/13)	66% (38/58)
45%-49%	14% (2/14)	10% (1/10)	20% (2/10)	20% (2/10)	16% (7/44)
< 45%	0% (0/10)	0% (0/5)	20% (1/5)	0% (0/8)	4% (1/28)

PROBABILITY OF REPUBLICANS HOLDING THEIR SEATS AT DIFFERENT
LEVELS OF REPUBLICAN REGISTRATION

Percent Republican Registration	1980	1978	1976	1974	Combined 1974-80
39% and Above	100% (21/21)	95% (18/19)	79% (15/19)	74% (17/23)	87% (71/82)
36%-38%	33% (4/12)	44% (4/9)	38% (5/13)	36% (5/14)	38% (18/48)
30%-35%	35% (7/20)	29% (7/24)	4% (1/23)	5% (1/21)	18% (16/88)
< 30%	0% (0/27)	4% (1/28)	8% (2/25)	9% (2/22)	5% (5/102)

NOTE: The percentage figures represent the percent of seats held by
Democrats (the upper table) and by Republicans (the lower
table) of all seats at that registration level. Figures in
parentheses are raw numbers.

the kind of challenge they get or the amount of campaign contributions
they receive. Consequently, the legislator and his campaign operatives
will go to great lengths to get the most minute and trivial improvements
in registration even though they know that it may not appreciably affect
the electoral makeup of the seat.

However, there are several problems with using registration figures
as a measure of the political impact of a redistricting plan. Depending
on the method of collection, the figures themselves may be inaccurate
and biased, since some of the people who are on the registration rolls
for a given area will have since moved or died. Various states and counties have different methods for dealing with a "deadwood" bias, but it
is evident that areas with higher levels of transiency—areas with

younger populations, high concentrations of apartment dwellers, and heavily ethnic concentrations—will have a greater amount of over-reporting. This means that unless the rolls have been purged recently, there will be an overestimate of the number of voters in the area, and in particular an overestimate of Democratic voters.

An even more serious problem, however, is that there is no exact relation between registration and expected voting behavior. Registration means different things in different areas. In California, for instance, registered Democrats in the western end of the San Fernando Valley are more conservative and disloyal than those in south-central Los Angeles, while coastal Republicans and Republicans in the Silicon Valley area are more liberal than those in parts of Orange and San Diego counties. Registration figures do not indicate what sort of Democrats or Republicans the voters are nor whether they are loyal or not. Moreover, with the rise in the numbers of independent and decline-to-state-affiliation voters, one has to try to factor in the impact of a large group of nonaligned voters. In California, both the Democrats' and the Republicans' percentage of the vote has dropped in the last decade, from 57 percent for the Democrats and 38 percent for the Republicans in 1970 to 53 percent for the Democrats and 34 percent for the Republicans in 1981. In some areas of California, the decline-to-state-affiliation vote is in the 13–15 percent range and significantly affects the political makeup of the districts. As a result, many of the coastal seats, seats with large state universities in them, and seats in the Bay Area are far more liberal than they appear in terms of registration.

The risk-averse nature of reapportionment decisions makes a third kind of statistic attractive: loyalty measures. The idea behind loyalty measures is to determine what the baseline level of support is, which is typically defined as "What is the worst that I could do in this district?" The worst that a legislator can do in his old district is, by definition, the weakest result he has had during the period of time he has held the seat. That would typically come in a bad year in terms of national or statewide races or, more idiosyncratically, in a year when he was challenged by a competent opponent. Once again, however, the more difficult task is projecting into a new area: "What is the worst that I could do in this new district?" A common way of answering this question is to look at how some particular weak candidate or group of candidates did, but this measure may not tell the legislator exactly what he wants to know. For instance, several legislators in the California Assembly were very much persuaded that the Yvonne Burke and Mervyn Dymally races in the general election of 1978 were good loyalty measures, because both had done poorly throughout the state. Upon closer examination, the reason that both ran poorly statewide may have been that they were black. In short, the so-called loyalty scores may have

TABLE 14 *Simulated Races for the 39th Assembly District*

Candidates From AD:	RESULTS FOR OLD DISTRICT 39			Candidates From AD:	RESULTS FOR OLD DISTRICT 39		
	Dem	Rep	Dem-Rep		Dem	Rep	Dem-Rep
4	40415	27694	12722	47	43100	28643	14458
5	34283	46969	-12686	48	38866	32750	6115
6	41186	39224	1962	49	45406	0	45406
7	46561	30644	15917	50	36216	27086	9129
10	43665	34373	9292	51	21499	42930	-21431
11	45934	20889	24944	52	36281	35175	1106
12	40712	32254	8459	53	33818	38283	- 4464
13	42291	0	42291	54	45423	23564	21859
14	60680	0	60680	55	44507	30965	13542
15	35286	43946	- 8660	56	42983	19819	23165
16	38313	34271	4042	57	45950	28040	17909
17	32048	39241	- 7193	58	40968	40362	606
18	42609	23860	18749	59	46883	0	46883
19	37364	21151	16213	60	48884	21504	27380
20	20027	57283	-37257	61	25557	41664	-16106
21	38047	35872	2175	62	28751	42069	-13318
22	31409	42457	-11048	63	54781	19832	34949
23	40757	36706	4052	64	34560	43251	- 8691
24	39368	40161	- 792	65	43866	31852	12014
25	56467	0	56467	69	29388	36030	- 6642
37	35395	31616	3779	70	30242	28580	1662
38	43883	25504	18379	71	47856	27970	19885
39	37975	33736	4239	72	56313	20628	35685
40	48356	22245	26111	73	48014	31145	16869
41	22465	41630	-19165	76	29961	41665	-11704
42	41028	31235	9793	77	43633	32896	10737
43	43688	25638	18050	78	50040	32458	17582
44	41603	24506	17097	79	46249	35491	10759
45	39094	26561	12532	80	52245	25983	26262
46	46025	25950	20075				

NOTE: Each column indicates the race that was simulated in Assembly District 39, beginning with the candidates in the 4th Assembly District and ending with those in the 80th Assembly District.

been measuring a racial bias that would have little meaning for most white candidates.

A more sophisticated approach to measuring loyalty uses the projection model discussed earlier. The question the legislator would like to have answered is: What is the range of potential results that can be expected in a particular district, and in particular, what is the worst that can happen? Since the expected vote model gives a method for projecting races into new seats and areas, it is possible to simulate a whole range of races in any one district. Obviously, many of the problems pertaining to such projections are magnified when candidates and races from one end of the state are projected into races in another, but the point here is not to test the marketability of particular candidates, but only to probe the responsiveness of the seat to different kinds of races, some weak and some strong. Projecting the weak races—where a weak race is defined as one in which the candidate's party did poorly—into

TABLE 15 *Number of Democratic Wins by District*

Assembly District	No. of Democratic Wins Under New Plan	No. of Democratic Wins Under Old Plan
39	44	45
40	46	46
41	12	14
42	Collapsed------------------------	
43	46	46
44	51	54
45	52	54
46	50	54
47	58	58
48	59	59
49	58	58
50	58	58
51	16	17
52	Collapsed------------------------	
53	47	53
54	52	58
55	58	54
56	57	57
57	51	47
58	27	31
59	49	51
60	45	46

NOTE: Every pairing of candidates in the 80 AD races are simulated in the districts 39-60. Entries in the table are the number of times the Democrat wins.

a seat gives the absolute loyalty of the district. The average number of votes across all the simulated races gives the expected mean for a candidate from a given party. Finally, it is possible to compute the number of races won by one party as opposed to another, which gives us a means of comparing the strength of various districts.

An example of one such simulation is provided in Table 14. It shows the simulated results for the 39th Assembly District. Since some of the districts fell outside the Assembly's version-2 data set, there were projections for only fifty-nine out of the total of eighty pairs of candidates. The output was set up so that the first column gives the race being simulated, the second gives the projected total for the Democratic candidate, the third gives the projected total for the Republican candidate, and the last gives the margin between the two. In this case, the Democrats won forty-six out of the fifty-nine simulated races. Most of the races they lost had Republican incumbents, but four had Democratic incumbents—the 15th, 17th, 24th, and 53rd Assembly Districts.

A similar simulation in the other districts yields a comparison of their relative strength under a given plan or across several plans. For instance, Table 15 shows the number of Democrats who won in each of the districts examined earlier. It compares the number of wins under the status quo and under one of several alternative plans considered. Thus, the 39th AD dropped a little in strength under the new plan, while the 55th and the 57th increased their strength measurably.

Conclusion

Ultimately, all of the methods commonly used to measure the partisan impact of plans are flawed in serious ways. They are inaccurate, perhaps biased, and in any case do not exactly measure what the legislator wants them to measure. This raises an important point: namely, that the art of gerrymandering is inherently constrained by the poor quality of the data available. Computer technology and improvements in the collection of political statistics have added some precision, but the ability to describe new areas, let alone predict future behavior, is limited.

9

Gerrymanders

The popular understanding of a gerrymander tends to lump several species together. The press and the public usually equate gerrymandering with drawing the lines in an unfair manner, with unfairness sometimes defined as denying the opposite party its rightful share of seats, sometimes as destroying the responsiveness of the system by entrenching incumbents, and on yet other occasions as weakening the political power of minorities. In fact, a gerrymander can be all of these things, although not simultaneously. It can be both partisan and racial or bipartisan and racial, but it cannot be partisan and bipartisan at the same time in the same area. Each form of gerrymandering has a particular technical definition and its own logic. What is less well understood, however, is that the natural tendency of the legislative reapportionment process is to move in the direction of incoherent, self-interested particularism. A gerrymander is order imposed on an otherwise disorderly process. If it were left unguided, legislative reapportionment would move towards pluralistic chaos. A gerrymander is a rational redirection of territorial trades in order to achieve some end—which is not to say that gerrymanders are good, but only that they have a coherent logic.

This chapter will examine the logic of various types of gerrymanders—the partisan, bipartisan, and affirmative action varieties—and show how the pluralism of the system resists the imposition of that logic. We will look at how each is defined, and why a party would undertake one type of gerrymander as opposed to another. We will also consider how the incentives of individual legislators often differ from those of their party, and why legislators might therefore oppose the party leadership's plan.

The Partisan Gerrymander

Distorted shapes, it was argued earlier, do not necessarily indicate that a plan is a partisan gerrymander. They do reveal intent—either an intent to maximize seats for a party, or to follow city and county lines, or to protect minorities, or to respect communities of interest—but the observer has to look closely to see what the intent was. If, then, shape is not the best indicator of a partisan gerrymander, what is?

Perhaps the best way to answer this question is to try to understand what the goals of a partisan gerrymander are.[1] The definition of a partisan gerrymander is a plan that gives an unfair advantage to one party over the other. The way that a party secures an unfair advantage is by maximizing the ratio of its efficient seats to the other party's inefficient seats. Efficiency in this sense means lessening, and inefficiency means increasing, the number of wasted votes. Suppose that A and B are candidates for some seat. A defeats B by a vote of 100,000 to 50,000. In the strictest sense, A has a surplus of 49,999 votes. Suppose, further, that there is a seat next door with candidates C and D, and that candidate C belongs to the same party as A, and D to the same party as B. If C loses to D by 10,000 votes, and assuming that some substantial fraction of those 49,999 voters who supported A voted along party lines, then it could be said that A's surplus was wasted from the party's perspective.

The first task, then, is to determine a level of efficient strength from a party perspective. As discussed before, every registration level has attached to it some probability of being Democratic and some probability of being Republican. The most efficient distribution would be the one that guarantees the highest expected value for the party. Since, for reasons of contiguity, many redistributions are not possible, this will be an empirical determination involving the expected values of various alternative options.

The efficient distribution may involve making previously safe seats riskier.[2] Imagine a three-seat legislature that has Democratic registrations with the following distribution:

---

1. A somewhat different, more mathematical approach to the description of a gerrymander is taken by Phillip Musgrove, *The General Theory of Gerrymandering* (Beverly Hills, Calif.: Sage Publications, 1977).

2. David Mayhew makes the point that spreading a party's resources increases the party's risks:

> The reason is that parties with absolute control over districting tend to be very greedy. A controlling party normally concedes a minimum of very safe districts to the

X	Y	Z
65.5%	65.5%	40%

On the basis of previous data, the two seats with the 65.5 percent Democratic registrations would be virtually certain to remain Democratic; under this scenario, the Democrats would have two sure seats and one sure loser. Quite simply, the strength of seats X and Y would be wasted. Gerrymandering in a partisan manner would mean redistributing some of the strength of X and Y to Z, as in the following way:

X	Y	Z
57%	57%	57%

Now, instead of two absolutely certain seats, there are three seats with good but not certain prospects: the risk has been spread over all of the seats. Earlier data analysis showed that the probability of holding a Democratic seat at a 57 percent registration level in 1980 was 80 percent, so that each seat now has a 20 percent probability of becoming Republican. This creates a higher risk for the incumbents in X and Y seats, and for the party itself. The probability of holding both X and Y is now 64 percent, the probability of losing all three seats is less than 1% but greater than zero, and the probability of holding all three seats is 51 percent. In other words, higher efficiency comes with higher risk, not only for the party but also for the incumbents in X and Y. This is an extremely important point to remember: it is a crucial impediment to a partisan gerrymander.

How does one implement the principle of maximizing efficiency in the controlling party? First, all seats in the gerrymandering party that are above the efficient level must be weakened where possible so that the excess partisan strength can be used to shore up a weaker seat in the same party or to make a seat in the other party more marginal. Obviously, if a safe seat from one party is surrounded by other safe seats in the same party, or even by safe seats in the other party, then the excess strength can do little good, and it constitutes unavoidable inefficiency. The point was made earlier that the Democratic seats in Los Angeles were inefficient and would remain so in any new reapportion-

---

opposition and then tries to salvage as many as possible for its own adherents. In this latter effort there is a tendency to spread electoral resources too thinly.

See David Mayhew, "Congressional Representation: Theory and Practice in Drawing the Districts," in Nelson Polsby, ed., *Reapportionment in the 1970s* (Berkeley: University of California Press, 1979), p. 277.

ment unless the reapportioner resorted to wildly noncompact shapes. The same could be said of certain Republican districts in Orange and San Diego counties.

Just as there will be seats that are hopelessly over the efficient level, there will be seats that are hopelessly below it as well. Good areas should not be wasted by being left in seats that cannot possibly be won. Rather, they should go to seats where the addition of good areas can have a significant impact. The choice will also be determined by the prospects of a complementary trade in the sense defined earlier: either with a seat in the same party that can afford to give up good territory, or with a seat in the other party with good areas in it.

Thirdly, the procedure must be reversed wherever possible for seats in the opposite party. In other words, the objective is to weaken the other party's marginal seats to the extent possible and to strengthen its safe seats. Sometimes, this will occur by adhering to the first two rules. In the process of making its marginal seats safer, the gerrymandering party may make the other party's safe seats safer by removing areas that are favorable to the gerrymandering party's incumbents. Or when the gerrymandering party brings its safe seats down to an efficient level, it may simultaneously weaken a neighboring marginal seat from the other party. Such coincidences of goals are not always possible, however. The first two rules can conflict with the third. The gerrymandering party might have to strengthen a marginal seat of the opposition in order to strengthen one of its own marginal seats. Ideally, if the gerrymandering party could disregard the wishes of its incumbents, it would make this decision by calculating which option gave it the highest probability of winning a seat.

Finally, the party that would gerrymander in a partisan fashion must try to create new seats and collapse old ones in a manner that maximizes party strength. As discussed in Chapter 2, demography and displacement dictate the general regions that require the creation of a new seat or the collapse of an old one. Decisions about which particular seats should be collapsed and where new seats should be placed can affect the partisan balance of a state. This does not mean that the gerrymandering party should never collapse one of its own seats, since it must look at the effect that a collapse or creation would have on the other seats in the area. When a seat is collapsed, others must absorb it, and ideally this absorption should strengthen weak seats in the gerrymandering party or weaken weak seats in the other party. Similarly, creating a seat means taking areas away from other seats, and the gerrymandering party would want to do this in a manner that is consonant with the previous principles.

The Party's Decision to Implement a Partisan Gerrymander

Obviously, there are a great many reasons why a controlling political party might want to implement a partisan gerrymander. Activists and ideologues will always tend to favor any measure that ostensibly strengthens their party. However, given that there are risks and higher campaign costs associated with a strategy that in effect attenuates the strength of the controlling party, it would be useful to consider the rational calculus behind this decision. In other words, what factors should a controlling party consider?

First, the party should consider whether it has a sufficient number of votes in its legislative caucus to pass a reapportionment bill without the support of the minority party. This will depend on how many votes are needed to pass such a bill and on the size of the controlling party's legislative margin. For example, a reapportionment bill in California requires a simple majority in both houses, so that the majority party needs to have more votes than the minority party in both houses and also control of the Governorship. Failing to hold one of the houses or the Governorship—as was the case in the 1970 reapportionment—would diminish the chances of successfully passing any bill the minority party opposed. A two-thirds vote requirement would mean that the majority party would have to have a large margin over the minority party—such as in a one-party state—or would have to successfully court some minority party dissidents. Having the required number of votes, however, still may not be sufficient politically, since the majority party would have to allow for defections from its own ranks. This might mean that it would have to have the constitutionally mandated number plus some margin of safety.

Assuming that it had the votes to impose its will, the second consideration is whether the party has the resources to fight in the more efficient seats it would be creating. The safe seats in the majority party that have been weakened in order to shore up the marginals may cost the gerrymandering party more money in the next election if, by weakening the seats, it inadvertently encourages strong candidates from the opposition to run. Against that consideration are the marginal majority party seats that have been strengthened, which may discourage some strong opposition candidates who would otherwise have run. However, since both of these kinds of seats will have majority party incumbents in them, they will not cost the party nearly so much as will attempts to win weakened minority party seats. Because challengers have to spend more than incumbents, the gerrymandering party has to be prepared to spend a lot of money to unseat the minority party's incumbents. Weakening the opponent by a few registration points will not per se guarantee a victory for the majority party. It must be prepared to overcome the minority party incumbent's natural advantages—name recognition, proven track record, and the like—in order to win the seat in the next election, or wait until the seat becomes open, by which time the gerrymandered advantage may have eroded.

The third factor in the calculation is the majority party's estimate of long-range political and demographic trends. If it believes that future electoral or demographic tides will flow in its direction, then the party will be more willing to take chances by creating more competitive seats. For instance, suppose that a controlling Republican faction thought that the Reagan mandate was a harbinger of a realignment in the 'eighties, and that the electorate would increasingly swing in its direction. Believing this, they would be much more inclined to want to create as many competitive seats as possible, thinking that these marginal seats will grow more Republican over time. On the other hand, if the Democrats believed the same thing, they would be more inclined to be more cautious and to make sure that they held on to the seats they already had. Similarly, demographic considerations such as whether the areas of growth or decline are in Democratic or Republican strongholds and whether existing trends will continue should affect the party's thinking.

For instance, beliefs about demographic trends very much influenced the thinking of the California reapportionment participants in 1980. There were two major sources of population growth in California in the period 1970–1980. One was the influx of older, white retirees into counties such as San Diego, Orange, and Butte, and the other was the tremendous growth of the Mexican-American population, particularly in southern California. Since the retirees tend to participate in the electorate at a higher level than the Hispanics—whose ranks include many nonvoters—some observers maintained that the parties would have to compete for an older, more conservative voter in the 'eighties. Others thought that the Hispanics could be registered and mobilized into an effective political force in California. Opinions on this point greatly influenced the reapportionment decisions of both parties in 1981.

What the preceding discussion suggests is that a party might not consider a partisan strategy to be worthwhile even though it has the opportunity to implement one. While the Assembly's final plan was partisan with respect to the number of Republicans who were collapsed, it was not partisan in many specific instances. Consider its decision about northern California, for instance. The opportunity to draw partisan lines there was particularly good. Northern California had gone through a transformation in the 'seventies. The Democrats at one time or another had held all but one of Assembly seats 1 through 9, but by 1980 it held only five of them. The question was whether the lost seats could be won back. Two of them—the 8th and the 9th—were marginally Republican, and it seemed that they might be brought back into the Democratic fold with assistance from reapportionment. The 8th had a Democratic registration of 55 percent and included a working-class stronghold in Solano County called Vallejo. There were several proposals about how best to weaken the Republican hold on the 8th, but the most promising seemed to be to keep the seat in Vallejo, remove some of its strongest Republican areas, and then push it into the more liberal areas of Sonoma County. Similarly, the 9th was a marginal seat—its low Democratic registration of 48.7 percent was offset by an abnormally large and liberal decline-to-state-affiliation of 14 percent—and the Republican grip on the district could be made even weaker by taking it into San Francisco County to pick up the residual 87,000 population created by the collapse of one of its seats.

There was a fair amount of support within party circles for an aggressive strategy in northern California. The alternative was to leave the 9th alone—since it had the required population already and did not have to be affected by a ripple—and to make the 8th a safer Republican seat by using the Vallejo area to shore up the already Democratic 4th. As these proposals were discussed, several key considerations came to the foreground. First, it was obvious to the Speaker and to others who would have to help finance any campaign against the Republican incumbents in these two seats that the aggressive proposal would cost a lot of money. Democratic challengers would have to take on Republican incumbents, whom it would take a lot of money to unseat. A challenger necessarily has to spend heavily to overcome the incumbent's inherent name recognition advantage, and the Republicans would no doubt counter with money of their own if the races looked close. Given the relative financial disadvantage of the Democratic party, it was not obvious that it should get into cost-escalating races with the Republicans over these seats.

Secondly, as the proposal was studied more, it became apparent that some Democratic incumbents would be made worse off by the aggressive strategy. In particular, the 4th Assembly District would not be able to take the loyal Democratic area of Vallejo, and the Democrats in San Mateo and Santa Clara counties would be pushed further south into less favorable areas by the displacement ripple set off by bringing the 9th into San Francisco. Obviously, the question was whether birds in the hand were worth more than ones in the bush. The Assembly Democrats had to choose between strengthening their own incumbents and going after the other party's seats.

Finally, there was the question of what the long-range results of the aggressive strategy would be. Certainly, there was no guarantee that by going up against well-financed incumbents, the Democrats could capture these seats in the next election. If they waited for the Republican incumbents to retire, then the chance of winning the seats would have to be postponed a number of years, by which time the contrived advantage could have dissipated. In the interim, several Democratic incumbents might have to fight tougher battles to stay in office, which would further increase the cost of the 1982 elections and might result in the Democrats actually losing more seats because of their increased vulnerability. If the Reagan policies were to prove popular and the demographic trends in northern California were to continue to bring in older, white voters, then the aggressive strategy could easily backfire. Perhaps it was better simply to draw in the wagons and wait out the bad political weather. In the end, a consensus among the Assembly leaders emerged that the best strategy was the cautious one, and the bipartisan alternative was chosen.

Individual Legislators and the Partisan Gerrymander

The implications of a partisan gerrymander are different for the parties than for the individual legislators in both parties. To begin with, as has been observed at several points, individual legislators will tend to prefer the least possible change, and this will constrain the quest for partisan efficiency considerably. In addition to different perspectives on displacement, the incentives of the legislators with respect to partisan strength will also run counter to the parties' objectives. Those in safe majority-party seats may accept some amount of weakening to help out a fellow party member or to destabilize a legislator in the opposing party, but they will differ from the party about what an acceptable level of risk is, and they will usually resist attempts to bring their seats to strictly efficient levels. Similarly, the marginal majority-party legislator will often want to be strengthened to a level above the efficient amount in order to minimize risk, and this will also hinder the majority party's plans.

The effects of a partisan gerrymander will be most severe for the minority-party incumbents in weakened marginal seats. Safe minority-party seats that are made safer will not resist the added partisan strength (although the incumbents know it may increase the probability of a primary challenge). Consequently, if the minority party is going to fight the partisan gerrymander successfully, it must ensure that its members—most of whom will be made better off by the majority party's plans—look at the broader party perspective and not at their own self-interest. This requires considerable party discipline.

Curiously, the majority party, too, must fight off the self-interest of its members if it is to succeed. As was noted earlier, disregarding displacement issues for the moment, all trades between legislators of the opposing parties will naturally be complementary: the best areas for the legislator in one party are the worst areas for the legislator in the other. If the legislators act in their pure self-interest and follow their natural risk-averse inclinations, they will tend to engage in mutually beneficial trades. A partisan gerrymander can be implemented only when majority-party legislators are willing to do such things as refuse to take good areas from an opposing party legislator in order to keep him weak, or even to give up good areas to weaken a minority-party incumbent. Thus, the partisan gerrymander will work only if majority-party legislators do not always act in their immediate self-interest and minority-party legislators do. This explains why party activists and hard-line reapportionment staffers have often observed that gerrymandering would be a lot simpler if the plan did not have to secure the votes of the legislators.

Pluralist Tensions and the Partisan Gerrymander

Clearly, it follows from the previous discussion that one obstacle to the partisan gerrymander—assuming that a party decides that a partisan gerrymander is in its interest—is the clash of individual and party incentives. If legislator A needs to pick up a lot of new area in order to shore up his seat, then he may be willing to take more than his required displacement. However, if he takes more than his required displacement from another legislator, B, then B will have to pick up more territory, too. Even if B is a member of the same party, there is no obvious obligation on B's part to give up more territory to A than is absolutely necessary. In short, A's decision to incur more risk may require B to incur more risk in at least two ways: first, B has to pick up areas that he may not be known in; and second, he may be sharing some of his strength with A in order to make A stronger. Becoming a little weaker from the standpoint of partisanship and taking on unfamiliar ground will increase the probability of a strong challenge for B, and it is natural that B might resist the added burden.

Another obstacle to partisan gerrymandering is that it is very hard to alter the partisan composition of a district in any substantial way under the Supreme Court's "one man, one vote" doctrine, except through

TABLE 16 *Impact of Territorial Gains on District Partisanship*

Average Democratic Registration	Amount of Voters Added				
	10,000	20,000	30,000	40,000	50,000
75%	56.8%	58.3%	59.6%	60.7%	61.6%
70%	56.3%	57.5%	58.4%	59.2%	60.0%
65%	55.9%	56.6%	57.3%	57.8%	58.3%
60%	55.4%	55.8%	56.1%	56.4%	56.6%

extreme displacement. One study of New York suggests that whatever partisan advantage the controlling party gets from reapportionment tends to erode quickly over time with changes in the composition of districts.[3] Hence, partisan gerrymandering is technically difficult because time and demography can undo the reapportioner's craft. However, partisan gerrymandering is constrained in another fundamental way—namely, that substantial changes in partisanship require substantial amounts of displacement. To strengthen a weak seat, the incumbent must either drop a considerable amount of bad area or pick up a considerable amount of good area. This means that three conditions must obtain: (1) the incumbent must be willing to take a lot of new territory and/or to give up a lot of familiar territory; (2) someone else must be willing or forced to take or give up a lot of territory; and (3) the areas involved must be significantly bad or good. Small amounts of very good areas or large amounts of only marginally better areas will not do the trick. Consequently, plans to bolster a weak seat can be foiled by several obstacles: the incumbent might prefer the certainty of voters who know him to more partisanly favorable but unknown voters; neighboring legislators might not want to give up the needed amount or type of territory; and the area available to the legislator within the confines of contiguity might not be sufficiently strong.

The difficulty of bolstering a weak seat can be demonstrated with another hypothetical example. Consider the case of a district that is 55 percent Democratic and 35 percent Republican and has 100,000 voters. How many additional voters at what level of registration would it take to raise the registration to 60 percent Democratic, assuming that voters were only added and not taken out? The vertical axis of Table 16 lists the average percentage of Democratic registration of the area being

---

3. See Howard A. Scarrow, "The Impact of Reapportionment on Party Representation," in Bernard Grofman, Arendt Lijphart, Robert B. McKay, and Howard A. Scarrow, eds., *Representation and Redistricting Issues of the 1980s* (Lexington, Mass.: D. C. Heath, 1982).

added, and the horizontal axis of the table lists the number of voters being added. The entries in the table are the levels of registration attained when a given amount of territory at a given level of registration is added to the initial population. Clearly, raising a 55 percent Democratic seat by 5 registration points requires a great deal of good area to be added. Only three entries get the seat to the desired 60 percent level. In no case does this goal demand fewer than 40,000 voters, which amounts to two or three times that number of people, depending on the voter-population ratio in the area. Moreover, it would require a registration level of at least 70 percent Democratic, which pretty much restricts the choice to highly loyal—and usually ethnic—neighborhoods. Needless to say, favorable conditions such as these are not usually available. It should be said, however, that the more typical strategy would be to try to strengthen the seat by a combination of losing very bad and picking up very good territories. The incumbent would still have a large total displacement, but it might consist of gaining only 25,000 voters at 70 percent Democratic and losing another 25,000 at 40 percent Democratic. Mixed strategies like this are more practical, since (1) not many seats can afford to take 100,000 new people and still satisfy the principle of one man, one vote, (2) it is easier to find 25,000 voters at a high level of registration than 50,000, and (3) a neighboring Republican legislator would under normal circumstances gladly accept 25,000 voters at 40 percent Democratic registration.

Partisan gerrymanders can also be foiled by the fact that legislators have other goals. Sometimes, legislators have very idiosyncratic goals: keeping their house in the district, or picking up a relative, or including a key contributor. Often, concerns that are petty from the party perspective matter far more to the legislator than the partisan strength of the district. He may, for instance, be less concerned about the problem of whether his successor can win than are the activists or party leaders. Quite simply, the best laid plans of partisan men can easily fall prey to the narrowness of the legislators' perspectives.

Partisan Plans and the Distribution of Power

Partisan plans are difficult to achieve for all the aforementioned reasons. However, there is an even more overriding misunderstanding about partisan reapportionments that needs discussion. It is widely assumed that the reapportionment process can so transform the entire distribution of political forces in a state that a Republican state becomes a Democratic state, or vice versa. If this reasoning is correct,

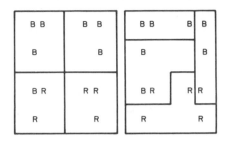

FIGURE 24 *Changing Incentives of Seats*

when Democrats control the legislature, reapportionment should be followed by increases in Democratic representation and therefore in liberal, "Democratic" legislation. Similarly, when Republicans control, there should be increases in Republican representation and therefore in conservative, "Republican" legislation. Partisan gerrymandering should result in partisan policymaking.

However, the logic is not quite so simple. Picture a country with four districts, each with three voters (see Fig. 24). There are two parties, the Blues and the Reds. Under the first plan, the Blues have two seats and the Reds have two. Under the second plan, the Blue support is more efficiently distributed to give them three seats. The Blues now have a majority in the legislature, and the legislation should become more bluish. However, upon closer examination, it is clear that the Blues had two very safe seats under the first plan and now have two marginal seats under the second. The representatives of these seats have to adjust to the fact that they are more marginal. They may have to moderate their positions to accommodate the influx of new voters. The median position of their districts will have changed, and the representatives will have to accommodate their positions to these new medians. Concentration of strength makes ideological extremity feasible; dispersion of strength in the interests of efficiency can put more members of a particular party in office, but does so only by changing their district incentives. In real-life terms, creating a marginal Democratic seat out of a Republican area in the Central Valley of California might bring a conservative Democrat into office who is very different from the party's central-city ethnic candidates. Creating a marginal Republican seat out of a Democratic area in Alameda County would bring a different kind of Republican into the legislature than one from Orange County.

In short, reapportionment cannot make magical transformations in the state's political composition. From the perspective of the parties, reapportionment cannot make a silk purse out of a sow's ear. It can increase the party's delegation, but there are limits to how far it can alter the public's policy preferences. The designs of a majority party can be moderated by the presence of legislators from the opposite party in the legislature or by sizable blocks of opposition-party voters in its districts. Policy transformations through reapportionment are hindered by the dilemma that heightened power in the legislature can be offset by the changed voter composition in the districts. Partisan gerrymandering can produce a more extreme skew in the distribution of seats in the legislature, but at the price of less skew in the distribution of opinion in individual seats. Parties in their turn can be moderated in their policies by having fewer representatives in the legislature or internally by having a broader spectrum of voters to represent. For the ideologue, partisan gerrymandering may actually not be worthwhile.

The Bipartisan Gerrymander

Political activists usually expect a partisan gerrymander. When their party is in power, they want the lines drawn in a way that maximizes their party's strength over the opposition; and when their party is out of power, they will work to oppose what they expect to be the blatant gerrymandering of the other side. Activists focus on a redistricting plan's implications for their party. For the average citizen, gerrymandering means something very different—if anything at all. It means selfish and greedy legislators protecting themselves from the vicissitudes of electoral fortune. An incumbent's reapportionment, in the public's mind, is a form of corruption with legislators on the make; only what they are getting is votes and not money. Political scientists and reform groups worry about the implications of reapportionment for the competitive democratic system. Does redistricting weaken the responsiveness of legislators to the voters? Does it contribute to the incumbency advantage?

Although it is not always recognized as such, this meaning of a gerrymander is bipartisan. Unlike the partisan gerrymander, the bipartisan gerrymander does not pit one party against the other. There is no attempt to increase the ratio of efficient seats in one party to inefficient seats in the other. Rather, all incumbents are protected; or to put it another way, all seats are made inefficient. Legislators engage in complementary trades of the sort discussed earlier—Democrats giving to Republicans their worst (i.e., most Republican) areas, and Republicans giving to Democrats their worst (i.e., most Democratic) areas. Displacement is equally shared. Seats are collapsed only where there are retirees and individuals who have declared for higher office New seats are created to compensate each party for the old ones that had to be collapsed. No party comes out of reapportionment with an advantage gained from the new lines.

Bipartisan reapportionment is easier for legislators to talk about than to bring off. In fact, a bipartisan reapportionment is a far from trivial achievement. Redistricting inevitably brings out latent tensions between the parties. Disagreements over definitions and notions of equity manifest the fundamental problem, which is that unless the conditions are right, bipartisan agreement on a matter so central to the welfare of the parties can break down.

The Rules of a Bipartisan Gerrymander

In many ways, the bipartisan gerrymander is the mirror image of the partisan gerrymander. The primary goal of the partisan gerrymander, as stated earlier, is to maximize the number of efficient seats in the majority party and the number of inefficient seats in the minority party. The bipartisan approach reduces the number of efficient seats in both parties, and by so doing, protects as many incumbents as possible. This means that incumbents in both parties will have more "wasted votes," as previously defined, and that they will be less threatened by challengers from the other party. Another way of looking at this is to say that since incumbents acquire higher margins of safety under the bipartisan approach, this is a risk-averse strategy. It avoids the danger of overextending the party's resources and protects the party's base against adverse political tides. It also—and this is not inconsequential—costs the party less money.

The other rules of the bipartisan gerrymander also differ in a mirror-image way from the partisan approach. Where in the latter case the controlling party tries to shore up its weak seats, in the former case it attempts to boost the strength of all weak incumbents in both parties. Thus, it resists the temptation to use wasted strength to weaken the marginal seats of the opposition party. Intraparty trades can often be more difficult than trades across parties. While trades between safe and marginal seats from the same party can be complementary as long as the safe seats stay above some reservation level of safety, there can be disagreements between the legislative leaders and individual legislators about what an acceptable level of safety is. The bipartisan plan can be undermined by these latent tensions.

Secondly, the controlling party would not necessarily try to lessen the waste of seats that are well above the efficient level, especially since one of the main motives for doing so—to weaken marginal seats in the other party—does not exist. Instead, there would be more trades between the safe seats of opposing parties, since there would be no incentive to hold back, and no amount of waste would be too great. In this sense, the bipartisan gerrymander is the ideological activist's nightmare. So many wasted votes! So many opportunities to make life difficult for the other party squandered!

The third rule is that incumbents of the minority party should be treated no differently from majority-party incumbents. The partisan reapportionment reversed the first two rules for the minority party by strengthening its safe seats and weakening its weak seats, but this is forbidden in a bipartisan setting. The important point is that if the first two rules are modified in any way, then the modification must apply to both parties equally. If there is a state requirement of a certain number of competitive seats, then they should be divided equally or by some other mutually agreed-upon rule. Or if geographical and demographical considerations make the first two rules hard to implement, then any adaptation to these constraints would have to be mutually agreed upon.

Lastly, there must be mutual agreement on how to handle the collapse of old seats, the creation of new seats, and, more generally, the problem of displacement. In the partisan gerrymander, seats are collapsed and created so as to maximize the probability of the majority party winning seats. Obviously, the treatment of these problems in the bipartisan gerrymander has to be more evenhanded, but it is not obvious what that would mean specifically. In the end, fairness must be defined as what the parties agree upon, but one general resolution of the problem would be an equal-sharing rule. Of course, an odd number cannot be divided equally—unless a very marginal seat is defined as neutral, which in practice it rarely, if ever, is—and so problems will inevitably arise. For instance, if there are three seats to be collapsed, how can it be done evenly? A fourth could be collapsed to make the number divisible by two, but collapsing in areas where it is not demographically required can cause enormous displacement for neighboring incumbents. Another plausible "fairness" rule would compensate each collapse with a new seat of comparable partisanship; but of course, this is hard to do, and even when it can be done, many would maintain that a new seat is riskier per se. The basic rule has to be that the new plan should make the least possible change in the status quo distribution of partisanship. But as one can readily see, there is ample room for disagreement, since it is the nature of reapportionment that no new plan will ever get back to the status quo exactly.

A Party's Decision to Pursue a Bipartisan Plan

What conditions will encourage a majority party to choose the bipartisan path? Certainly, not having a sufficient number of votes in the majority party to pass a partisan plan is one. This condition can occur easily in a competitive two-party state when there is a two-thirds voting rule for a reapportionment bill; and it can even occur when there is a simple plurality rule, if party strength is exactly even or the margin of the majority party is so small that one or two defections could cause the bill to be defeated. One hypothesis, then, is that the smaller the majority party's margin, the higher will be the probability of a bipartisan settlement.

Equality or near equality of party resources will also favor a bipartisan plan. When one party—especially the majority—can afford to spend considerably more than the other on elections, then it will perceive the risks and value of competitive seats very differently from the other. The party with the resource advantage will want to attenuate its strength and minimize its wasted votes as much as possible. It will be less hesitant to go after the other party's marginal seats, since it will be able to outspend its opponents. Even a minority party with a resource advantage will favor competitive seats, as the experience in California amply demonstrates. Both the Rose Institute and the Republican Assembly Caucus made a point of emphasizing that their plans for redistricting the state would create more marginal seats than the Democratic plan.[4] They claimed that this was in the interests of good government, but few were persuaded that that was the true motive.

Lastly, a bipartisan plan will be fostered by uncertain perceptions of what the future will bring politically and demographically, and made more difficult when the trends favor one party. The first situation can occur because the trends are indiscernible or contradictory or too fickle to be predicted. Being equally uncertain, both parties would have an incentive to be risk-averse and to settle for a safe, bipartisan plan. If there are discernible trends, however, it is important that neither party believe that it will be favored by them, since a favored party will be encouraged to take more risks and try to win more seats—to assume, in effect, an "imperialist" attitude. Reapportionment imperialism can be defined as trying to make political gains from the reapportionment process, and not being satisfied with the status quo. A party will be less satisfied with the status quo if it thinks that things are going its way than if it thinks that general conditions are against it.

---

4. See responding arguments in *Assembly of the State of California v. Deukmejian*, S.F. 24348, 24349 (February 1982).

This was clearly reflected in the thinking of various participants in the California struggle, where the Republicans believed that they should make gains from reapportionment, and the Democrats were split between the cautious ones who shared the Republicans' perception and the imperialists who thought that the Reagan mandate would fizzle and the Democrats should be in a position to get the most politically out of Reagan's shortcomings. In this sense, the bipartisan coalition was undermined not by the treachery of the Speaker, but by the pressure of the hard-liners in both parties who thought that the opportunity was right to make gains by taking risks in reapportionment. If the Republican perception had been shared by all the Democrats, then the caution of the latter might have complemented the confidence of the former: the Democrats might have conceded a few seats in order to bolster the remaining ones. As it was, no one was willing to concede anything, so the fate of every marginal seat was hotly contested.

In fact, viewed from the perspective of these three conditions, it is not surprising that bipartisanship failed in California at all three levels: the two houses of the state legislature and the U.S. Congress. The first condition was violated because the Democrats had the votes in both the Senate and the Assembly to draw the lines the way they wanted. The second condition was also absent, because the Republicans had a large resource advantage and wanted to create as many competitive seats as they could. Finally, only one faction of the Democratic party felt the need to pursue a cautious strategy, while other Democrats and Republicans believed that they should be in a position to capitalize on national and statewide trends.

Apart from the general conditions that promote or discourage a bipartisan reapportionment, there are always specific problems that must be resolved if there is to be a consensus between the two parties. To begin with, a bipartisan reapportionment is facilitated if individual legislators look after their self-interest and are unwilling to make themselves worse off in order to weaken an opponent. Trades between incumbents of opposing parties will never be noncomplementary in the sense defined previously, although the incentives will sometimes be mixed because of incompatible displacement needs. Therefore, as long as incumbents from two parties trade their worst areas to each other, they will make each other better off. If the incumbents adhere to this principle, they will make partisan imperialism more difficult for the party leaders.

However, while trades across parties are never absolutely noncomplementary, the incentives can be mixed because of divergent population needs. This was certainly a major stumbling block in the Assembly experience. By employing a stricter displacement rule for Democratic than for Republican incumbents, the Democratic bill stirred up considerable Republican anger. However, if the Democrats had counted every seat that acquired more than one-third new population as a "collapsed" or "quasi-collapsed" seat and had tried to impose some rule of equal sharing on the two parties, this would have complicated the intraparty negotiations greatly. Displacement problems will always be particularly acute in states that have experienced considerable growth or decline, and it may be that this inevitably makes it more difficult to achieve bipartisan agreement.

The inability to find a formula to handle issues such as displacement, collapses (i.e., the ultimate form of displacement), and new seats is thus another obstacle to a bipartisan plan. The simple formula to "take care of incumbents" does not solve the problem; parties can even disagree about who is or is not an incumbent, for there is an advantage to defining incumbency strategically.

An incumbent is a legislator presently sitting in a seat. When the interests of two seats are at odds, then the greater burden in an incumbent's bipartisan reapportionment should be placed on the seat without an incumbent. In the simplest case, this means that new seats— which by definition have no incumbent as yet—should get less desirable areas than seats with incumbents. New seats should get what is left over after all the bargaining by incumbents is done. A strategy of this sort will rarely cost a party any votes, since legislators will not feel strongly enough about the new seats to vote against the bill for that reason alone. The price in terms of disfavor with the leadership or even in terms of what could happen to their own seats is too high to warrant anything but a verbal protest. More often, this rule is especially unpopular with activists, party operatives, and, most especially, would-be candidates who must worry about trying to win the open seat in the next election. However, since they do not have a vote, there is little they can do to oppose the natural shortsighted incentives of the legislative reapportionment process.

The case of the new seat versus the sitting incumbent is thus relatively uncomplicated. Similarly, the leadership might try to impose the rule that sitting incumbents have priority over retirees. Typically, some number of legislators will have declared their intent to quit the legislature at the end of the session; and by so doing, it could be argued, they have forfeited their right to have a say in the lines of the new district. But many retirees will want to designate their successors, and hence will feel an obligation to ensure that the new district includes their successor's house and that it is winnable for him or her. In some instances, this concern for the successor masks the real motive, which is to hedge one's own bets in case one decides to run another time. Or, more simply, the desire to designate a successor may originate with the need for a final symbolic display of power, or in a genuine fondness for the successor, or simply in a community expectation motivating the retiree to guard the interests of his old district. Whatever their motives, retirees who feel this way can in effect remove a valuable option.

Another possibility is to favor the incumbent who does not plan to run for higher office over the one who does. This, for example, was the decision rule proposed by the Assembly Republicans in the 1981 reapportionment. The logic behind this rule is analogous to the logic of picking on the retiree's seat. Since the higher office seeker is looking to move up, he has given up the right to dictate what the seat should look like. However, again there are problems. The candidate for higher office, like the retiree, may have some concern for his successor. He will certainly be more inclined to want to preserve his options in the event that he cannot raise enough money or finds himself running too far behind in the preliminary polls. But, most importantly, there is a fundamental weakness in this rule, which is that the partisan balance can be affected by the strategic timing of decisions to run for higher office. If a party can persuade its own legislators to hold off announcing their candidacies until reapportionment is completed, then it will always benefit from the application of this rule. Similarly, the individual legislator who keeps his intentions secret will be in a better position to hedge his bets than one who openly and honestly declares for higher office. The Republicans in the California Assembly were more skillfully prepared in this regard than the Democrats were. By enforcing a unit rule and coordinating their tactics, they were able to keep their members from declaring for higher office until the reapportionment bill was passed. Since the Democrats had no comparable discipline, there were several Democratic incumbents who had announced that they were running for higher office, and the Republicans argued that these were the natural seats to collapse. Definitions can therefore be used to make gains in a bipartisan setting.

For this reason, there will be no easy way to decide who gets preferential treatment and who does not. Certainly, the bipartisan plan has to take care of as many of the incumbents who want to return as possible, but there will be some who cannot be protected, and they must be encouraged to retire or run elsewhere. At the same time, there will be other seats that the parties will want to protect even though the incumbents do not plan to return, in order to preserve the existing distribution of partisanship, particularly when there is no sufficiently compensating seat for the one that is collapsed. The key question has to be: What will be the distribution of seats after this reapportionment, and how close will it come to the status quo? Of course, the distribution of seats in the status quo may be unsatisfactory to some partisans, and they may be right, but this perception is unlikely to be universally shared. The only conceivable equilibrium for a bipartisan plan is the status quo, since no other solution will be accepted by both parties.

One last obstacle to be overcome in order to formulate a bipartisan plan comes from within the majority party's own ranks, where some will propose solving intraparty trading problems by exploiting the seats of the opposing party. This is particularly true of displacement issues, since, as has been observed several times, the partisan needs of opposing parties are usually compatible. It will always be less desirable to alienate an incumbent of one's own party than one from the other party, since it can mean losing his vote on other issues as well. If a legislator belongs to the other party, the probability of getting his support on other bills is lower anyway, and so less is lost by alienating him on reapportionment. This is where political skill matters, since it is no simple matter to persuade legislators from a majority party that they should get less preferential treatment than members of the minority party. The majority party's temptation to take care of its own first and foremost will always be great, and therein lies a major obstacle to bipartisan plans.

The Affirmative Action Gerrymander

Most people who talk of gerrymandering mean one or the other of the two types discussed so far (without, of course, sharply distinguishing them from each other). The third type to which this chapter is devoted seeks to reverse the discrimination of the political system against the minorities, and in that sense favors them as a group. It is as controversial as are the other two types. Those who are concerned about the ability of minorities to have an effective voice in American government see the affirmative action gerrymander as a necessary step towards counteracting the normal biases of power and money in American government. Those who think that the lines can and should be drawn in a manner that favors no group, even the disadvantaged, and those who think that minorities already have too many advantages see the affirmative action gerrymander as no better than its partisan or bipartisan cousins.

The goal of the affirmative action gerrymander is to maximize the political strength of minorities to the extent possible. As a community leader in East Los Angeles put it: "Quite simply, we expect what everyone else expects: fair representation. We would expect a plan that gives us some parity with our population."[5] The affirmative action plan tries to give minority groups a proportion of representation in the legislature that is as close as possible to their proportion in the population.

Of course, racial minorities run up against the same biases in the single-member simple-plurality (SMSP) system as does an opposition party—namely, that the system is not designed to give proportional results. Therefore, the affirmative action gerrymander must try to make the SMSP system resemble as much as possible a proportional representation system. This means that the goal of the affirmative action plan will occasionally conflict with other values inherent in single-member systems: compactness and observance of city and county lines and communities of interest, to name just a few. This is because minorities do not always reside in nicely compact areas. Their communities do not always coincide with city lines. And sometimes the community of interest between minorities violates urban-rural, coastal-inland, and other kinds of traditional communities of interest. In other words, the needs of the affirmative action plan can conflict with other representational values, and reasonable people can consequently disagree about its merits.

In several ways, the affirmative action gerrymander has a great deal in common with the two gerrymanders discussed previously. Incumbents will sometimes find it in their interest to oppose the affirmative action plan. The SMSP system will make the goal of proportionality difficult to achieve. People will disagree about the value of using the redistricting process to help minorities. Our observations regarding the effects of uncertainty on behavior, the difficulties of measurement, and the accommodation of ripple effects apply to affirmative action gerrymandering just as much as they do to the other two types. However, there is one crucial distinction between the affirmative action gerrymander and the other two: the affirmative action plan must take into account the fact that minorities participate in the political system at a lower rate than do non-minorities. This problem is illustrated by the data in Table 17, which shows the breakdown of Assembly seats in California by the percentage of the district population that is registered to vote. The numbers in the rows indicate the different levels of total registration, and the second and third columns divide the seats into those with non-minority populations greater than 50 percent and those with minority populations greater than 50 percent. First of all, it is important to appreciate the range of registration, since it includes a district that is 17 percent registered and another that is 73 percent registered. Sec-

5. Testimony of David C. Lizarraga, President of The East Los Angeles Community Union (TELACU), before the Assembly Committee on Elections and Reapportionment (East Los Angeles, February 20, 1981), p. 49.

TABLE 17 *Percent Registered by Minority and Non-Minority Categories*

Percent Of Population Registered To Vote	Minority Population < 50%	Minority Population ≥ 50%	Total	Percentage
61+	3	0	3	3.7%
56–60	14	0	14	17.5%
51–55	15	3	18	18.7%
46–50	13	1	14	16.2%
41–45	12	1	13	15.0%
36–40	9	2	11	11.0%
31–35	0	2	2	2.5%
26–30	0	4	4	5.0%
21–25	0	0	0	0
<20	0	1	1	1.2%
	66	14	80	

ondly, the data clearly show that the seats that are most severely un-derregistered have minority populations greater than 50 percent. Most political science research on this subject indicates that the reason for this phenomenon is not racial per se, but the disproportionately lower income and education levels of the minority communities.[6] Minority leaders also argue that a pervasive feeling in the poorer areas that voting is meaningless further contributes to voter apathy and lower participation rates. The point is that while the equal population doctrine is oblivious to the number of voters in a given area, the goal of proportionality requires that some attention be paid to differential voter-population ratios.

The Twin Sins of Dispersion and Concentration

The goal of the affirmative action gerrymander is to increase the representation of a given minority or minorities. This can either mean a higher proportion of elected officials who belong to that

6. Raymond Wolfinger and Stephen Rosenstone, *Who Votes* (New Haven: Yale University Press, 1980), pp. 13–36; and Norman Nie and Sidney Verba, *Participation in America* (Cambridge: Harvard University Press, 1976).

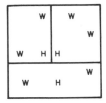

FIGURE 25 *Dispersion of Minorities*

particular ethnic group, or maximizing the strength of a group so that it can have a major say in the policy stands that the representative takes. As a spokesman for MALDEF put it: "It is not our position that an 'Anglo' cannot represent the Hispanic community, but we would at least like a fair opportunity to, as a community, have some 'palenca' or political influence."[7]

Defining an acceptable level of political influence is not as simple as it might seem. What is the minimum population that a group needs in order to have political influence? How do we know that a community has been gerrymandered into a weaker position? If the standard of a minority seat is not simply the presence of a minority incumbent, then what is it?

The most common method of definition is to identify the extremes. A minority can be gerrymandered by being either overly concentrated or overly dispersed. Overdispersion is the typical tactic of the Democratic party. To shore up its surrounding seats, a controlling Democratic party will take slices of a community and share the wealth of loyal minority voters—known in the trade as "gold." This denies the ethnic politician the base to run from, but strengthens the Democrats. Speaking about the experience of the Hispanic community in California, Richard Santillan has said: "The Democratic political leadership during periods of redistricting has deliberately dispersed Chicano voters throughout many districts in order to maximize the number of Democratic candidates who would be guaranteed a significant number of Chicano 'hip-pocket' votes."[8]

The method of overdispersion can be easily demonstrated. Imagine a state with nine voters in it, one-third of whom are Hispanic and living in the same barrio (see Fig. 25). In this figure, lines have been drawn so that each of the districts gets one-third of the Hispanic barrio. This serves to shore up the Democratic registration of the three White seats, but greatly reduces the possibility that an Hispanic will get elected to

7. Testimony of John Huerta before the Assembly Committee on Elections and Reapportionment (East Los Angeles, February 20, 1981), p. 18.

8. Testimony of Richard Santillan before the Assembly Committee on Elections and Reapportionment (East Los Angeles, February 20, 1981), p. 41.

FIGURE 26 *Concentration of Minorities*

any of the districts and even that the Hispanics will have the controlling voice in determining the policy stand of any representative. In Figure 26, all three Hispanic voters have been put into the same seat, giving the Hispanics representation in the legislature. Even if only two of the Hispanics were put together, this would give them a chance at having influence in the district.

If the strategy of divide and conquer is the gerrymander of the party of the left (because it wants to share the loyalty of the minority community), then overconcentration is the gerrymander of the party of the right. Since minority groups have been overwhelmingly Democratic in the past, the presence of minority groups in Republican seats can cause some discomfort to Republican incumbents. Hence, for the very reason that a partisan Democratic gerrymander attempts to share the support of an ethnic community among several seats, Republicans will oppose such a tactic in order to minimize Democratic strength.

An example of overconcentration would be the following: Assume that the state just considered had four instead of three Hispanics in a population of nine. Again, they are concentrated geographically in one area (see Fig. 26). One option would be to put three Hispanics into one district and the fourth into a second district that would be two-thirds Anglo. The effect would be to give the Hispanics one safe seat but no controlling voice in the other. This option could be described as over-concentrating the strength of the Hispanics, since it limits their influence to one seat. However, a second option would be to put two Hispanics each in two separate seats, now giving them a controlling voice in two seats instead of just one.

The key to maximizing the strength of minorities is avoiding the twin sins of dispersion and concentration. As one minority leader put it: "To our friends in the Democratic party, I am here to tell you that no longer will we submit to plans of 'divide and conquer.' . . . To our friends in the Republican party, I am here to tell you that no longer will we allow you to lump us all into one district so that you may fatten up in the suburban Republican districts."[9] In essence, an affirmative action plan

---

9. Testimony of David C. Lizarraga, p. 50. (See note 5, above.)

tries to moderate between two extremes. This rule of ethnic strength is identical in principle to the rule of partisan maximization, which is to use the strength of a group as efficiently as possible. If that calls for concentrating the group more, then concentrate; if it calls for dispersing more, than disperse. Use whichever tactic results in a larger share of seats.

Determining Sufficient Levels of Strength

Proportionality provides one obvious standard of the fairness of ethnic representation as a whole, since the number of seats held by a given minority group can easily be compared with their numbers in the population. However, problems arise when attempting to use this measure. First of all, a minority group that has the power to control a given district might still elect a non-minority representative. There is no automatic guarantee that ethnic groups will vote along ethnic lines. Secondly, even if they do, since lines are drawn on the basis of population, not registration, a controlling number of minority people in a given district may not translate into a controlling number of voters. Obviously, if there are fewer voters for a given number of people in minority communities, then measures of strength based on population alone will exaggerate the electoral power of the minority community. Population may be the standard the courts require the reapportioners to use, but the minority interest group that seeks to maximize its electoral strength needs a measure based on voters.

How, then, can a minority group know when it has sufficient strength to control a district? To begin with, the component parts of the minority population must be defined. Every racial and ethnic population will consist of voting and nonvoting individuals. The voters will further divide along party lines into Democrats, Republicans, minor parties, and independents. A district will consist of component racial or ethnic populations. For example, District 1 might have some number of Whites, Blacks, and Hispanics. On the basis of population alone, there could be two definitions of controlling strength. One is that the number of people in a given minority group—say, Blacks—is greater than the number of *any* other group in the district. The other is that the number of Blacks is greater than the sum of *all* other ethnic and racial groups in the district. The assumption behind the first measure is that no two groups will perfectly coalesce against the majority group, and therefore it is sufficient to be stronger than any of the others. Conversely, the assumption behind the second measure is that they might coalesce, and hence it is important to be stronger than the sum of the other groups. The second rule thus calls for having 51 percent of the population in a district.

However, as was mentioned before, population can be a deceptive measure of political strength. The population of the Blacks in our example could be greater than that of the Whites, and at the same time the number of White voters could exceed the number of Black voters in the district. Thus, the best rule is to compare the number of the voters in the various ethnic and racial groups. The Blacks could be assured of a seat if the number of Black voters were greater than the number of voters in any other groups, or, using the alternative measure, greater than the sum of the voters in any other groups.

Even this, of course, is no guarantee, for two reasons. First, the voting component of the groups consists of Democrats, Republicans, and others. In the general election, the minority candidate need worry only about defeating the Republican candidate, and if the seat is heavily ethnic or racial in population, this will not be a major concern. The real threat in such seats will be a divisive primary in which an incumbent must worry that a candidate with the support of a coalition of other racial or ethnic groups might defeat him, or that he will face challenge from within his own community, and that this will divide his vote sufficiently to enable a candidate from another group to win. So the examination should be taken one step further: it is necessary to look at the number of ethnic or racial group voters in the predominant party. In the case of the largest minorities—the Blacks and the Hispanics—this is the Democratic party. Hence, returning to the previous example, it is necessary to know whether the number of registered Black Democrats exceeds the number of voting Democrats from other groups.

The desire to be able to estimate minority strength in a district leads quickly down a path of greater refinement of measurement. In the end, there is still the possibility of a divisive primary, in which several candidates from the dominant ethnic group split the group's vote and allow another group to win control. Obviously, reapportionment can do little to prevent this occurrence except decrease as much as possible the number of voters who do not belong to the dominant minority. The uncertainties surrounding minority representation partly explain why Hispanic leaders in California were hesitant to try to define what an Hispanic seat is. It was important to make the rank and file think that they would get something out of reapportionment for their lobbying efforts, but the Hispanic leaders could not really promise them that they would get more Hispanic representatives. However, without some tangible return, many would question whether getting involved

V_m NV_m NV_m	V_{nm} V_{nm} V_{nm}
NV_m NV_m NV_m	V_{nm} NV_m V_{nm}

FIGURE 27 *Seats with Nonvoters Included*

V_m V_{nm} V_{nm}	V_{nm} V_{nm} V_{nm}

FIGURE 28 *Seats with Nonvoters Excluded*

in reapportionment mattered. The course the leaders followed was to work out the definition in specific cases rather than in general principle. Still, some misunderstanding was inevitable on this point.

The idea that a minority group must look at its voting strength in order to judge its ability to control a seat leads to an interesting irony. While minorities benefit from having their whole populations counted in reapportionment, when assessing how well off they have been made by a plan, they must look at voters and not population. They benefit from having whole populations counted, because each nonvoter from their group replaces a potential voter from the other groups. This point can be illustrated by a simple, exaggerated example. Let Vm and NVm be minority voters and nonvoters respectively, and Vnm and $NVnm$ be non-minority voters and nonvoters. It is conceivable that counting nonvoters in the redistricting populations would produce the situation shown in Figure 27. Although the minority voters consist of only one-sixth of the electorate, they have one of the two seats in this example. Taking the nonvoters out diminishes the prospects of minority control (see Fig. 28). In either case, the definition of control depends on the voters and not the nonvoters, but including the nonvoters enables the minority to hold a seat in this example. However, if two voting non-minorities were substituted for a nonvoting minority, then minority control in the seat would disappear even though the minority population exceeded the white population by two to one. Control must be measured by the number of minority voters, but the inclusion of non-voters can be beneficial to the minorities. To be sure, this example greatly exaggerates the advantage enjoyed by minorities when non-voters are counted, but it does illustrate the point about population-based and registration-based rules for measuring apportionment schemes.

Pluralist Tensions and the Affirmative Action Gerrymander

Like its partisan and bipartisan counterparts, a successful affirmative action gerrymander has to overcome various pluralist pressures in the reapportionment. One such pressure that the California case demonstrates well is the opposition of non-minority incumbents to attempts to establish a base of minority power in their districts. The San Jose situation is an example of this. The white Democratic incumbent legislator, John Vasconcellos, was understandably hesitant to let the Hispanics establish a power base in his district. This may at first seem odd, since one might think that a Democratic legislator would relish the idea of getting a large block of loyally Democratic voters in his district. This, however, ignores the problem of the primary threat. Obtaining a higher percentage of minority voters will drive the Democratic incumbent's registration up and insulate him or her further from the threat of defeat at the hands of a Republican challenger. In this sense, minority voters are coveted by many Democratic non-minority incumbents. However, the non-minority Democratic incumbent will not want any one minority to have a base sufficient in size to pose a primary threat. The "optimal" level of minority population for the non-minority Democratic incumbent is just below the level at which the minority group controls the district. Like the minority group itself, the non-minority Democratic incumbent must calculate this on the basis of voters and not population. Thus, the optimal population level of minorities in the nonwhite Democratic incumbent's seat might be higher than 50 percent of the total district population if there is an extremely low minority population-voter ratio, but will always contain less than half of the registered voters in the district. Nonvoters will not hurt the non-minority Democratic incumbent.

The non-minority Democratic incumbent must also decide whether he or she is safe in a situation of divide and conquer—i.e., where the number of non-minority voters exceeds the number of any one minority group but not the sum of all of them—or whether he or she is safe only when the number of non-minority voters is greater than the sum of all minority group voters. Still, the non-minority Democrat wants the number of minority voters to be as close to the margin of credible challenge as possible, since the more minority voters, the stronger the non-minority Democratic incumbent will be against a Republican challenger. A non-minority incumbent in a seat with a large homogeneous (i.e., single) ethnic block of voters will want to see that that ethnic block does not exceed the critical level; and when it does, that some of the ethnic voters are shaved off. If the Democratic non-minority incumbent has several ethnic groups, he or she will either make sure that the sum of ethnic voters is below that critical level—if there is some danger of coalition among the minority groups against him or her in the primary—or that if one group is becoming too predominant, that more non-minority or minority voters of another group are added. Thus, the rules for the non-minority Democratic incumbent are:

1.   Determine a critical level of minority challenge from either a single minority or a coalition of minority groups.

2.   Be sure that neither the group nor the coalition exceeds that level.

3.   Increase the number of minority voters to as close to that critical level as the incumbent feels comfortable with.

The California case also amply demonstrates that Republican incumbents do not want too many minority voters, either. When the Assembly plan consolidated the Hispanics in several Republican districts—a possibility they had not foreseen—the Republicans were outraged. Whereas the Democratic incumbent worries about the primary, the Republican worries about the general election. Small numbers of minorities, especially nonvoters, are tolerable, particularly if the seat is safely Republican. However, as the number of minority voters becomes larger, the threat of defeat in the November election increases. Thus, the more marginal the Republican seat, the lower the tolerable level of minority population will be. This is because a small increase in the minority population of a marginal seat can shift the balance between the Democrat and the Republican. Conversely, the safer the seat, the higher the tolerable level of minority population will be, since their presence will not disturb the partisan balance of the district in a significant way. It is of course easier for a more highly registered Republican seat to absorb less registered minorities than it is for seats that are predominantly minority—and usually Democratic—to absorb non-minority Republican population. The rules for the non-minority Republican incumbent are:

1.   Accept a level of minority population that will not substantially affect your probability of defeating a Democratic challenge.

2.   Absorb as much unregistered minority population as possible.

Non-minority incumbents of both parties will find it in their self-interest to oppose the goals of an affirmative action gerrymander. The minority group will want to have its population distributed as efficiently as possible, but the Democratic non-minority incumbent will want to keep the minority population just a shade below that efficient level: high enough to get their loyal votes and low enough to keep them from challenging in the primary. The Republican non-minority incumbent will want to keep the number of minority voters as low as possible, but at any rate will tolerate minority strength in relation to the partisan strength of his seat. In any case, this will be well below the efficient level needed for an affirmative action gerrymander.

Non-minority incumbents, however, are not the only ones who will object to affirmative action gerrymanders. Surprisingly, the incentives of minority incumbents can also be at odds with those of an affirmative action gerrymander. This is because risk-averse minority incumbents will want to increase the number of minorities in their districts above the efficient level. For instance, a Black incumbent with more than 50 percent Black voters in his district might request that any new areas added to the district by reapportionment further increase the Blackness of the district. He might fear that the addition of non-Black voters will weaken the racial character of the seat, and that his incumbency would be threatened. The incumbent's edginess is quite understandable. Typically, the incumbent knows what the Black population is in his district and may even know how many of them are registered. However, he cannot be sure that the addition of more highly registered non-minority voters will not make him vulnerable. The non-minority population will have more voters and perhaps more money, and the incumbent must fear that a divisive primary between two minority candidates could open the way for the better financed non-minority candidate. Risk aversion on the minority incumbents' part dictates that more than the efficient level of minorities be added to their districts.

A simple example will illuminate the problem. Assume that there are two districts. Both are identical in size, but one has a minority voter population of 30 percent, and the other of 72 percent. The efficiency rule of the affirmative action gerrymander dictates that the minority incumbent in the district with 72 percent minority population should give up some so that both can be at 51 percent. This would give the minority community two probable seats rather than one certain one. However, the incumbent will see that he has to get 21 percent non-minority population in exchange, and that the margin of his group over other minorities—and worse, over non-minorities—will decrease. Moreover, if the non-minority population he is adding has a higher ratio of voters to population than the minorities, then the risks associated with holding that seat will seem very high. Non-incumbent minorities or others who are more interested in taking a shot at two seats even at the risk of losing them both will prefer the option of two seats at 51 percent; the incumbent will prefer the option of 72–30 percent.

Other minority groups are, then, a third source of opposition to the affirmative action gerrymander. When the seat is reasonably homogeneous, there will be very little problem. Control by the largest minority group will be indisputable. However, when there are several minority groups in the same district, then the issue of how different proposals affect the strength of one group relative to another will matter greatly. Recall that the rule for the controlling minority group is to increase its numbers so as to maximize its share of voters relative to any other group or any coalition of other groups. Thus, an affirmative action gerrymander that naively maximizes the strength of all minorities relative to non-minorities and ignores how redistricting influences the relative size of the minority groups that compose the sum is courting disaster. Only if there is some prior agreement between the groups about shared policy agendas and about the rules for competing for control will a minority maximization rule succeed. Otherwise, the minority groups will see the intended affirmative action gerrymander as "pitting minorities against one another."

Conclusion

The partisan plan is a risky strategy. The majority party spreads its resources as efficiently as possible in the hope of winning as many seats as it can. By so doing, it raises the risk of losing seats that it currently holds and incurs the higher costs of fighting elections next time. The partisan plan is encouraged when one party has a resource advantage and/or thinks that political trends are going its way. At the individual level, legislators in the majority party have to be willing to make sacrifices for the good of the party, and this creates an inevitable tension between the perspectives of the party and the individual legislators.

The bipartisan plan is a risk-averse plan. It makes the incumbents from both parties safer and divides the burden of displacement as evenly as possible. The key to a bipartisan plan is a set of conditions that increases the uncertainty of both parties and makes them less willing to spread their resources thinly. At the individual level, bipartisan trades will occur when members of opposing parties trade in a complementary way and do not act against their self-interest in order to weaken their opponents. One of the trickiest issues in a bipartisan reapportionment is the sharing of collapses. The most stable rule for sharing collapses would seem to be an equal division rule, since all others are subject to strategic manipulation.

The affirmative action gerrymander is a plan that tries to reverse the discrimination against minorities that is inherent in a single-member, simple-plurality system. It follows many of the same principles discussed earlier about how to make minority-party support efficient. To ensure control of the seat or even a dominant voice, a minority group must look at its share of registered voters in a district in order to assess its clout in the primary and general elections. Non-minority Democratic incumbents will try to keep the number of registered minority voters slightly below the efficient level in order to get their support in the general election but not be threatened by them in the primary. The non-minority Republican wants to keep the number of minority voters well below the efficient level. Minority incumbents, on the other hand, will want to have a number of minority voters that is above the efficient level.

10

Reform in a Pluralist Setting

Most proposals for reapportionment reform take a public interest approach. Their goal is typically to ensure the protection of the public's interest as defined by some set of formal, or good government, criteria. The typical reform measure proposes to assign the task of redistricting to a commission with the mandate to draw lines that conform as closely as possible to formal standards. The purest public interest approach would require that the members of a reapportionment commission be apolitical, either in the sense that they should not be actively affiliated with the Democratic or Republican parties, or that they should be appointed by the courts or some suitably nonpolitical body.

Within the context of political theory, the public interest approach has a Rousseauvian tone. The public interest of reapportionment is like Rousseau's common good: it is what is best for all members of the polity even if they themselves may not recognize it as such. The formalist vision is of a reapportionment system that is equally fair to all participants and that preserves the important democratic values which all citizens benefit from, such as competitive seats and responsive legislators. In this sense, the public interest approach distinguishes reapportionment from other political issues normally brought before the legislature.

A competing tradition in political theory–and one that is more consistent with American institutions–is the Madisonian approach. Since it is less optimistic about the capacity of individuals and interest groups to come to agreement on important issues, it tries to provide an institutional framework for the resolution of inevitable disagreements. In addition, the Madisonian approach is more skeptical about human nature and the ability of individuals to rise above the perspective of their narrow self-interest. There is room for people to act altruistically, but Madisonian institutions do not depend upon such behavior for their proper functioning. Pluralism is a modern variant on the Madisonian theme. Pluralist institutions are agnostic with respect to ultimate truths and values, allowing policies to be created by the competition among various groups. The fundamental problem that is thought to plague a pluralist democracy—the tyranny of the majority—is resolved in Madisonian principles by means of institutions that protect fundamental rights and allow the formation of group coalitions to advance specific policies.[1]

An approach to reapportionment consistent with the pluralist point of view does not assume, as does formalism, that there is one overriding public interest. Rather, it assumes that the interests of poor and rich, Black and White, Hispanic and non-Hispanic, rural and urban, and the like will diverge on a particular solution to reapportionment as they do on many other issues. It does not try to mask the fact that reasonable people can disagree about how to draw the lines, even if it is disturbing to contemplate the idea of disagreement about the rules of political competition. To the extent possible, the process of reapportionment should be neutral on the question of ordering redistricting values and should allow choices between values to emerge politically through the process of negotiation and compromise between various groups. The institutions of redistricting, in other words, should encourage groups to come to agreement without predetermining the nature of the settlement.

So stated, this is the ideal of a pluralist reapportionment. But at the same time, one must recognize that the ideal may be unattainable in pure form, since the choice of institutional framework itself will create incentives that encourage certain kinds of settlements and discourage others. This in turn will affect key reapportionment values.

For instance, consider the question of whether a commission should be given a two-thirds or a majority voting rule. The two-thirds rule will eliminate highly partisan settlements in most states. Unless the partisan imbalance of the redistricting body is enormous—as in one-party southern states—the majority party under a two-thirds rule would have to secure the votes of the minority party. These concessions would lead to a reapportionment that would more closely resemble a bipartisan than a partisan gerrymander. As noted already, the bipartisan gerrymander results in somewhat less competitive, more homogeneous

---

1. I am referring, of course, to such classic works as Robert A. Dahl, *Who Governs* (New Haven: Yale University Press, 1961); idem, *A Preface to Democratic Theory* (Chicago: University of Chicago Press, 1956); and Nelson Polsby, *Community Power and Political Theory* (New Haven: Yale University Press, 1963).

districts, whereas the partisan gerrymander leads to more competitive and heterogeneous seats. Thus, the institutional incentives, as defined by the voting rule, direct the reapportionment settlement towards, or away from, certain values of representation—namely, more or less competitive and homogeneous districts. This being the case, the only way that the redistricting process could retain some of its agnosticism with respect to the contrasting values of competitiveness and homogeneity would be to allow the parties to enter into an agreement every ten years on whether to use a two-thirds or a majority rule for reapportionment. Since the position a party would take on this issue would depend on its electoral expectations—i.e., a party that thinks it will be in the majority at reapportionment time will favor a majority rule, and one that expects to be in the minority will favor a two-thirds rule—this agreement should be made well in advance of the actual reapportionment date. Thus, the parties will have to choose from a position of ignorance as to whether they will benefit or not from the rule. If the parties are risk-prone, they will probably choose majority rule; if they are risk-averse, they will probably choose the two-thirds rule. In any event, renegotiating the voting rule issue every ten years would be one way to avoid the binding of future participants in reapportionment to value judgments made in the past.

The Choices of Reform

Though the first—and most important—institutional choice is the voting rule to be used by the redistricting body, there are other choices as well, and they, too, affect the probabilities of certain kinds of outcomes. The size of the redistricting body is one of these. A small commission would have lower negotiation costs than one that includes all members of the legislature. Quite naturally, the more people who have to vote on the final lines, the more positions there will be in need of reconciliation. Given the inherent complexity of reapportionment, the lower negotiation costs of small decision bodies are attractive. See Table 18.

On the other hand, large decision bodies have two key characteristics that cannot be lightly dismissed. One is that there are so many viewpoints that have to be represented in reapportionment that it may be valuable, in a pluralist context, to have a large decision body. This would especially be true if people applied the same standards of descriptive representation to the reapportionment commission that they apply to the legislature. If this were the case, then Democrats would want their share of Democrats on the commission, Republicans would

TABLE 18 *The Institutional Choices of Reapportionment Reform*

Institutional Choice	Options	Consequences
Voting Rule	Simple Majority or Two-Thirds	Partisan or Bipartisan Outcome
Size of Decision Body	Large or Small	High Negotiation Costs, Degree of Descriptive Representation
Partisanship of Reapportioners	Partisan or Nonpartisan	Partisan Fairness
Self-Interest of Reapportioners	Legislators or Nonlegislators	Resistance to Change, Idiosyncratic Changes
Normative Constraints	Fixed Formal Criteria or Flexible Standards	Responsiveness to Changing Political Climate

want their share of Republicans, Blacks would want their share of Blacks, Hispanics would want their share of Hispanics, and so on. The smaller the decision body, the harder it would be to provide each of the interest groups with its own reapportionment representative.

In defense of the small commission, one might say that there is no reason why each group would have to have its own representative, but there are several objections to this. First, if the members of a polity want descriptive representation in their legislature, it would not be illogical for them to want to have the reapportionment body also be descriptively representative. Since reapportionment is a political issue, these groups might want their interests defended by someone they can trust—i.e., one of their own who is responsive to their community— just as they might on other political issues. Choosing a small decision body precludes the option of descriptive representation and violates the principle of pluralist agnosticism towards representational values. A large decision body, on the other hand, preserves the option of descriptive representation, but does not preclude other options at the same time. If in twenty or thirty years, the demand for proportional representation dwindles, there is no reason why the large decision body could not be constituted on some other principle.

The third choice is between political and nonpolitical members of the commission. We need not dwell at great length on this issue, since it has been discussed in several places in this book already. First, it is doubtful that any reapportioner would ever be above partisan suspicion, regardless of the stringency of the selection criteria applied. The experiences of the court masters in 1973 and the Rose Institute's model plan in 1980 show how in one major state at least, no one who has yet produced a statewide plan is exempt from allegations of partisan bias. Some Republicans felt that when the California Supreme Court took over the 1973 California reapportionment, it implemented a more effective Democratic gerrymander than the Democratic legislature's own plan. Similarly, the Rose Institute was unable to persuade most Democrats of its nonpartisanship, especially when its model plan happened to remove twice as many Democratic incumbents from their seats as Republicans. This is illustrative of the point that regardless of what is in the reapportioner's heart and mind at the time the lines are drawn, many people will judge the fairness of a plan by its outcome—i.e., its effect on the parties. This leads to a second objection to an apolitical reapportionment board: namely, that since all reapportionment plans inevitably have an impact on the parties, there is no such thing as an apolitical plan; and if plans are inevitably political, it is better to confront the political fairness issue openly rather than shove it under the rug of ostensible neutrality.[2]

Assuming that the reapportionment board should be politically constituted, what is a fair distribution of partisanship? One standard might be proportionality with registration in the state. Thus, if one party has 58 percent of the registered voters, another party has 32 percent, and the rest of the voters belong to minor parties or are unaffiliated, the reapportionment body might reflect these proportions (in addition, of course, to ethnic and other considerations). It might be objected, however, that registration does not necessarily reflect voting behavior, or the strength of a party in the legislature, as was discussed earlier. Thus, another option would be to make the reapportionment body proportionate to the partisan distribution in the legislature, or, alternatively, to use the legislature itself. This, of course, leads back to a legislative reapportionment, but it would seem to be the simplest method of achieving proportionality.

The dangers of not having some sort of proportional composition rule are twofold. One is that the majority party could be overrepresented on the board, and that it would have the power to force its plan on the minority party, even with a two-thirds voting rule. The converse danger is that the minority party would be overrepresented and would extort election gains through the reapportionment process. By pegging

---

2. Robert Dixon writes: "All district lines drawn on an apportionment map are political lines in the sense that they group or separate partisans of one persuasion from fellow partisans in the same area." Robert G. Dixon, Jr., *Democratic Representation and Reapportionment in Law and Politics* (New York: Oxford University Press, 1968), p. 18.

membership in the reapportionment body to a principle of proportionality, the probability of both kinds of distortion is reduced.

Another important institutional choice involves the self-interest issue raised by Common Cause. Common Cause contends that a conflict of interest is created when legislators have a vote over their own districts. This contention deserves closer examination. The interest at stake in reapportionment is electoral support: legislators will try to get districts that are more to their liking and that will enhance their prospects of reelection. However, the interest of getting friendly voters should be distinguished from that of personal monetary gain and other non-electoral benefits, and it is not clear whether the effect of the former is pernicious or beneficial. To some extent, benefiting electorally from a reapportionment bill is not all that dissimilar from the electoral reward a legislator receives for any other piece of legislation. In the former, support increases because the reapportionment bill gives the legislator more voters who agree with him on issues; and in the latter, he gets more votes because the voters approve of his actions in office. In addition, of course, the conflict of interest charge assumes that all or most legislators get what they want, or that they always want to get partisanly stronger. Since neither of these conditions hold for all members of the legislature, nor even for all members of the controlling party, it is not the case that all legislators will be confronted with these kinds of conflict of interest situations.

Aside from the question of whether the conflict of interest in reapportionment is really what is normally meant by conflict of interest in government, or whether it is merely the electoral incentive in another form, is its effect pernicious or beneficial? There are really two consequences of allowing legislators to vote on their own lines. One is that the lines in some cases will reflect the idiosyncratic preferences of the legislators. For instance, legislators will sometimes request to have the lines diverge to pick up amusement parks, athletic stadiums, the houses of key contributors, mothers-in-law, and the like. While such requests are a nuisance, their effects on representation or partisan balance are minimal. Not all legislators make such requests, and not all of them get what they want. Those that do must often pay the price in terms of displacement and partisan weakening. For the most part, requests of this nature are irrelevant to the key issues of reapportionment, which is precisely why they seem so irritating to the staff and party leadership.

The more important effect of allowing legislators to vote on their own lines is that legislators are more likely to be resistant to change than persons whose careers are unaffected by reapportionment. This follows from the earlier discussion about displacement and risk aversion. Legislators, who have typically made a substantial investment in building up name recognition and trust in the areas they have represented, will not want to give up familiar voters unless their electoral position would improve significantly by so doing. It is the inertia they create that makes it difficult to realize in an uncompromised manner the goals of gerrymandering in any of the senses described earlier. A commission composed of activists or allegedly dispassionate experts would have less investment in the status quo and consequently would be less resistant to radical alterations in district lines. In this sense, allowing legislators to participate in reapportionment puts the brake on major departures from the status quo and hands over the ultimate decision on district lines to individuals with a vested interest in district continuity. That interest in continuity is not necessarily deleterious to the democratic process. Name recognition and familiarity make it easier for voters to know what the incumbent stands for and what he has done: from a policy perspective, the voters are more informed and their votes are more meaningful. At the same time, the party infrastructures are not unnecessarily disturbed, and the working relations between city and county officials and legislators are not weakened. There are good reasons, therefore, for letting legislators preserve the continuity of their districts.

The final major institutional choice is whether and what kind of reapportionment criteria should be imposed on the process. A pluralist reapportionment should not make a permanent commitment to any one set of criteria, other than those prescribed by the U.S. Supreme Court—i.e., "one man, one vote" and the protection of minorities. Rather, the decision about values should be reached politically by negotiations among the members of the reapportionment body. Those members should be aware that they cannot realize all formal reapportionment criteria simultaneously, and that only certain of these criteria are mutually compatible. Hence, the reapportioning body will inevitably have to agree to an ordering of the criteria, and it is conceivable that this ordering could vary from decade to decade as social and political priorities change. The ordering should be determined by the same voting process as that used for determining the final lines: namely, by a two-thirds or majority rule vote.

It would also be desirable, although probably unlikely to occur, to make the values of redistricting as consistent as possible with the goals of representation. The connection between the two can be seen in Table 19, where various aspects of representation are displayed with those reapportionment values that are most consistent with them. The first contrast in this scheme is that between professionalism and amateurism. A professional legislature is one in which the legislators' jobs are full-time and the legislators have extensive resources at their disposal. The opposite would be true for an amateur legislature. If legislators are

TABLE 19 *Representation Characteristics and Redistricting Values*

Representation Characteristics		Redistricting Choices
Professionalism	Amateurism	Competitiveness of Seats
Heterogenous Voter Mandate	Homogenous Voter Mandate	Communities of Interest, Protection of Minorities
Working Government Majority	Proportional Representation	Protecting Minority Communities, Political Fairness, Communities of Interest
Strong Party Responsibility	Weak Party Responsibility	Continuity, Coincidence of State Legislature and Congressional Lines

to be professional and if people are to be induced to choose politics as a full-time career, then the importance of the electoral incentive will increase. The partisan strength of a seat will affect a legislator's job security, and it is only natural that legislators—like any other jobholders—will not want to lose their jobs. At the same time, if the public wants to have able and talented people in the legislature, then it must not impose unreasonable risks on its legislators. The dilemma is that some measure of responsiveness is necessary in order to get legislators to act in desirable ways and to get the legislature to reflect changes in public opinion. The trend towards professionalism in the legislature conflicts with the electoral incentive.

There should be room over time for a polity to adjust itself with respect to the proper degree of legislative professionalism. If the legislature seems out of step with changes in the climate of opinion, then perhaps the trend towards professionalism has gone too far, and reapportionment can be used to redress the shift. If, on the other hand, it becomes hard to attract and hold good people in the legislature, then a polity might want to strengthen the electoral standing of its legislators to ease the burden of electoral insecurity. The point is that when the reapportioning body considers whether to increase the number of marginal seats, it ought to weigh the effects of electoral insecurity against legislative professionalism. It should also realize that the ability to cope with a competitive situation may be unevenly distributed in society—that the burden of fighting expensive campaigns may be more easily shouldered by those with the advantages of wealth and power. One of the motives behind a professional legislature was to take government out of the hands of those who could afford to be amateur politicians and open politics up as a career for those from less privileged positions in society. In this sense, a wholesale retrenchment from professionalism might be class-biased.

A second issue of representation affected by reapportionment is whether the representative should be responsive to a single, homogeneous interest or to the common, or median, preference of society. The first situation would produce legislators who defend the narrow interests of their districts; policies in such a legislature emerge from the clash of divergent perspectives. Reapportioners would take care to ensure that communities of interest were preserved, that ethnic and racial groups were not mixed, and that like-minded voters were grouped together. The legislative mandates would be clear, and the median preferences of individual districts would be skewed in various directions away from the median preferences of the polity as a whole. The responsibility of each legislator would be to the district, and not to some common or modal good.

The other approach would be to make districts as heterogeneous as possible, so that the median preference of each district is as similar as possible to the median preference of the polity. The simplest and most effective way to achieve this would be to have each member of the legislature run at large; but under a district system, the districts themselves would have to be fashioned to approximate median opinion. Obviously, any attempt to do this will be greatly constrained by residential patterns, but reapportionment—particularly with a loosened compactness requirement and little regard for displacement—could significantly shift individual districts in that direction. It should be obvious from previous discussions that minorities in particular will oppose any change that pushes the system towards the median preference of society, and that this choice is therefore another variant of the classic Madisonian tension between majority rule and minority rights.

A related representation issue that has been mentioned at several points is the choice between a political system that regularly produces working legislative majorities and one that gives proportional, descriptive representation to all groups in society. The advantage of the former is that single-member, simple-plurality systems tend to exaggerate seat strength, with the result that the governing party gets working majorities that are disproportionate to its electoral strength. It also, by the cube rule, exaggerates small shifts in public opinion, so that the opposition party can come to office with a clear mandate. Designing districts to protect minorities or to preserve homogeneous interests in the name of descriptive representation will weaken the working majority feature of the single-district system. It is conceivable that a pluralist polity might change its mind on this issue over time, as the agenda and concerns of politics shift.

Finally, reapportionment affects the role of parties in representation. Parties give coherence and organization to political competition. They simplify the choices at elections and lower the information costs for voters, especially those who do not have the leisure or background to follow politics and public issues closely. They provide a framework for cooperation among legislators and between legislators and their supporters, which is especially important to those candidates and groups who must depend on organization to offset the advantages of wealth and notoriety. The formalist, or good government, school never mentions the preservation of parties as one of their criteria, and yet that may be as important to the functioning of fair and effective representation as any of the other criteria. Reapportionment affects the parties in various ways. Obviously, the partisan composition of reapportionment decision bodies is one of these. The preservation of district continuity is another, since it enables stable cooperative ties to solidify. In addition, to the extent possible, the districts of offices at different levels should overlap—as the court masters tried to do in California in 1973— so that the grass-roots organizations can rationalize their structure: i.e., campaigns at the Congressional and state legislative levels can be coordinated more easily. These measures in some small way would help shift power to our decimated party system.

Improving Legislative Reapportionment

The conclusion of this study is that in various ways the procedure that leaves reapportionment in the hands of the legislature is very compatible with the pluralist foundations of American government. A legislature is large enough to provide descriptive representation on reapportionment matters. It is proportionately political, as defined earlier. The conflict of interest that legislators are allowed to exercise tends to make them cautious and resistant to change, and this in turn protects the continuity of districts. Since this is a conclusion that many people will initially resist, we will consider the standard criticisms of legislative reapportionment once more and ask whether, and to what extent, this kind of reapportionment can be improved.

It must be pointed out that some of the public's complaints are irresolvable and inherent in the process of reapportionment per se. What most people would like to see happen—i.e., having the politics taken out of reapportionment—cannot happen. To the extent that the public and the press continue to believe that it can happen, they will continue to be distressed by what they perceive as the "seedy, decennial rite" of redistricting. However, accepting that there will be inevitable conflicts and that the solution has to be political, one can still try to make reapportionment more consistent with pluralist ideals.

One reason that reformers look to commissions to solve the reapportionment quandary is that they have little faith in the public's ability to protect its own interests, and so they perceive the need for a blue-ribbon panel to fulfill the guardian role. In theory, since legislators are elected by the public, they can be held accountable at election time for the lines they draw. However, if the public is uninterested or uninformed—because of the esoteric and complex nature of the issues involved in reapportionment—then it will not be able to guard its own interests. The danger, of course, is that in trying to protect the public's interest on an issue in which there are many different public interests, rather than only one Public Interest, the commission will protect some of these interests but not others.

To the extent possible in a pluralist society, the public should protect its own interests, and the political system should facilitate the public's awareness of the many diverse interests in reapportionment. For this reason, the role of secrecy in reapportionment should be minimized. Some amount of secrecy is necessary for successful negotiation. If all proposals under consideration are always known, the progress of the bargaining will be slower and, for fear of alarming key legislators, some possible options may never be considered. However, excessive secrecy makes it hard for the public to hold legislators responsible for their votes. A compromise between these two extremes might be the following. Negotiations could still be held in secret, but there would be two periods of public disclosure prior to voting on the final bill. First, legislators and interested groups would be required to file as public record their requests for district changes. These could then be examined by the press and made known to the rest of the public. Needless to say, there would be no guarantee that their formal requests would be the same as those made privately to the committee, but it would make it risky for them to submit false proposals if their requests were also submitted to the courts if and when the legislature failed to pass its own bill.

The second period of pre-vote disclosure would come one to two weeks before the bill was to be voted on. There should be a hearing for each district at the state legislative and Congressional level, which the legislator must attend to answer questions about the bill. There should also be strict requirements about the kinds of information that would have to be made available—i.e., maps, registration figures, etc.—so that the press will be able to publicize features of the districts completely. This would identify legislators clearly with their new districts and give them time to reconsider the consequences of their vote.

Publicity is crucial for making people aware of their interests, but even so, one must realistically expect that many will not know or care about reapportionment. In a pluralist system, an apathetic majority will defer to the interests of coalitions of groups with intense concerns; and while one must be pessimistic about the prospects of widespread public involvement, heightened publicity will facilitate the involvement of interest groups and better enable them to bring pressure upon legislators to get what they want.

At the same time, as the process becomes more open, there will be an even greater tendency towards overall incoherence than before. One way to introduce rationality into the process would be to divide the negotiations into two stages, the first of which would involve the broad outlines of districts and the issues of collapses and new seats, and the second of which would involve the detailed street-by-street negotiations. During the first stage, the leaders of the state legislative bodies and the Congressional delegations would be required to hammer out lines that coincided with one another to the extent possible. One might even require that the number of seats in one house be exactly divisible by that of the other. During the second stage, the fringes of districts could be altered by in-house negotiations with the members. This would partly answer the obvious objections that the normal procedure of legislatures is not to interfere in the business of the other house and that the negotiations would be hopelessly complex. It would allow each legislative group some degree of autonomy over its own districts, and, by keeping the nickel and diming separate from the larger issues, the first-stage negotiations would become more manageable.

Finally, the prolonged nature of the reapportionment struggle causes problems. By dragging on for years, redistricting typically becomes extremely expensive and wearisome. Ideally, all participants should treat their involvement as a social contract in which they accept the risks of loss as well as gain. If a party does not act to change a majority-rule redistricting system, then it should accept the inevitable partisan injustices if it fails to become the majority party; and if it accepts a bipartisan rule, then it should live with the risk of minority extortion if it becomes the ruling party. Realistically, this will not happen, and thus the system should close off all unnecessary routes of appeal. There should be one court review of a plan's constitutionality, and no other means of holding up a plan passed by the legislature. This will end partisan bickering and force the parties and legislators to get on with the business of government.

Doubtless, these proposed changes, which make reapportionment more consistent with a pluralist approach, will not satisfy reformers with formalist ideals. A pluralist approach cannot create unanimity where there is none to begin with. It cannot even create the comforting facade of agreement that a commission offers. It only promises a tolerant, open way for a polity to resolve its disagreements. But that would be a considerable achievement in itself.

Index

Activists, political, 159; attitudes toward gerrymanders, 155, 161; influence of radical electoral reform on, 12–13

Adjustment areas, and splitting of city or county lines, 24–25

Aesthetic criteria, 33–51; indirect value of, 33, 43; problems caused by, 35–41, 46; relationship with good government criteria, 32, 33–34, 35, 42–51, 69. *See also* Compactness

Affirmative action gerrymander. *See* Gerrymanders, affirmative action

Aggregate fairness, 29–30. *See also* Fairness in reapportionment

Alabama, 66

Alameda County, 23, 24, 99, 158

Alatorre, Richard: as Chairman of the Elections and Reapportionment Committee, xii, 81, 82, 83, 86, 87, 89, 90, 92, 93–95, 96, 97–98, 101; negotiations with legislators, 106, 108, 109–110, 112, 130

Antelope Board of Trade, 72

Asian communities, 48, 70

Baker, Gordon E., 5*n*, 40*n*

Baker v. Carr, 4, 40*n*, 55, 56, 70

Balitzer, Alfred, 53*n*

Bargaining in reapportionment, 120–134; case studies of, 104–117, 128, 129, 131; complementary and noncomplementary conditions in, 123–125, 126; demographic factors in, 121–127; failure in, 99–101; partisan strength in, 121, 123, 125, 128; persuasion in, 127–132; power

of legislative leaders in, 128, 130–132, 134; recommendations for improvement of, 189–190; secrecy in, 84–85, 189; skills required for, 132–133; typology of positions in, 121–127

Beloff, Max, 56*n*

Berman, Howard, 61*n*, 81, 86, 87, 88, 98

Berman, Michael, 86, 89

Bicker, William E., 5*n*

Binderup, Douglas, 64*n*

Bipartisan coalitions, reasons for failure of, 97–101, 160, 163

Bipartisan gerrymanders. *See* Gerrymanders, bipartisan

Bipartisan reapportionment commissions, 3, 4

Black communities, 115; compared with Chicano districts, 92, 93; in the Democratic party, 71–72; distribution in California, 46–48, 71; protection of the political strength of, 70–72. *See also* Minority communities; Racial communities

Black legislators, 14, 81, 130

Blackmun, Justice, 56

Border district near Mexico, 96

Brown, Willie: bargaining strategies of, 106, 114; as Speaker of the California State Assembly, 81, 86, 87, 89, 92, 93–94, 96, 98, 102

Budget of California, 86

Burkean theory of representation, 15, 65, 68

Burke, Yvonne, 143

Burton Congressional plan, 136

Cain, Bruce E., 13n, 33n
California: distribution of partisan support in, 43–44; minority communities in, 46–48, 70–72; rural areas in, 70
California coastline, linear reapportionment ripples illustrated by, 19–20
California Democratic party, 44; control of the Assembly Speakership by, 81. See also Democratic party
California reapportionment, 5, 6, 81–103; absence of a bipartisan coalition in, 98–101; attitudes of legislators toward, 104–119, 127–132; control and construction of data for, 83–87, 111; criteria based on Proposition 6 in, 17, 23, 41n, 60–61; distribution of territorial trades in, 126–127; Elections and Reapportionment Committee in, 81, 82, 87, 92, 98, 102, 105–115 passim, 107, 120, 129, 130; gerrymandering in, 88–89, 152–154; hearings on, 60–61; Hispanic role in, 81, 82, 89, 90–96, 98, 101, 103, 115, 130, 137, 152, 172–173; interhouse rivalries in, 84–85; and non-minority incumbents, 174–175; partisan struggles in, 82–83, 84, 87–90, 92, 93–94, 98–101, 183; reform proposals for, 4, 13–14; role of the Assembly Speakership in, 81, 82, 86, 87, 88, 92, 97, 102, 114, 120, 130, 131; types of seats traded in, 125–126; voter deviations in, 58–59
California State Senate, political data holdings of, 83–84, 85
California Supreme Court, 188; on criteria for reapportionment, 41n, 42n; and Hispanic representation, 48, 90, 94, 95; and partisan bias in reapportionment, 183; 1973 reapportionment by, 48, 58–59
Californios for Fair Representation, 90, 91, 92, 95–96. See also Hispanic community
Carillo, Pedro, 95n
Carter, Jimmy, 141
Case studies of political reapportionment, 6, 81–103, 105–115
"Cautious seats," 122
Census data, 9; inaccuracy of, 28–29; integration with political data, 83, 85
Chavez, Cesar, 95
Chicano districts, 89, 92, 93, 96, 169

Cities, number of seats relative to population size of, 16
City and county lines, respect for, 117; in California Assembly reapportionment, 23, 41n, 60, 97, 103; vs. compact districts, 35, 37, 41–43, 44, 46; conflict with equal population requirement, 70; conflict with preserving communities of interest, 72; evaluation of, 60–63; vs. line splitting, 24–25, 42, 46, 61–62, 70; and protection of minority political power, 71, 74; in redistricting criteria, 11, 15, 41–42; relationship with competitive seats, 73; remedy to prevent line splitting, 42; and single vs. multiple representation, 62–63
City of Mobile, Alabama, et al. v. Bolden, 66
Claremont, in Los Angeles County, 61–62
Coalitions: bargaining power of, 131–132; bipartisan, 97–101, 160, 163
Cohen, Eleanor, 62n
Collapse of old seats, 27–30. See also Seats
Colorado, reapportionment in, 82
Common Cause, 12n; on compactness, 32; on nonpartisan reapportionment, 135n; reform proposal of, 4; on self-interest of legislators, 1, 184
Communities of interest, 108; counties as, 16–17, 63–64; defined, 63
Communities of interest, preservation of, 63–67; and compactness, 33, 37, 39–40, 43, 48–49; compatibility with competitive seats, 72; conflict with the equal population requirement, 70; conflict with respect for city/county lines, 72; in criteria for redistricting, 11, 15; critique of the value of, 63–66; crucial role of, 14; and linear ripples, 19–20; and protection of minority political strength, 71; racial and ethnic communities in, 66–67; rationale for, 39, 63–64; remedy for, 40
Compactness, 10–11, 13; and communities of interest, 33, 37, 39–40, 43, 48–49; in the fair distribution of partisan support, 43–44; and good government criteria, 32, 33–34, 35, 42–51; historical reasons for, 32–33; indirect value of, 33, 43, 50; intrinsic value of, 34, 50–51; minority populations and political representation influenced by, 35–37, 40–41, 43, 46–48, 50–51; partisan skew in, 35–38; popular attitudes toward, 102–103;

remedies for the problems caused by, 35–43; vs. respect for city and county lines, 35, 37, 41–43, 46

Competitive seats: conflict with equal population requirement, 69–70; conflict with the protection of minority political strength, 71–72; disadvantages of, 68; effect of gerrymandering on, 180–181; in reform strategies, 67–68; relationship with preservation of communities of interest, 72, 74; vs. respect for city and county lines, 73

Computers, 5, 31; compared with qualitative data, 136–137; disadvantages of, 137–138, 146; in nonpartisan reform strategies, 3; objectivity of, 136; role in California reapportionment, 83, 87; in the Tabula Rasa method, 10, 11

"Condor" district, 94, 101

Conflict of interest in legislative reapportionment, 1–2, 52, 184–185, 188. *See also* Legislators

Congressional districts: equal population requirement for, 55, 56; value of the single vote in, 57

Constitution, U.S., 55, 66

Constraints: on gerrymanders, 155–157, 163–166; of linear ripples, 20–21, 22; of redistricting criteria, 11–12

Consultants, xi, 88–89, 114, 115, 129

Contiguous districts, 10–11; interdependency with redistricting, 17–18; and ripple dispersal, 21–22

Contra Costa County, 14, 23, 24

Cortese, Dominic, 96

Costs, 22; of data construction for reapportionment, 85; of gerrymandering, 151, 160; incurred by competitive districts, 68; of political campaigns, 153; of radical change of the electoral system, 13, 14; and the value of compactness, 33, 50

Counties: number of seats relative to population size of, 16; single vs. multiple districts in, 16–17; splitting of, 23–25. *See also* City and county lines, respect for

Courts: deviations from the ideal population permitted by, 25, 55–60; displacement augmented by, 19, 25. *See also* California Supreme Court; U.S. Supreme Court

Cranston, Alan, 111

Criteria for redistricting, 10–12, 13, 15; in California, 17, 23, 41n, 48; consistency with the goals of representation, 185–186; ordering of, 12, 73–74, 185; selection of, 185. *See also* Good government criteria

Dahl, Robert A., 180n

Data required for reapportionment, 83–87. *See also* Political data

Deddeh, Waddie, 96

Deegan, John, Jr., 3n, 75n

DeGrazia, Alfred, 117n

Delay tactics in reapportionment, 89–90

Democracy: and legislative reapportionment, 179, 185; political conflict in, 5; vs. removal of incumbents by redistricting, 12

Democratic party: and the distribution of partisan support, 43–44; minority representation in, 67, 72, 95, 169–170, 174–175; registration figures in, 141–142, 143; vs. Republicans in reapportionment, 20, 82–83, 84, 87–90, 92, 94–95, 99–102

Demography, 9–31, 89; in bargaining on reapportionment, 109, 110–111, 121–127; and the collapse of old seats, 27–30; in gerrymandering, 152, 154. *See also* Population

Deukmejian, S. F., 162n

Displacement, 17–27; causes and sources of, 17–19; crucial role in bargaining, 120, 121, 122, 123; debated in California reapportionment struggles, 99, 101, 108, 113; in gerrymanders, 156, 159, 161, 164; minimizing of, 19, 20, 24–27; one-third rule for, 21–22, 113

District planning: bipartisan approach to, 3, 4, 159–166; compactness in, 32–51 (*see also* Compactness); complexity of, 9; equity in, 30–31, 51; fairness in, 3–4, 16, 27, 33, 38, 51, 73–77, 130; methods for, 10–27; objective approach to, 13–14; partisan strategies in, 148–159; political impact of, 135, 138–146; sequential construction of districts in, 11; statewide effects of, 17, 22, 24, 135; two-thirds vs. majority voting rule in, 180–181, 185

Dixon, Robert G., 4n; on criteria for redistricting, 135n; nonpartisan reapportionment evaluated by, 52–53; on the political nature of reapportionment, 183*n*; reform strategy proposed by, 3

Downs, Anthony, 117*n*

Downsian electoral model, 117–118

Dudley, Juanita, 71*n*

Dymally, Mervyn, 143

Electoral system: and geographic basis of legislative districts, 38–39; minimized disruption of, 15–16; radical change of, 12–15; representation of minority political parties in, 36–37, 46, 50; two-party stability in, 50–51

Engstrom, Richard L., 75*n*

Equal population requirement, 11, 55–60; conflict with competitive seats, 69–70; effect on minority political strength, 70; evaluation of, 56–57; vs. good government criteria, 69–70; and voter deviation ranges, 57–59

Equal size of districts, 30–31, 39*n*

Equity for minorities, 51. *See also* Minority communities

Ethnic communities, 21, 24, 129; protection of, 66–67, 71, 130; representation of, 67. *See also* Minority communities

"Expected vote model," 139–141, 144

"Fadargol," 2

Fairness in reapportionment, 16; in bargaining by legislators, 130; based on the ratio of seats to votes, 3–4, 74–77; in bipartisan gerrymanders, 161; and compactness, 33, 38, 51; for dispersed minority groups, 51; in good government criteria, 53, 73–77; population needs vs. displacement in, 27; role of political data in, 135; in seat collapse, 29–30

Fenno, Richard, 13*n*

Ferejohn, John A., 13*n*, 33*n*

Fiorina, Morris P., 13*n*, 33*n*

Florida, 55

Foley, Tom, 82

Folsom, city lines of, 60

Forrest, Edward, 10*n*

Frankfurter, Felix, Justice, 56

Gaffney v. Cummings, 55–56

Game theory, 131

Geographical regions, as communities of interest, 63, 70, 72

Gerrymandering, 2, 11–12, 27, 147–178; vs. compactness, 32, 33; for district residence of legislators, 112; "good government" solution for, 11–12, 52–77; of Hispanic communities, 89, 90, 174–175; origins of the term, 32; popular view of, 32, 147, 157–158, 159; racial, 66, 72

Gerrymanders, affirmative action, 66, 166–178; and assessment of minority political strength, 170–173; effect of pluralism on, 174–177; goals of, 166–167, 168–169; maximization rule for, 166–167, 170–171, 177; overdispersion vs. overconcentration in, 169–171; summarized, 177–178

Gerrymanders, bipartisan, 147, 159–166; frequency of, 124–125; homogeneous districts caused by, 180–181; obstacles to, 163–166; reasons for, 162–163; strategies in, 160–161, 177

Gerrymanders, partisan, 148–159, 177, 181; constraints on, 155–157; effect on legislators, 155–157; efficient level of party strength for, 148–150, 154; political impact on policymaking, 157–159; reasons for, 88–89, 151–154

Gisler, Stan, 60*n*

Gomillion v. Lightfoot, 66

Good government criteria, 52–77; conditions required for, 53–54, 68–73; conflicts among, 68–73; criticism of, 53; critique of preserving communities of interest, 53–67; defended by legislators, 117; evaluation of the equal population goal in, 56–60; evaluation of respect for city and county lines in, 60–63; fairness in, 53, 73–77; political nature of, 54, 62–63, 64–68; preservation of political parties not included in, 188; ranking of, 73–74; as a reform strategy, 11–12, 179; relationship with compactness, 32, 33–34, 35, 42–51

Governorship of California, 100, 151

Grass-roots political organizations, 13

Grofman, Bernard, 4*n*, 5*n*, 75*n*, 156*n*; on fairness, 3–4; on good government criteria for reapportionment, 53

Hallett, Carol, 81, 89, 95, 101

Hardy, Leroy, 5*n*, 104*n*

Hernandez, Richard, 93
Hess, Sidney, 10n
Heterogeneous districts, 63, 64, 73; and the median preference theory of representation, 187
Hispanic community, 24; alliance with the Rose Institute, 91–92; distribution in California, 46–48, 71; gains in the California Assembly reapportionment plan, 71, 103; political strength of, 70, 71, 89, 103, 130; relationship with the Democratic party, 71–72, 92, 169, 174–175; role in the California Assembly reapportionment, 48, 89, 90–96, 98, 101, 103, 115, 130, 137, 152, 172–173, 174–175
Hispanic legislators, 81, 82, 98, 130. *See also* Alatorre, Richard
Homogeneous districts, 74, 75, 106, 118, 176; and competitive seats, 73; and Democratic non-minority incumbents, 174–175; effect of bipartisan gerrymanders on, 180–181; and preserving communities of interest, 39, 48; representation of, 63, 64–65
Huerta, John, 72n, 91n, 103, 169n

Ideal population, 109, 110, 120; allowable deviations from, 25–27; attitudes of legislators toward, 105–106; calculation of, 9, 15; and displacement required by demographic changes, 17
Imperial County, 71
Imperialism in reapportionment, 162–163
Incrementalist redistricting method, 15–22; and methods to contain ripples, 22–27
Incumbent legislators, 1, 12; advantages of, 67–68; attitudes on affirmative action gerrymanders, 175–176; bargaining skills of, 132; and bipartisan gerrymanders, 161, 164–165; continuity of the districts of, 184–185; and the creation of new seats, 164; effect of minority political strength on non-minority incumbents, 174–177; and Hispanic strategies for representation, 92–93, 95, 96; and political data, 132, 136; and radical change in the electoral system, 12, 13, 14; role in negotiations on reapportionment, 99, 100, 102; and seat collapse, 28, 30 (*see also* Seats). *See also* Legislators

Indiana, reapportionment in, 82
Institutional choices of reapportionment reform, 181–188. *See also* Reform strategies

Jacobson, Gary, 68n
Jewell, Malcolm E., 104n
Jewish communities, 66, 88, 93
"John Steinbeck" seat, 94, 137
Johnston, R. J., 75n

Kern County, 72, 95
King, Anthony, 13n
Kirkpatrick v. Preisler, 55
Kline, Fred, 102n

Lancaster, California, 72
Latinos, 47
Lee, Eugene C., 65n
Legal issues in redistricting, 4. *See also* California Supreme Court; U.S. Supreme Court
Legislative reapportionment: adverse effects of, 2; central issues in, 53, 69; compared with the Downsian electoral model, 117–118; criticism of, 1–2, 4, 9, 27, 52–53, 188–189; evaluation of, 184–185, 188–191; political nature of, 5–6, 53–54, 62–68, 73, 77, 183; process of, 104–119; recommendations for the improvement of, 188–191. *See also* Reform strategies
Legislators: bargaining skills of, 132–133; case studies of, 104–117, 128, 129, 131; conflict of interest of, 1–2, 52, 184, 188; impact of partisan gerrymanders on, 154–155, 157; neighboring districts of, 106–107; persuasion of, 127–132; prospects for statewide careers, 109–110; reasons for opposing redistricting plans, 105–112; residence of, 100, 107, 112, 117; responsiveness to their constituents, 2, 62–63, 64–66; risk-averse strategies of, 116, 119, 128, 143, 155, 160, 176, 184–185; selection of constituents by, 105–106, 107, 108, 117–118; self-interest of, 1, 115–116, 117, 125, 155, 163, 184–185
Legislature of State of California v. Reinecke, 22n, 42n, 60n, 63n
Linear ripples, 19–22. *See also* Ripples in reapportionment

Lizarraga, David C., 167n, 170n
Los Angeles, 126; Hispanic community in, 93–94; minority communities in, 46–48, 71, 93; municipal incorporation in, 44, 46; political strength in urban and suburban areas of, 72; protection of minority political strength in, 71
Los Angeles County, 21, 48, 49; collapse of seats in, 99–100, 101; communities of interest in, 72; distribution of partisan support in, 44, 45, 139–140, 149–150; projections of voting behavior in, 139–140
Lowry, Mike, 82
Loyalty measures, 143–145

Madisonian approach to reform, 179–180, 187
Mahan v. Howell, 55
Malan, Rian, 136n
March, James, 15n
Marin County: district size of, 63–64; district splitting of, 17
"Martyr" seats, 122
Mayhew, David, 148n–149n
McCarthy, Leo, 81, 87, 97, 99
Media coverage, 14, 92–93; California reapportionment plan interpreted by, 102–103; value of, 190
Mexican-American Legal Defense and Education Fund (MALDEF), 91, 103, 169
Mexico, border district near, 96
Miller, Gary, 44, 46
Minority communities, 13, 21, 28; and affirmative action gerrymanders, 66, 166–177; assessment of political strength of, 171–173; concentration vs. dispersal of, 46–48, 169–171; effect of compact districts on political representation of, 35–37, 41, 43, 48, 50–51; legal and political protection of, 66–67, 70–72, 90, 99–100, 130; and the median preference theory of representation, 187; minority vs. non-minority representatives of, 67, 95, 169; political strength of, 70–72, 90–96, 170–176; and the proportional standard of fairness in seat allocation, 75–76; in reapportionment reform strategies, 180, 182; remedy for the population division of, 41; role in California reapportionment, 89, 90–96, 98, 103, 105–106,

115, 130; splitting of, 89, 90, 94, 96, 130; voting by, 75–76, 90–91, 167–168, 173
Missouri Congressional plans, 55
Monrovia, 46
Monterey, 48, 137
Moretti, Bob, 1, 97
Mori, Floyd, 99
Morrill, Richard, redistricting plan created by, 13–14
Municipal incorporation, 44, 46
Musgrove, Phillip, 148n

Nagel, Stuart S., 10n
Naylor, Bob, 61n, 102
New York, reapportionment in, 116, 156
Nickel and diming strategies, 110–111, 129
Nie, Norman, 168n
Niemi, Richard, 3n, 75n
"Needy" seats, 121–122
Nonpartisan reform strategy: criticism of, 52–53, 73–74; described, 2–3, 52; necessary conditions for, 53–54, 68–73

"One man, one vote principle," 54, 55, 137, 155, 185; rural representation diminished by, 70; value of, 56–57
Orange County, 88, 102, 126, 150
Ordeshook, Peter C., 56n
O'Rourke, Timothy G., 5n
"Overage," 15
Owen, Guillermo, 3n, 75n

Palmdale, California, 72
Pareto improvements, 122–123
Partisanship: in California reapportionment, 82–83, 84, 87–90, 92, 99–101, 102, 183; decline in, 67–68; in reform strategies, 182–183
Partisan skew, remedy for, 35–38
Partisan strength: in bargaining positions, 121, 123, 125, 128; distribution of, 43–44; efficient level of, 44, 76, 148–150, 154, 160
Partisan strength, assessment of, 138–146; "expected vote model" in, 139–141, 144; loyalty measures in, 143–145; of minority groups, 171–173; in registration figures, 141–142, 148; simulation of, 144–145
Pasadena, 46, 71
Peele, Gillian, 56n

Peer group pressures, 130
Personality, role in bargaining, 133
Persuasive techniques used in redistricting, 127–132
Pettit, Bruce D., 83n
Pitkin, Hannah, 64n
Pluralism: compatibility with legislative reapportionment, 179–191; effect on gerrymandering, 147, 155–157, 174–177; single-member simple plurality systems, 43, 50, 51, 167, 177, 187
Policymaking, effect of partisan gerrymanders on, 158–159
Political conflict, and the nature of reapportionment, 5, 53
Political data, 116, 135–146; in bargaining strategies, 132–133; computerized, 83, 85, 86–87, 136–138, 146; discrepancies in, 111; effect on gerrymandering, 146; "expected vote model" for, 139–141, 144; merger with census data, 83, 85; qualitative form of, 136–137; registration figures in, 141–143; role in assessing partisan effects of redistricting, 138–146; technical and partisan problems in, 83–87
"Political formula" reform strategy, 3–4
Political impact: of partisan gerrymanders, 155–159; of reapportionment, 135–146
Political leaders: bargaining power of, 113, 128, 130–132, 134; improved quality of, 12, 186; job security of, 116, 119, 186; power in reapportionment, 113, 128, 130–132, 134; role in partisan gerrymanders, 154–155
Political nature of reapportionment, 5–6, 53–54, 62–63, 64–68, 73, 77, 183
Political parties: decision-making and incentives to implement gerrymanders, 88–89, 154–155, 162–166; grass-roots organizations in, 12–13; preservation of their role in representation, 188; racial and ethnic representation in, 67; and stability of the two-party system, 50–51; weakened by legislative reapportionment, 2, 12–13
Political parties, minority: disadvantages of, 50; effect of compact districts on, 35, 36, 37, 41, 43, 50–51. See also Minority communities
Political power of partisan gerrymanders, 157–159

Polsby, Nelson, 4n, 5n, 149n, 180n
Population: allowable deviations in, 25–27, 87; in criteria for redistricting, 10–13; equality of, 11, 55–60, 69–70; highest population deficit rule, 28–29; ideal, 9, 15, 25–27, 105–106, 109, 110, 120; ripples, 17 (see also Ripples in reapportionment); role in the incrementalist redistricting method, 15–17; surplus and deficit in, 15, 17, 20, 29, 120. See also Demography
Precincts, 85, 111, 116
Professionalism, legislative, 119, 186–187
Progressive movement, 65
Proportional representation, 75; minority party representation in, 36, 50–51, 167, 171
Proportional standard of fairness in seat allocation, 74–77
Proposition 6, role in California reapportionment, 17, 23, 41n, 60–61
Public interest, role in reapportionment, 179–180, 189
Publicity on reapportionment, 92–93, 190. See also Media coverage

Quality of politicians, 12, 186
Quinn, Tony, 89n

Race: in California politics, 14; and reapportionment, 48, 66–67
Racial communities: legal and political protection of, 66–67; political strength of, 70–72. See also Minority communities
Rae, Douglas, 3n, 36n, 37n
Ranney, Austin, 13n
Rawls, John, 73, 74
Reagan, Ronald, 88, 100, 154; on reform of reapportionment, 2–3
Referendum tactics, 89, 101
Reform strategies: choices in, 2–4, 181–191; compatibility with pluralist ideals, 189–191; creation of competitive seats in, 67–68; "good government" criteria in, 11–12, 53–74, 179; nonpartisan, 2–3, 52–53, 73–74, 181–183; and partisan proportionality of reapportionment commissions, 183–184; in a pluralist setting, 179–191; proposed by the Rose Institute, 13–14, 162, 183; public interest approach in, 179–180, 189; and pub-

lic pre-vote disclosure on reapportionment bills, 189–190; realistic expectations of, 6, 188–191; relative to the goals of representation, 185–188; selection of criteria in, 11–12, 185–186; size of the decision-making body in, 181–182; two-thirds vs. majority voting rule in, 180–181, 183, 185

Registration: in assessment of partisan strength, 141–143; and distribution of partisanship in reapportionment commissions, 183; in gerrymandering, 156–157; of minority communities, 167–168; points, 113, 114, 128, 157

Representation: Burkean theory of, 65, 68; comparison of single and multiple, 62–63; consistency with reapportionment criteria, 185–188; descriptive, 64, 68, 182, 187, 188; in a highly competitive system, 68; median preference theory of, 65–66, 68, 187; of minority communities, 35–37, 41, 43, 48, 50–51, 67, 70–72, 90–97, 166–169, 187; of racial and ethnic communities, 66–67; role of political parties in, 188; of rural areas, 70

Republican party: vs. Democrats in California reapportionment debates, 20, 82–83, 84, 87–90, 92, 94–95, 99–102; and the distribution of partisan support, 43–44; and minority groups, 91–92, 95, 170, 175–176; political strength in suburbs, 72; proposal for reapportionment reform submitted by, 4; registration figures of, 141–142, 143; relationship with the Hispanic community, 91–92, 94, 95; rules for non-minority incumbents in, 175; and seat collapse, 29; strategy used in California reapportionment, 87–90, 97, 100, 162, 165

Reynolds v. Sims, 39*n*, 55, 58, 59, 63*n*

Richardson, H. L., 2, 90

Riker, William, 56*n*, 131, 132

Ripples in reapportionment, 17–27; circular, 23; containment of, 22–27; defined, 17; dispersal of, 21–22; and the equal population requirement, 69, 70; linear, 19–22; self-contained, 23

Risk-averse strategies, 116, 119, 128, 143, 155, 160, 176, 184–185

Robinson, Richard, 87

Rose Institute, 5*n*; alliance with the Hispanic community, 91–92, 95; political

data of, 84, 86, 87; on preservation of city and county lines, 74*n*; redistricting plan proposed by, 13–14, 162, 183; relationship with the Republican party, 84, 86, 87, 91, 95, 162

Rosenstone, Stephen, 168*n*

Rural districts: effect of compactness on, 48–49; vs. urban districts, 63–64, 70

Sacramento County, 23

"Safe" seats, 122

Salinas Valley, 94, 137

San Bernardino County, 61, 72

San Diego County, 71, 88, 95, 96, 102, 126, 150

San Francisco, 126

San Francisco County, 153; compared with Marin County, 64; and displacement, 26–27; and seat collapse, 30

San Jose, Hispanic community in, 89, 90, 95–96, 174

San Luis Obispo County, 20

San Mateo County, 27

Santa Barbara County, 94, 103

Santillan, Richard, 169

Scarrow, Howard, 3, 4*n*, 5*n*, 156*n*; on good government criteria, 53

Seats: collapse of, 21, 27–30, 93, 97, 99–100, 109, 150, 161; competitive, 67–74 *passim*, 180–181; effect of compact districts on, 35–38; and fairness based on the ratio of seats to votes, 74–77; partisan strength of, 121; trading of, 18, 22, 23, 127–132; typology of, 121–127

Secrecy in reapportionment, 84–85, 189–190

Security Pacific Bank, 91

Simplification of reapportionment procedures, 10–22

Simon, Herbert, 15*n*

Single-member simple plurality systems (SMSP), 43, 50, 51, 167, 177, 187

Solano County, 153

Sonoma County, district unification of, 16–17

Sonoma State University, 85, 86

Speakership of the California State Assembly, 1, 14; role in reapportionment, 86, 87, 88, 92, 97, 102, 114, 120, 130; struggle for control of, 81, 82, 132

S-shaped curves, 4, 75

Stanislaus County, 23, 24

State districts, and the equal population requirement, 55, 59–60
Strategic trades, 18, 19
Suburbs, 72

Tabula Rasa redistricting method, 10–15; compared with the incrementalist method, 15; and creation of compact district lines, 34–35; described, 10–12; problems caused by, 12–15
Taylor, P. J., 75n
Technical requirement for reapportionment, 83–87, 105. *See also* Computers; Political data
Texas Congressional planning, 55
Torrance, split city lines of, 61
Transportation: and compact districts, 33, 50; and respect for city and county lines, 61
Tufte, Edward R., 3n, 75n

"Underage," 15. *See also* Population
United Jewish Organization v. Carey, 66
Urban-rural differences: among communities of interest, 63–64, 70; conflict with the equal population requirement, 70; role of suburbs in, 72; and the value of compactness, 39–40, 43–44, 48
U.S. Supreme Court, 155, 185; on communities of interest, 39, 63; equal population doctrine of, 55–60, 70, 105; on racial discrimination in legislative districts, 66

Vallejo, California, 153
Vasconcellos, John, 95, 96, 174
Ventura County, 94
Verba, Sidney, 168n
Virginia, 55
Voting: apathy in, 2; compared with legislative reapportionment, 117–118; decline of partisanship in, 67–68, 110, 143; deviation ranges in, 57–59; doctrine of vote dilution in, 56–57, 60, 75; and fairness based on the ratio of seats to votes, 74–77; participation of minority communities in, 75–76, 90–91, 167–168, 173; predicting the results of, 139–141, 144, 152; relative to registration figures, 143; in rules for reapportionment, 180–181, 183, 185; value of the single vote in, 56–57, 60; "wasted" votes in, 160, 161

Walker, Dan, 61n
Warren, Justice, 55
Washington state, reapportionment in, 82
Waters, Earl G., 67n
Weaver, James B., 10n
Wells v. Rockefeller, 55
Wesberry v. Sanders, 55
White v. Weiser, 55
Wildgren, John K., 75n
Wolfinger, Raymond, 168n

Zelman, Walter, 103

Compositor: Wilsted & Taylor
Printer: Braun-Brumfield, Inc.
Binder: Braun-Brumfield, Inc.
Typeface: Palatino